KEEPING THE FAITH

through the UN-thinkable...

by Tamra Jean

a real life account

KEEPING THE FAITH
through the UN-thinkable...

Self-published by: Tamra Jean
ISBN: 979-8-9853186-4-7 (Paperback); 979-8-9853186-0-9 (E-Pub)
Cover and Interior Design: The team at WhereTheSpiritOfTheLordis.com
Photography: Almost all photographs were taken with Tamra's own cell phone during her journey, (only a few purchased online).

ALL Scriptures are quoted from the **Concordant Literal New Testament** ©1983, and the **Concordant Version of the Old Testament** ©2012, by the Concordant Publishing Concern, and are used with their gracious permission, (unless otherwise noted or when quoting another source which includes a Scripture). Please note all underlines in Scripture quotes are my own additions, for emphasis.

When definitions are added within a Scripture quote, (in parenthesis), the source will be noted, either *"CLKC"* (extracted from the **Concordant Literal New Testament with keyword concordance**) or *"Thayer"* found in the Thayer's Greek Lexicon at BlueLetterBible.org. When neither is noted, the definition is my personal understanding or opinion... (Please do spirit check this for yourself, as I am only human.)

The author of this book does not issue, provide or prescribe medical advice nor any technique as a form of treatment for physical, spiritual, emotional, or medical problems without consulting a qualified physician, either directly or indirectly. The heart and purpose of this author is only to offer information of a general nature to help you with your spiritual and your emotional well-being. In the event you use any of the information in this book for yourself, the author and the publisher assume no responsibility for your actions. (Phew... glad that is done, now let's live for Yahweh {God}!)

TABLE OF CONTENTS

INTRODUCTION

How do you live by faith and
by the Word of the Living Yahweh {God},
in today's world?

How do you stand true to Yahweh {God}
when everything seems stacked against you?

How do you forgive... the unforgivable?
(Not just with words, but truly, deep in your heart.)

And further still:

What do you do when family turns against you?

Is it "too radical" to give every breath to Yahweh {God}, being in His presence at all times, even while doing all things? I mean, instead of simply going to church, praying and worshiping Him for an hour, and then going home and *knowing deep inside that your level of trust in Yahweh {God} and true peace* is so much less in everyday life?

What is it about churches today that just does not seem to quite "fit" with what the ***Bible's correct translation*** *really says?* Even that question *sounds or feels* almost blasphemous, but *how can I be a faithful follower of Yeshua {Jesus} when religion does not seem to add up?*

Do miracles still happen, or did they die 2000 years ago, along with Yeshua {Jesus}?

Yeshua {Jesus} said, "*...what a cramped gate and narrowed way is the one leading away into life, and few are those who are finding it." (Matthew 7:14)* He does not say it is unachievable. *What if you could be one of "**the few**"? What does it take to steadfastly walk with Yahweh {God}, seemingly "alone" to the very end of the "**narrow way**"?*

Have you ever wondered such things?

What would all of this look like in life today?

These and other questions would swirl through my mind like a tornado in Texas...

And Yahweh {God}, in His **grace** and **mercy**, sent *angels* (as I call them) along my path, or me along their path, to help me, to guide me as He Himself opened my eyes to see Him, in Truth! Thank You Father!

My deepest desire, my prayer to our Father in Heaven, is that you will be encouraged and inspired by what faith can do as you read the events I have lived through and share in this book. Many of them were difficult, (to put it mildly), and holding fast to the Truth seemed a white-knuckle walk at times. However... as Yeshua {Jesus} Himself said:

Jesus said to them, "With men this is impossible, yet with God all is possible."

Matthew 19:26

IF I were to tell you, that I truly live in PEACE today, in a peace I had not known, the peace of Yahweh {God}, you probably would not believe me, (especially after reading what you are about to read). I would NOT have believed me either... in the early, unsure steps of my journey.

So be encouraged *while* you read this... you may relate to one or more of the difficult experiences I share, perhaps even experiences similar to those which have brought you to where you are now, possibly to becoming as stuck as I was. I pray that my learnings, touching your heart, might just help you climb "out of that box" that has held you captive too.

Now to Him Who is able to do superexcessively above all that we are requesting or apprehending, according to the power that is operating in us, to Him be glory in the ecclesia and in Christ Jesus for all the generations of the eon of the eons! Amen!

Ephesians 3:20-21

Whether you have anyone (or *no one*) in your corner, standing with you... know this: I, along with Yahweh {God} of course, am now your biggest fan! I know you can do this... I know you can live through anything and everything that may be happening, right now. Even if you do not believe it... please believe me. Lean on my faith... until you gain more of your own. (I leaned on the faith of others throughout my journey! Many of whom are listed in *Hebrews 11*, as well as helpful angels Yahweh {God} sent along my path.)

I pray the eyes of your heart are opened to see the Father as I *now* see Him, a trustworthy, omnipotent (all-powerful), omniscient (all-knowing) Abba, Papa, Daddy. Let me tell you this is a STARK contrast to how I "knew" Him to be from church and religious teachings I had adhered to from a toddling 2-year-old and on to a 32-year-old (when my journey took a few, much needed, sharp turns!)... I thought He was always angry, looking down at me from heaven with continuous disapproval and disappointment, just waiting to scold me at every step. THIS is NOT Yahweh {God}. And those were *only a few* of the multitudinous lies I believed... as you will soon read.

Now, this... this ***IS*** Yahweh {God}:

...yet God, being rich in mercy, because of His vast love with which He loves us... vivifies us together in Christ (in grace are you saved!) and rouses us together and seats us together among the celestials, in Christ Jesus, that, in the oncoming eons, He should be displaying the transcendent riches of His grace in His kindness to us in Christ Jesus.

Ephesians 2:4-7

"Worthy art Thou, O Lord, our Lord and God,
To get glory and honor and power;
For Thou dost create all,
And because of Thy will they were, and are created."

Revelations - The Unveiling of Jesus Christ 4:11

> **For in grace, through faith, are you saved, and this is not out of you; it is God's approach present, not of works, lest anyone should be boasting.**
>
> *Ephesians 2:8-9*

I endeavor to be like the Apostle Paul…

> **For I am not daring to speak any of what Christ does not effect through me for the obedience of the nations, in word and work, in the power of signs and miracles, in the power of God's spirit…**
>
> *Romans 15:18-19*

I stretch out my hand to you, dear reader, giving my heart and my prayers, sharing the Scriptures that I held fast to, like holding Yeshua's {Jesus'} robes, sometimes by only a single, thin strand. I share my past experiences and my learnings… including both mistakes leading off the path to following other gods, as well as the choices that directed me to walking in the footsteps of the Father, *Keeping The Faith* in my incredible life of purpose, fulfilling the divine destiny for which I was created!

I pray that I am walking worthily of the calling with which I was called *(Ephesians 4: 1-2);* and I humbly share my journey that it may help you on yours… for while this is a "wicked eon" (wars, battles, plague and pestilence, unkind and down-right wicked people, unjust court systems, and more) that we live in, there **is a realm** you can walk in where nothing can touch you. Let's walk in THAT REALM, shall we!

Yahweh {God}, my Father in Heaven Himself, led me to write and share this… He CEASELESSLY FLOWED all of these words down to me (and to my faithful friend who helps me!) in just over three months.

So Yahweh's {God's} opinion is all that matters. He may have been "wondering" how I could possibly think that I would be able to help others with my head buried in the sand (and tape over my mouth). I can now hear Him saying, *"Courage, daughter of Mine."*

"God never said it would be easy, He said He would be with us."
Barbara Brown

If you get offended with anything in this book, dear reader, please know that I myself got offended at times along my journey, (one instance of which you will read about in chapter one in the first four paragraphs of the book)! However, after I humbled myself, I opened myself up to gratitude which eventually led to peace… for the rest of my life! So, may I suggest you consider doing the same… with anything you yourself may be offended by. Humbly submitted for your prayerful consideration.

I share a few times throughout this book, that "I felt fear" writing this… or "I was worried how to write about *this.*" Well actually, I believe it took SO long to even begin writing this, simply because I did not want to share ANY events of my life with ANYONE, let alone delve back into memories best forgotten! (Yet, my prayer has been to help others, as Yahweh {God} sent others to help me, His answer to which I am called...) I now see, (AFTER saying *"Yes"* and finding the courage to write all of the following), that the ONLY way to help others, is to *speak* the truth! To *share* the truth! Knowing some will not embrace it with open arms, and that is ok. Knowing also that many will embrace it, and be encouraged on their own walk. I know that if I help just one of His lost sheep on their path to the One TRUE Yahweh {God}, I will rejoice and it will all have been worth it.

I pray that one is you.

Father in Heaven,
Praise Your Holy Name!
I thank You for my life...
for every single day of it.
Thank You for being so patient with me,
as I learn Your ways.
Thank You for giving me the courage, resolve and words to write this...
I offer my life to You Father, just as I prayed as a young teen, "Use me for Your will, Father," so I continue to pray...
every step of mine, every click of the mouse, every word I type and every word I speak is for You and You alone!
And, let me be "an angel" with a helping hand to others on this journey...
I pray You heal every single beloved creation of Yours, every child of Yours who reads Your words here, heal them from the top of their heads to the tips of their toes.
Open the floodgates of heaven, Father, and pour out Your glory, Your peace, Your love, Your light, and Your healing over us!
I Praise You and You alone!
In Yeshua's {Jesus'} Holy Name,
Amen. Amen. And Amen.

May Yahweh {God} fill you with wisdom and peace.

Blessings beyond...
Tamra

P.S. As you have already seen above, (and when you hear me speak), I call "God" by His true Hebrew Name, **Yahweh!** (And in some cases **Yah**, as in Exodus, Psalms and Isaiah.) I have chosen, out of the utmost respect for Him, to call Him by His real name, along with Yeshua {Jesus}. Throughout this book, I add in brackets {God} and {Jesus} to help bridge the gap in learning their original and true, Hebrew names.

P.S.2. Also, dear reader, please remember to have on your own panoply of Yahweh {God} (*Ephesians 6:13-17)* as you read this book, as well as when you read or listen to anything I quote, reference or point you to. No human on earth is perfect, and as it is written, "test the spirits to know whether they are of God," *spirit-checking* as well as *Scripture-checking* what anyone teaches or even simply speaks or writes.

Yet be testing all, retaining the ideal.

1 Thessalonians 5:21

Beloved, do not believe every spirit, but test the spirits to see if they are of God...

1 John 4:1a

FOREWORD

"Your dedication to your faith is awe-inspiring. Truly. I love how you walk, talk and breathe your faith." This is what I said to Tamra just the other day.

How I met her is testament to how small Social Media has made the world become. We began talking tens of thousands of miles apart in different countries, different nationalities and very different walks of life. But still, we connected through our shared experiences of church, religion, and our ongoing deconstruction (I believe this process never ends, nor should it).

When it comes to church, like me, Tamra has gone through seasons of enlightening, or awakening. It usually starts with questions, and hers already started at a remarkably young age. Maybe, just maybe, some of the clichés we have been taught in church were man-made along the way, and ended up doing more harm than good?

Now, the first tell-tale sign of pushback will probably be: *"Do not question - you should have child-like faith."* Well, a person who believes having child-like faith is equivalent to not asking questions, has obviously never met a child before. I have always maintained that I have never questioned Him, only what I have been taught to believe about Him. And so, Tamra's journey to finding Him for herself (not traditions handed down by others), began.

She takes us on her journey of when her life collapsed to ground zero. While sifting through the rubble, she identified beliefs and mindsets that were actually holding her back and left them discarded. She then takes advantage of the blank canvas to create a new life of fulfilment and well-being.

Equally, when she lost relationships and everyone she once trusted rejected her, she cultivates new friendships with people who were on a similar path as herself and accept and appreciate her for who she is.

You will probably find a common theme among people who have done great things - people who inspire others, who are great leaders, influencers, who others look up to, and who have that "something" others want. Most of them have been through awful hardships and unthinkable injustices, but chose to be strong and to always keep going. Then, they turn and help others.

Tamra's passion is contagious. In spite of her circumstances, she never loses her passion for Yahweh {God} and His word. It is the one constant throughout her journey. Some people live their entire lives never being this passionate about anything and it definitely encouraged me to reignite my passion for broken people, and being a safe haven for whoever needs it. Accepting others without condemnation in my heart can bring about healing. Especially the kind of hurt that condemnation caused.

No matter where you are in life... I trust this book will awaken something within your spirit and encourage you to keep going, to continue seeking Jesus, the Author and Finisher of your faith.

R Lessing
New Zealand

Chapter 1

IN EVERYTHING BE GIVING THANKS…

We aren't born grateful… we must BECOME IT!

Be rejoicing always. Be praying unintermittingly. In everything be giving thanks, for this is the will of God in Christ Jesus for you.

1 Thessalonians 5:16-18

"Find one thing you are grateful for... truly grateful for, Tamra," she said.

"What! ARE YOU SERIOUS?" (I SHOUTED, though only in my mind.) I was angry. I was livid for three days. Yes, three whole days. I managed to keep my voice and composure calm(*ish*) through the rest of our conversation...

Later I thought: *"Did you NOT hear what I just shared with you? Most people say 'Oh... my dear, poor girl...' when I tell them what happened to me at age 17. I was raped. At knifepoint."*

After those three days of stewing in anger... I humbled myself a little, and decided that maybe I would try it. I would try to find one thing that I could be grateful for. Maybe she was right? What if this Barbara Brown knew what she was talking about? After all, what I had learned so far about this woman spoke volumes:

> She has three Masters Degrees in science and education, she is an author, ordained minister, businesswoman, speaker, adviser to world leaders and wellness advocate, helping people re-awaken and restore their original design, and fulfill the purpose for which they were created. She has brought the "Realm of the Miraculous" to palaces, boardrooms, and churches all over the world... She is the most sold-out, radical follower of Yeshua {Jesus} I had ever met!
>
> Yahweh {God} has performed miracles through her, including giving sight to a blind boy. Yes... restoring the blind eyes of a young

boy to full eye-sight. The kind of miracle you read Yeshua {Jesus} and His disciples performing.

> **"Verily, verily, I am saying to you, he who is believing in Me, the works which I am doing he also will be doing, and greater than these will he be doing, for I am going to the Father. And whatever you should be requesting in My name, this I will be doing, that the Father should be glorified in the Son."**
>
> *John 14:12-13*

So, I humbled myself a little more still and began looking, looking into the past. THIS TIME, looking with a fine-toothed comb for something, ANYTHING **positive** I could take away from this horrific experience.

For probably the millionth time, literally, this nightmare I had lived through re-played through my mind, moment by moment, like a photographic memory flip-book of the horrific experience:

It was winter in a small town in Minnesota, in January. Snow was on the ground and piled on the sides of the roads by snowplows. It was freezing, freezing cold. I had just gotten home from working at the local movie theatre. It was around midnight, (on a school night!).

Blake, (as I will refer to him in this book), came out of nowhere, walking up behind me as I was about to get out of the car. (My parent's classic 80's, light blue station wagon, that they allowed me to drive sometimes, kept in good condition by all the weekly chores of wash and wax us kids had to do. The front seat was the one-seat bench type, light blue plush "leather" look, betrayed only by its vinyl feel. A couple of the creature comforts no longer functioned, but it was drivable.) He asked me for a ride home. Blake was a boy I had previously dated in high school. Yes, it seemed strange that he had appeared suddenly at my house. An uneasiness crept upon me. Surely I could trust him... why wouldn't I? So, while it was already late, and I had an important English paper to hand in the next day at school, I reluctantly agreed.

I drove towards his house, and he asked me to park in the mall parking lot so we could talk first. I did. (I was SUCH a people-pleaser, even at this young age. I really wanted to tell him NO, but sadly did not have the guts to.)

As we pull in, he points to a light pole to park by, the light burnt out (a detail I only registered afterwards). I leave the car running, hoping it would be a short talk. The heater isn't working, and it is freezing. Literally! Ice forming on the *inside* of the windows.

He pulls out a cigarette to smoke. I remind him, sheepishly, that there's no smoking in my parent's car. He opens the door, steps outside, and lights up his cigarette.

At that very moment, I feel THE STRONGEST URGE to step on the gas pedal and DRIVE OUT OF THERE. Drive home. Now. RIGHT NOW. My foot feels like a brick, TRYING (by itself almost) to step on the gas pedal and get OUT of there.

However, the people-pleaser in me feels bad for Blake... bad because I would be leaving him stranded in the parking lot, (still a ways from his home), in the freezing cold.

So, I stay there, an eerie uncomfortableness thickening around me. Sat waiting for him to smoke his cigarette, so he could "talk with me"? I become more and more uneasy as the seconds tick by... still, I wait.

He finally gets back into the car and we talk, no real subject, no real point to it. He keeps looking all around. Out the back window. Out the side windows. Out the front window. Why, I can't tell, as strange as his attention was to what was *not* there. After a while, I finally, timidly, say that I need to go home now. I have school tomorrow.

He says ok, just take me home. Then he tells me he had moved. My heart sensing an even greater uneasiness at this, my very core not really believing him, I say ok and ask where he lives. He says he moved out into the country, and he would direct me.

Every time he tells me to make a turn, I feel more and more uneasy... He finally directs me to what at first looks a little like a driveway. It isn't. It is a dead end. He tells me to turn off the car. I obey. Before I even have a chance to let go of the keys in the ignition and glance at him, a large 10-inch blade of a chef's chopping knife is at my throat, swiftly withdrawn from the concealment of his winter coat. He demands that I take all my clothes off. I am paralysed with fear. Completely frozen. Deflecting his eyes to the knife, he threatens me in a deep gruff voice, "*Am I going to have to USE this?*"

Braced back against the seat back, trembling, I croak, "*No... no.*" He lays the knife on the floor in front of the seat, between his feet, just within reach. I gingerly, as slow as I can, take off my clothes, item by item, hoping the ordeal would end before having to remove the next. He removed his too at the same time. He tells me to lay down on the front bench seat.

Then he forced himself on me. I was a virgin. It hurt.

I remember little else that happened. All I can remember is that, straight afterwards, he started apologizing. I was so scared. What do you say to a guy who had just done this and is now apologizing?!? I truly thought he was going to kill me. And he still had the knife at his feet. All I could muster out of my mouth was, "*It is ok.*" He tried to talk to me "normally," like nothing had happened. The apologizing continued. He asked what he could do to make it right. I said, "*I have to go home, I have school tomorrow.*" Again, what could I say so as to not aggravate him to violence. I had no idea what else he was capable of. (We both had school tomorrow… the *same* school.) He said, *"Ok,"* and asked if I could drive him to a friend's house. I agreed. I did not care where I drove him to, I just wanted him OUT of the car. He kept apologizing. He asked again what he could do. I finally asked that he just get rid of that knife. Virginity and purity already gone, I certainly wanted the threat to my life gone too. So, when we got near his friend's house (still out on the country gravel roads somewhere, at least a twenty-minute drive from wherever we previously had been) he told me to stop the car. He got out, threw the knife deep into the corn field and returned to tell me he had thrown it away. He then walked off, up the road to his friend's house.

I drove away. I did NOT KNOW where "out in the country" I was. Not a clue. I just drove. I knew I would find a familiar highway eventually. Frankly, where didn't matter. That I kept driving, did. That I was alone, safe and free from the imminent threat was enough to keep me focused on the moonlit road ahead. When I did finally emerge back into civilization, I was MUCH further from home than I realized.

When I finally got home I woke up my parents (as I always would when I worked late, to give them the peace of mind of my safe return home from work). I was late, very late and only to avoid a scolding, I relayed to them what had just happened to me, brief as I could and avoiding as many of the details as possible. I remember them being frantic and emotional, naturally distraught at what they had just heard. Utter shock tempered an otherwise small-town, idyllic prairie-like household moment, with both my parents silently displaying a calm collectedness. My father all but maintaining a practical resolve only let slip by the welling of angry tears in his eyes. My mother more hysterical, while barely visible, moderating her countenance through a preconditioned upbringing in her own strict Lutheran childhood, still noticeable through tonal inflections in her voice. A parental, protective show of strength for my benefit. After a hug, a tentative hand on my shoulder, and a heartfelt, *"Oh my dear,"* in gentle consolation from them both, I pleaded my tiredness and a sole desire to go to sleep, if possible, to awaken to it all being just a bad dream. Not much else was said. By now, it was passed 3 o'clock in the morning, and of all concerns to have in that moment, mine was waking up in a few hours and getting to school, turning in my paper for English class. (I was a "straight-A" student, and high school Grade Point Average meant EVERYTHING to me at the time...)

I awoke to my 6:30 am alarm and got ready for school as usual. I went to all my classes, as usual. I handed in my paper just like the other kids. And later that day went to work, as normal... as normal as my outward appearance could possibly portray it. I simply wanted to pretend that nothing had happened, that it would all just go away.

My oldest sister (I will call her Stacey in this book) called me on the phone that afternoon on this "new" normal day. In her college years we became quite close. We would do many things together, bowling, shopping at the mall, and I would spend the night at her apartment on some weekends! Having heard secondhand from my dad what had happened to me, she was shocked I had not told her myself! Amidst my embarrassment and shame, the last thing I wanted was to share it with *anyone*, not even her... I, still not knowing what to do, felt lost. Completely lost. (Things like this DID NOT HAPPEN in real life. Only in the movies... and bad movies at that.) She asked if I had been to the police. I was surprised at her question. Why would I do that? It was engrained in me not to "tattle." Besides, I was petrified of what *he* would do if he found out I had told anyone. He would come and kill me for sure. He was definitely capable. And to the POLICE?!? No. I could not do it.

Understandably emotional, she insisted that I MUST go to the police. RIGHT NOW. I reluctantly agreed, and she then drove me to the police station. My dad, naturally, met us there.

Following my discussion with the police, Blake is brought to the station for questioning. He admits to everything, kidnapping, rape, etc. But, he states there was no penetration. (I personally believe that his lawyer, on hearing my testimony, guided his "statement" of guilt and thus, sadly, both testimonies concurred regarding penetration.) My testimony had not included it. I kicked myself for years for NOT KNOWING, for NOT asking the police when questioned what the word "penetration" meant, and for the incomplete testimony that resulted. I was a virgin. Yes, there was penetration, and it hurt. I just didn't know what it was called.

My dad then encourages me to testify against Blake in court. Once again, I reluctantly agree. I just want to "get on with my life." I just want this all to "go away."

Charged with the offense, and declared by the court as on remand, Blake is kept in custody until trial. Even so, since January 13th, I fear going to bed at night, even walls and bars not sufficient to ease my distress, still afraid of him raping me again. Or worse.

A few days later at school, a girl, my age, approached me and discretely showed me a town newspaper article about what had happened locally. There it was, in black and white, and though my name was not present, the offender's was published. She asked if it was *me* that this had happened to. I must have nodded, involuntarily. She continued to tell me that the same thing had happened to her, but she did not have the guts to tell anyone. She complimented my courage in going to the police.

Strong?!? Not the way I would have described my state through any of this. Looking back now, I realize that I had no self-esteem whatsoever. None. If my sister had not known, had not insisted, I probably would not have done so.

Once the school girl had told me of her experience, I consulted my guidance counselor asking if she would please use my experience to encourage everyone in my grade, (if not the whole school), to not allow abuse to silence their fear. If another girl at school had experienced sexual abuse, yet was too timid to speak out about it, how many more voiceless victims had been suppressing their own nightmares. I wanted to encourage EVERYONE (both girls and boys) that they CAN speak out! They CAN tell the truth! They CAN take those who hurt and abuse them to court, (and not just physical abuse either). My guidance counselor agreed to accompany me, but on the terms that it had to come from me, and just to those in my grade (I say "just," it was still over three hundred fifty students in all). Determination for this cause overcame my own, ever-present fear of speaking out myself.

Having left the Lutheran Church I was raised in when I was fifteen, I was now currently going to a Pentecostal church in a near-by town. I would go up EVERY TIME there was an alter call. I would cry and cry. I was so lost. I so desperately wanted life to return to normal. I so desperately wanted the night of January 13th to be deleted from my life. I wanted to feel safe when I went to sleep. I wanted to stop dreaming about the horrific incident with Blake. I begged Yahweh {God} to give me my life back, to heal me of the feeling of being "dirty," embarrassed and ashamed. (Little did I know at the time that Yahweh {God} WAS right there with me! He had His own plans for me other than for my life to be going back to any previous kind of "normal.")

I began to receive attention from members of the church and others at school when they found out what had happened to me. To be honest, (to tell the whole "ugly" truth about myself also), I began to like all the attention. And I started to become a victim, a rape victim, because people would give me pity. Some would say I was strong for going to court. The fact was, feeling I mattered in the world was the greater attraction. It had given me an identity, a presence, far away from that of the youngest "seen and not heard" child of five.

In court I testified on the witness stand to the entire story (with many, many more details than I was comfortable sharing). But, "nothing but the truth" was my opportunity to *speak* all the truth and in doing so began the process of letting go the feeling of accountability, on my part, for what happened. Blake was sitting right there. Just a few feet away. (I was petrified.) On the opposite side of the courtroom, I felt the welcome comfort of my parents, family and supporters who were sitting in the front rows. Naturally, the retelling, the re-*living* of the events of that night was interrupted by uncontrollable tears that I had previously bottled up. Despite the judge's compassion, offering a break before continuing. I declined. Even when, unexpectedly, I was shown Exhibit A, the knife. I had to continue. I had to just get it done and over with.

Blake was found guilty on the charges of kidnapping and *attempted* rape, but not rape itself. (Because of the "penetration" question and how I originally answered it at the police station.) He was sentenced to only four years in prison. Had I been humble enough to ask the meaning of penetration, and a conviction of rape, he would probably have received fifteen years.

Even with him behind bars, I did not feel any safer at night, when out alone, going home from… anywhere, frankly, nor going to sleep, knowing I was physically safe from him, but not from the memory.

Two months after the trial and within a week of graduating from high school in Minnesota, fueled by my desire to get away from this small town of memories, I moved to New England to live with my other sister (I will refer to her as Christina), who had also moved away four years previously.

"Find one thing you are grateful for… truly grateful for, Tamra."

That advice, the actual doing of it, pounded on the door of my mind every waking moment for days and days. What could I take as a positive from all this? I went through every detail over and over in my mind… LOOKING for WHAT IN THE WORLD I could be grateful for?!?

It became top of my priority list every day… a priority list of one.

Finally, (thank you, Father in Heaven), I **finally** saw WHAT I *could* be grateful for:

My foot feeling heavy as a STONE.
The URGE to drive away.
To drive home.

That weighty feeling, THAT was the spirit GUIDING me that night, *(trying, at least)* to save me from what was about to happen! That was Yahweh's {God's} way of reaching out to me. If only I could have recognized it. If only I could have remembered what I knew from the Scriptures:

Now they passed through Phrygia and the Galatian province, being forbidden by the holy spirit to speak the word in the province of Asia. Yet, coming about Mysia, they tried to go into Bithynia, and the spirit of Jesus does not let them.

Acts 16:6-7

"Now the consoler, the holy spirit, which the Father will be sending in My name, that will be teaching you all…"

John 14:26

I had dismissed the instructions of the spirit. I had said *"NO"* to the spirit's wisdom, sent to help *save me*. I had chosen to please PEOPLE AGAIN, instead of Yahweh {God}.

At the time, I did not know this was the spirit, back in 1995. I had yet to learn about the spirit and how Yahweh {God} talks to us. The Lutheran Church taught me that Yahweh {God} no longer communicates in any way (almost as if He is dead, as I understood it). *"He no longer does miracles. He no longer talks to anyone,"* I was taught, *"After the Apostle Paul, God stopped communicating to people."*

Praise Yahweh {God}!
I know now, TODAY, that was **all lies.**

At the same time as meeting Barbara Brown, I met Dr. Tom Taylor, who also has a deep personal relationship with Yahweh {God}, such that I am still seeking myself. His passion for Yahweh's {God's} word and for ONLY the truth reminds me of the Apostle Paul. An honest and humble teacher, an angel whom Yahweh {God} had me cross paths with, Dr. Tom Taylor helped me greatly along my journey. He has an alarmingly fresh perspective of the **Bible**, not "taught to him" by religion, literary experts nor the many, many books by the same; but instead, as part of a small dedicated group, he took a rigorous, fourteen year deep dive into the original Greek and Hebrew texts of the Scriptures with the sole purpose of finding the truth and sharing Yahweh's {God's} message that had been, and still is to a large extent, so lost in today's teachings and religious doctrines, a truth within the Scriptures which has been *"misinterpreted, misunderstood and misapplied."*

Then, years later, **led by Yahweh** {God} as He "**Lights Up the Scriptures**" through Dr. Tom Taylor, he held 183 weekly eye opening, *ear opening if you will,* "non-religious" **Bible** studies (which are all recorded on audio) for all truth seekers hungry to "hear and heed." I am entirely grateful for all the wisdom imparted from these studies. No matter your level of knowledge (or lack) of the **Bible**, dear reader, I encourage you to join me in benefitting from the revelations from these studies… *repeatedly.*

In one of these studies, titled *"172 - The Shorter the Leash, the Greater the Life,"* Dr. Tom Taylor relays an experience of the spirit communicating with him…

> *This training is all INDIVIDUALLY prescribed, if you will. In other words, my training is not your training, and your training is not my training. Maybe mine won't look like yours, but I'll bet it has some characteristics that are very MUCH alike. Let me give you an example:*
>
> *One day, I needed to get some ice-melt, and I was released in my spirit to run that errand… So, I got to the hardware store, (only about a 2 or 3-mile trip). After I got the ice-melt, I tried to go beyond that point, and my spirit became grieved, I mean palpably, I mean… just constriction in my gut, the FURTHER from home I went, actually the further from the hardware store I went! And fortunately, I recognized the signs and I turned around immediately, right in the middle of the street (Tom laughing), I just made a 3-point turn. And the CLOSER I got to home, in fact, about the time I got BACK to the hardware store on this return trip, my spirit eased. And I never forgot that experience, because it taught me how CRUCIAL it is that we LISTEN to the SPIRIT of our Father as He communicates to our own spirit. And more importantly than listening… is what we have studied many times before, called harkening, which is where WE are accountable for our part! Also known as obedience!*
>
> *Now, I do not really WANT to know what would have happened if I had kept going that day, and just gutted it out, gutted out the grieving in my spirit.*

Do we REALLY need that exercise?

Light Up the Scriptures study *"172 - The Shorter the Leash, the Greater the Life"* by Dr. Tom Taylor. (Time: 13:58 - 16:05)

Sadly... I DID find out what happened that night when I *did* ignore and grieve the spirit.

After finding something I was (or could be) grateful for, a new deeper, wider perspective of gratefulness itself... I chose, at that exact moment, to LEARN to HEAR and OBEY the spirit.

**"Today, if ever His voice you should be hearing,
You should not be hardening your hearts."**

Hebrews 4:7b

I became truly GRATEFUL for this lesson about the spirit. (It did not just happen overnight. It took a few years to lay roots in me and grow.) I held onto this! I began to FOCUS on THIS, just THIS!

As I said previously, I had become a victim. I had identified myself as "a rape victim" for years. Whenever I would share with people what happened (usually NOT in such detail as above), I would let tears of self-pity trickle down my face... and then receive much attention and worldly sorrow from everyone.

Today, (and for over eight years now), healed and matured from the need of pity, I am more amazed than anyone that I am able to share this story for self-*less* reasons, feeling almost like I am telling this about another person. Tears are gone along with the seeking or benefitting from pity. Yahweh {God} is so good! He has completely healed me.

He answered my prayers! Even amidst this horrific experience by the hands of wickedness, Yahweh {God} healed my heart, giving me the strength to use the telling of this chain of events in my life ONLY for the good, helping others to release themselves from the chain in theirs.

Now we are aware that God is working all together for the good of those who are loving God, who are called according to the purpose...

Romans 8:28

After sixteen years of worldly, waste-of-time, waste-of-money therapists, the true miracle pill to healing having been spoken, encapsulated in just seven words: *"Find one thing you are grateful for..."* began my journey from victim to victory, from healing to helping.

"With men this is impossible, yet with God all is possible."

Matthew 19:26

I am just radical enough to believe that Yahweh {God} is SERIOUS about what He has directed and inspired to be written in the Scriptures, including:

Be rejoicing always. Be praying unintermittingly. <u>In everything be giving thanks</u>, for this is the will of God in Christ Jesus for you.

1 Thessalonians 5:16-18

It does NOT say: "In some things be giving thanks…"

It does NOT say: "In happy things be giving thanks…"

It DOES say: "**In everything be giving thanks…**"

Everything. EVERY THING.

"Everything" according to Dictionary.com means, "every single thing or every particle of an aggregate or total; **all.**" (Dictionary.com) To that, I choose to say, *"Yes Lord, and Amen."*

I taught myself (with help from a few others) to BECOME thankful. We are not born thankful. It does not FLOW CEASLESSLY out of us the moment our heart starts pumping… it did not from mine, anyway. When I had become thankful, as natural as it is to take in each breath, peace flowed with it.

> **And let the peace of Christ be arbitrating in your hearts, for which you were called also in one body; and become thankful.**
>
> *Colossians 3:15*

How Barbara Brown was helping me is explained in detail in the *"Heart, Soul and Spirit Cleanse"* section in her book **Your Personal Roadmap to Whole Body Cleansing.** This radical, and life-changing process is just one part of the *"Six Steps to Rapid Healing"* which is described as follows (emphasis mine):

> To go free, simply "look God in the eye," and say, *"Thank You,"* for what you learned from your experiences and what you're learning now *(even if you don't know what it is!).* Reciting this statement may be all you are capable of at first, but, if you apply the preceding steps well, one day you'll truly feel thankful.

> **When your gratitude is greater than your pain, you'll be free. Healing then becomes inevitable and unstoppable!**
>
> **Your Personal Roadmap to Whole Body Cleansing,**
> By Barbara Brown, MSE and Dr. Tom Taylor, page 78.

I want to encourage you... that IT IS POSSIBLE to BECOME THANKFUL in all things. It takes time, an open mind and a determination to accept that what happens to you does not define you.

It is important, at this stage, to tell you that there is one unavoidable and fundamental step prior to this step in the *"Heart Soul and Spirit Cleanse"* shared above.

That is, Forgiveness.

I had, years past, already *forgiven* Blake. Truly. (I discuss more on how in the chapter on forgiveness.) So, regarding this specific event and the ability to forgive, I praise Yah {God} for the lessons that enabled me to break through this step. Thank You Father!

If I may humbly say, whatever your circumstance, whatever your "lessons or learnings in life" (from Yahweh {God}), IT IS POSSIBLE to forgive *and* to even become thankful.

> Maybe this is ONE REASON why Yahweh {God} allowed me to live through this... so that I could encourage you (from my own example) to BECOME THANKFUL.

> **Blessed is the God and Father of our Lord Jesus Christ, the Father of pities and God of all consolation, Who is consoling us in our every affliction to enable us to be consoling those in every affliction, through the consolation with which we ourselves are being consoled by God...**
>
> *2 Corinthians 1:3-4*

Around this time I met another wonderful couple, (whom I will call Deborah and Daniel), strong and steadfast in Yahweh {God}, creators of a non-profit organization, a non-religious group, (which I will call "Sold-Out-Seekers" here in this book, as they requested to be kept anonymous). They were true, sold-out seekers and followers of Yahweh {God} in more areas of life than I had ever known any person to be. I adored Deborah from the moment I met her. She was a *kindred spirit,* (you'll understand my application of that term if you have ever read the novel **Anne of Green Gables** by Lucy Maud Montgomery). Also her husband, Daniel, quickly became a "father in the faith" to me. His steadfast trust in (and reliance on) Yahweh {God} reminds me of Abraham's devoutness in the **Bible**.

Deborah always says: *"I would rather see a sermon than hear one."*

This is my "life sermon" to those on this path... Praise Yah {God}! Praise His Holy Name!

I often think of the life of Joseph as an encouragement that has helped me over the years. His trials and tribulations... (I encourage you to read the story if you do not know it, *Genesis chapters 37 and 39-50*).

What sticks out in my mind is what he said when he forgave his brothers. His kind and forgiving attitude, having realized that Yahweh {God} had a bigger purpose in mind when **He allowed** Joseph to be sold as a slave. Now, Yahweh {God} alone knows the purpose He has for *my* life… however, I have learned to also think and say:

You devised evil against me, yet Elohim, He devised it for good…

Genesis 50:20

As I have learned in life, His ways are not our ways:

For My designs are not your designs,
And your ways are not My ways, averring is Yahweh.
For as the heavens are loftier than the earth,
So are My ways loftier than your ways,
And My designs than your designs.

Isaiah 55:8-9

Other Scriptures I now find helpful and relevant include:

No trial has taken you except what is human. Now, faithful is God, Who will not be leaving you to be tried above what you are able, but, together with the trial, will be making the sequel (a way to escape, exit ~ *CLKC*) **also, to enable you to undergo it.**

1 Corinthians 10:13

I do admit, previously when I would read this Scripture I did not believe it. I now know that Yahweh {God} has a different view of "above what I am able" than I do. His is the truth, mine was my own definition of "the end of my rope," or sometimes my comfort zone. I am where I am today, writing what I am writing because of YAHWEH's {GOD's} definition, not mine, of this Scripture. Like ALL Scriptures, **"His word is truth."** *(John 17:17)*

"And you are clean, but not all." For He was aware who is giving Him up. Therefore He said that "Not all of you are clean."

…

These things saying, Jesus was disturbed in spirit, and testifies and said, "Verily, verily, I am saying to you that one of you will be giving Me up." The disciples, then, looked at one another, being perplexed concerning whom He is speaking.

John 13:10b-11 and 21-22

The other disciples had NO IDEA what Judas was about to do. Only Yeshua {Jesus} knew. And, Yeshua {Jesus}, in my opinion, knew all along… yet He treated all twelve the same. THAT IS LOVE. That is an attitude of surrender, on Yeshua's {Jesus'} part. What an example…

"For if you should be forgiving men their offenses, your heavenly Father also will be forgiving you. Yet if you should not be forgiving men their offenses, neither will your Father be forgiving your offenses."

Matthew 6:14-15

I would guess that you, dear reader, just like myself, are not perfect. So let us choose to forgive, so we may ourselves be forgiven. (Let he who has no sin, cast the first stone. *Read John 8:2-11)*

Honestly, I was not planning on sharing in such detail what happened to me (and this is a condensed story). I do not want any pity or attention, I got over the need for that through this process many years ago. I was simply going to share literally one sentence: I was raped at knifepoint. However, when I discovered these following reports, I was led to share what happened in more detail to show that any trauma, of whatever nature or degree, to either gender, is healable… and freedom awaits:

> … hundreds of thousands of men experience domestic violence each year…
>
> Data from the National Crime Victimization Study between 2003 and 2012 show that men account for about 24 percent of domestic violence survivors. Domestic violence against men is real and takes just as many forms as domestic violence against women—physical, sexual, reproductive, financial, emotional and psychological.
>
> Domestic violence—whether against women or men—often goes unreported. Men in particular may decide not to report violence by an intimate partner to law enforcement for fear of being labeled the instigator or not believed.
>
> DomesticShelters.org article *"Men Can Be Abused, Too"* (gathered on Nov 10, 2021) at: DomesticShelters.org/articles/statistics/men-can-be-abused-too

And also:

> Across their lifetime, 1 in 3 women, around 736 million, are subjected to physical or sexual violence by an intimate partner or sexual violence from a non-partner – a number that has remained largely unchanged over the past decade.

> This violence starts early: 1 in 4 young women (aged 15-24 years) who have been in a relationship will have already experienced violence by an intimate partner by the time they reach their mid-twenties.
>
> World Health Organization (WHO.int) *article* ***"Devastatingly pervasive: 1 in 3 women globally experience violence"*** (gathered on July 7, 2021) at: WHO.int/news/item/09-03-2021-devastatingly-pervasive-1-in-3-women-globally-experience-violence

My heart is to give any and all practical help, from my own life, of how to go from anger/hurt/fear to *gratitude,* **to live in freedom** and be a living Scripture today. Saying *"Yes"* to our Creator, trusting Him and His ways... EVEN WHEN it is not how we would have written the script of our life story.

I am very aware that there are many others who have been through even MORE HORRIFIC events than this and, even, with less or no family support. I pray for you, I pray sharing my story may give you confidence to share yours, and that you too may come to find gratitude in EVERYTHING in your life.

I pray you, dear reader, will stand on my shoulders, learn from both my failures and my fruition, my stumbling and my steadfastness, and hear and follow your own leading of the spirit of Yahweh {God}! Blessings beyond...

Whether you are male or female, if you have experienced any kind of abuse (verbal, emotional, physical... any kind and from anyone including gang members, father, mother, spouse, partner, children), a loss of a loved one, on the painful end of gossip, bullying... to literally anything about which you are unhappy or depressed or suffering pain:

Father, Yahweh {God} in Heaven,
I pray for healing in your heart, mind, soul, spirit and body. I pray He open your eyes to see the wisdom and possibility in His words, "become thankful."
I speak freedom and release from bonds of sins of others in this world. I speak peace into you, in every area of your life.
I pray He flow into you the spirit of my heart, and of the heart of Yahweh {God}... may the fruits of His spirit take root in you, and grow strong and deep in Him.
In Yeshua's {Jesus'} holy Name,
Amen.

Now the fruit of the spirit is love, joy, peace, patience, kindness, goodness, faithfulness, meekness, self-control...

Galatians 5:22-23

compassions
self-control
pitiful
meekness
kindness
righteousness
faithfulness
goodness
patience
joy
Love
peace
THE TRUTH
the Fruits of the Spirit
One Yahweh and Father of all,
Who is over all, through all and in all.
Galatians 5:22

Oh yes... and... that is not the ONLY thing in my life that I **learned to be grateful for.** Once filled with a "spirit of gratefulness" it becomes easier, including being thankful for typical everyday life occurrences. Here are a few other examples:

Thankful for all weather:

I am so grateful to Yahweh {God}, that as far back as I can remember (around age 7), I have always been happy with weather, whatever it was. 20-below in Minnesota winters, rain, thunderstorms, summer sun, you name it.

However, almost every person I have ever met in my life (save a handful) complain about the weather... constantly! If I may encourage you IF you ever are one to complain: BECOME thankful for it! If you do not like the weather where you live, then either choose to travel or work elsewhere in those seasons or move entirely. Stop complaining. Simple as that!

> For example: Amidst a snowstorm with friends... The van carrying three of us died in the middle of New England winter. Snow. Freezing cold temperatures. No engine. No heat. We all sang hymns of praise while waiting for help to come!

Thankful when making a wrong turn:

I am still working on this one. Not feeling guilty or beating myself up. I am BECOMING thankful for making a "wrong turn"! What if Yahweh {God} is saving me from who knows what if I had gone the other way? Or... what if I now get to take a "new route" and enjoy the scenery!

Thankful for hearing Yahweh {God}:

Grateful for Yahweh {God} bringing me to the end of myself, by way of every experience in my life. Yes, every experience. Thankful to finally seek and hear Him alone. What a journey... Easy? No. Worth it? Yes!

Thankful for positivity:

Writings and audios have helped me learn about positive thinking, positive speaking and more…

A few years ago I received an audio recording by Louise Hay titled, *"101 Power Thoughts."* Listening to this recording helps remind me to apply positive focus on all aspects of life, from other angry drivers to gratitude for my own feelings of joy and peace in the car, from frustration to peace, from stress to flowing feelings of life and love, as well as teaching me to move beyond medications and over-the-counter drugs!

Millions have learned to create more of what they want in their lives - more wellness in their bodies, minds and spirits through Louise Hay's healing techniques and positive philosophy. Her first book, **Heal Your Body**, was published in 1976, long before it was fashionable to discuss the connection between the mind and body.

Also…when someone is driving SLOWER than a turtle in front of me… Yahweh {God} may be saving me from, again, who knows what ahead. Or He could be simply encouraging me to, *"Slow down! Enjoy the scenery, Tamra! Enjoy the drive!"* Maybe Yahweh {God} is trying to tell me (via the vehicle in front of me on a thin impassable road) to slow down… **in LIFE!** Enjoy each and every sunrise… helping fellow faith keepers on their path… and ALL experiences in life, moment by moment!

Yeshua {Jesus} never RUSHED anywhere.

For everything there is a stated time,
And a season for every event under the heavens…

Ecclesiastes 3:1

Thankful for…:

Singing to my daughter (beginning at age 3 or 4), I would ask in song, *"And what are you thankful for…"* As a happy little girl, she would respond in song too! We would do this at home, in the car in the mornings on the way to school, ALL THE TIME! I wanted her to BE grateful always, as the **Bible** says:

> **Train up a youth in accordance with his proper way;**
> **Even when he is old he shall not withdraw from it.**
>
> *Proverbs 22:6*

Thank You Father!

Thankful when leaving:

I taught my daughter (at the age of 4) to be THANKFUL when we LEFT a park, instead of crying when it was time to leave.

Thankful for spilt milk:

My daughter's reaction to spilling milk on the table or floor pierced my heart. She seemed scared as if she would be yelled at, so I quickly learned to say, and truly mean it also, *"It is ok, darling. Now the floor (or the table) is ALL clean! Sparkling! Thank you!"*

Thankful for your location:

Similar to the weather discussion above… I have always been grateful for where I live. (I was taught at a young age NOT to complain!) So… if you do not like where you live, may I humbly suggest to BECOME thankful for it, or move! Live your dream!

<u>Thankful for your job or career:</u>

BECOME thankful for income! If you do not like it, either change your mind and START liking it, or change your job, or even your career choice.

> Contrary to "popular belief," changing jobs or careers is not as difficult as it seems, regardless of age. AND… it will be *more miserable* staying stuck, than breaking through the barrier of fear, and living through **change** to doing something you enjoy… and even LOVE! What would that look like compared to the continuous monotony of staying where you are, to counting down your last days wondering what could have been?

As an adult, I applied for weeks and weeks for accounting work (as I had a degree in accounting), and found nothing. I began working at the local supermarket, as I had bills to pay! I was joyous at work every day… looking through the eyes of gratitude! It did pay my bills, housed me and clothed me while carrying me forward to the next step.

<u>Thankful for health and strength:</u>

BECOME thankful for the healthy limbs, lungs, *life* that you DO have!

Previously, without a vehicle for six months, I walked or biked to the grocery store in storm, sleet or sunshine. I again SANG WITH GRATITUDE to Yahweh {God} that I had a bike and backpack… that I did not have to WALK (though perfectly healthy and able if I had to)!!!

<u>Thankful for the COVID-19 Pandemic (of 2020-2021):</u>

Regardless of how many millions around the world reacted to this… I decided to view it through positivity: it guided me to an even more quiet lifestyle in the country. After I stopped pouting about it, I decided to ENJOY IT! Even EMBRACE IT! And look what came of it… I have finally learned to LIVE in PEACE in my mind, body, soul and spirit, no matter the circumstances outside my control! I have finally learned to TRUST Yahweh {God}, even in the midst of my own lack of understanding.

I wrote this book (which I have been wanting to do for years…)! Such a WONDERFUL TIME in my life! What growth! What a blessing!

FIVE HELPFUL HABITS
That Led Me To Become Grateful

1 ~ Happiness Journal

I kept a "Happiness Journal" to help me focus my thoughts on the POSITIVES in my daily life!

2 ~ Throw out the Box

I stopped watching the News… in fact I turned OFF the television altogether.

- News is negative. Completely negative and full of fear.

  Bruce Lipton, Ph.D., a world renowned scientist, speaker, epigenetics specialist and best-selling author of **The Biology of Belief**, stated in an interview with Guy Lawrence:

> *What do you think about, watching the fear that is propagated every minute of the day on news stations, which are not news stations, they are now entertainment stations because they're selling ads... What is it all about? It is fear. The flu is coming. Well, it's not flu, it's called the COVID, is coming. It's gonna kill you. It's like, I'm a recipient at home. I just got fear. I go, Why is that relevant? Well, you just started to shut down the immune*

system. You are now opening yourself up for the fear to manifest itself.

And as long as you keep people in fear, you control them. Because fear shuts off the, "I'm open to the world," puts you into a spore and then says, "somebody else take care of this." And that's where we live.

Quote from a podcast with Bruce Lipton Ph.D. at:
BruceLipton.com/the-frontier-sciences-evidence-based-practises-principles-guiding-you-to-transform

- I actually placed a table cloth over the TV, to help me not even see it. Others thought I had lost my rocker… gone completely crazy. I did not care. I was a stay-at-home mom and this helped me stay positive and strong (and so I kept the television OFF).

Another book of Barbara Brown's includes a note which is written by a "redeemed" husband:

> **Cancel the newspaper, turn off the radio, and throw out the television.** My wife made it clear before we were married that she would not have a TV in the house (She hasn't had a television since the late 1980s), and I had to decide whether I loved her more than TV. It was a fast decision, which I've never regretted. We find that any print media or TV we happen to see when we're out is as brainless as ever; it's distracting and rarely leads anyone to Jesus.

GOD is GOD *and* We Are Not
by Barbara Brown, MSE, pages 189-190.

As the Psalm says:

> **I shall not set a worthless matter in front of my eyes…**
>
> *Psalm 101:3a*

The people in your life may not agree with this wisdom of turning off the media… maybe you need some different people in your life! People who DO agree with you!?!

3 ~ I Learned to NOT Gossip!

- I learned to speak less and less:

> **… <u>be ambitious to be quiet</u>, and to be engaged in your own affairs, and to be working with your hands…**
>
> *1 Thessalonians 4:11*

- I began speaking ONLY positively of others. And… gossiping takes TWO people, the speaker and the listener. It was hard, but I learned to say: *"Let's not gossip,"* or *"I do not want to hear about that person without them being here, thank you."*

4 ~ Complement NOT Criticize

I would look for things in others to complement them on… instead of picking out what I did NOT like about them.

- Example: I stopped people watching. When I do see others, I notice one thing that I do LIKE about them, (instead of listing all the things *"I would never do that," "I would never wear that"* or *"I would never do my hair like that,"* etc.)

5 ~ You are WHO you are WITH

- It is a known fact that: You become like whom you are around the most. Ask yourself, how are you being influenced? If you sense a gut feeling about it, that's your spirit talking.

> **…Are you not aware that a little leaven is leavening the whole kneading?**
>
> *I Corinthians 5:6*

- So… choose *wisely* who you spend time with. (And YES, this even includes family members.) You will hear all about how I weeded some out myself. However difficult your situation, however traumatic your experience, you are in charge. You are in charge of your life, your ears and your mouth! Weed wisely!

When you LOOK for things to "put down" (so you feel better about yourself)… you WILL find them.

WHEN you LOOK for things to be grateful for… you WILL find them.

Energy flows where thought goes!

And, you will truly feel better living in the positive, even if it is often just in your mind. That is where it must start to form. Dr. Tom Taylor (international speaker, author, bio-energetic expert, and creator of *"It's All About Energy,"* a free resource on learning how to make your body work for you... just to list a few of his credentials in addition to **Light Up the Scriptures**), teaches the most effective secret sentence starter that completely OPENS up your mind, bypassing any unbelief in your conscious or your subconscious, followed by an open-ended question to unlock the believability of the more positive perspective.

This secret sentence starter can be used, literally, to break through **every** obstruction:

"What if..." and following that up with, *"What would that look like?"*

For example:

> *"What if... I was in a career I loved, what would that look like?"*
>
> *"What if... the people around me respect my beliefs and don't try to change me? What would that look like?"*
>
> *"What if... I stopped wasting time on gossip, what would that look like?"*
>
> *"What if... I stopped watching TV, news, adverts, the media, what could I do with all my time now, in a more positive state? What would that look like?"*
>
> *"What if... I have faith for Yahweh {God} to show me His way, what would that look like?"*

You do not have to find the answers... simply ask the question, *"What if..."* Your mind and body WILL find the answers for you, some immediately, some in their own good time... your energy will seek them out! Your energy will change. Your *life* WILL change!

For the rest, brethren, whatever is true, whatever is grave, whatever is just, whatever is pure, whatever is agreeable, whatever is renowned -- if there is any virtue, and if any applause, be taking these into account (think of these things).

Philippians 4:8

I shall acclaim You, O Yahweh, with all my heart;
I shall indeed recount all Your marvelous works.
I shall greatly rejoice and be glad in You;
I shall surely make melody to Your Name, O Supreme.
…
Make melody to Yahweh, the One dwelling in Zion…

Psalm 9:1-2 and 11

Chapter 2

LEAVE THE DEAD CHURCH... TO FIND YAHWEH!

(Pssst... He is inside you!)

And, approaching, one scribe said to Him, "Teacher, I will be following Thee wheresoever Thou mayest come away."

And Jesus is saying to him, "The jackals have burrows, and the flying creatures of heaven roosts, yet the Son of Mankind has no where that He may be reclining His head."

Now a different one of the disciples said to Him, "Lord, permit me first to come away and entomb my father." Yet Jesus is saying to him, "Be following Me, and leave the dead to entomb their own dead."

Matthew 8:19-22

For years I had been attending on-and-off a (what I now call) "big box church." At the time it was the most "sold out" group of people I had encountered, utterly devoted to truly living EVERY DAY for Yahweh {God}. (Not the, *just go to church on Sundays, get your "hand stamped" and then back to everyday life of sin for the rest of the week* kind of people.) It was incredibly organized, I must say. There were Wednesday night and Sunday morning meetings of the whole church, with an elaborate (and brilliant) children's ministry also. Small groups were created consisting of those who were in similar life situations as yourself, to relate to. A "discipler" was appointed for every person, someone "older in the faith" to help train you, and to whom you would confess your sins, etc.

I loved Yahweh {God}. I loved worshiping Him, singing songs, praying. I had for most of my life... taught from a young age, actually hearing sermons from the womb! Thank You Father in Heaven!

Did I always reflect the childlike innocence of the faith? Oh no. Sadly, I strayed from Yahweh {God}, very far, for about two years, when I was in college in the same metropolitan city (back in 1997). Now I am truly grateful for life in the grace of Yahweh {God} because, if I had lived in the

Old Testament times, I would have been killed for my sins. One night I had a dream of a candle burning while all around it was black darkness, a thick darkness you could feel. And the wick was dreadfully close to the end, almost completely burned out.

> **Indeed El does speak once,**
> **And twice, yet no one regards it,**
> **In a dream, a vision of the night,**
> **When stupor falls upon men,**
> **In slumberings on their bed;**
> **Then He reveals matters to the ear of men,**
> **And He dismays them with admonitions,**
> **To withdraw a human from his deed,**
> **And that He may obliterate pride in a master.**
> **He keeps back his soul from the pit**
> **And his life from passing into the unseen.**
>
> *Job 33:14-18*

When I awoke I KNEW it was a dream from Yahweh {God}, telling me that, spiritually, He was about to COMPLETELY leave me because of my actions. The already flickering light to His path was about to go out. I was PETRIFIED. I did NOT want Him to leave me COMPLETELY. I KNEW what that meant:

> **…because, knowing God, not as God do they glorify or thank Him, but vain were they made in their reasonings, and darkened is their unintelligent heart.**
>
> *Romans 1:21*

So, I repented. I changed my ways. PRAISE YOU LORD! THANK YOU YAHWEH {GOD} for Your patience, mercy and love.

> **…if we are disbelieving, He is remaining faithful -- He cannot disown Himself.**
>
> *2 Timothy 2:13*

> **He shall not contend permanently,**
> **And He shall not hold resentment for the eon.**
> **He has neither done to us according to our sins,**
> **Nor has He requited on us according to our depravities.**
> **For as the heavens are lofty over the earth,**
> **So is His benignity** (mercifulness, kindness and
> bountifulness ~ *CLKC*) **masterful over those fearing Him.**
> **As far as the east is from the west,**
> **So He removes our transgressions far from us.**
> **As a father shows compassion over his sons,**
> **So Yahweh shows compassion over those fearing Him.**
> **For He knows our formation,**
> **Remembering that we are soil.**
>
> *Psalm 103:9-14*

Months later, I met a man whom I dated and, later, married (I will refer to him as Red). I later went back to that same church, which at the time is where I believed the true Yahweh {God} was worshipped. (Most of Red's family actually were very involved, and even a few being elders, in the "sister Spanish church" to where I attended.) Red eventually joined the church also.

Influenced by the "*American Dream* box," I prayed to Yahweh {God} for a child... I prayed for five long years, begging for a child. Yahweh {God} finally granted me a daughter, a precious little angel! Red and I decided to live on only one income, (his), so I could stay at home and raise my little girl myself.

A few years went by, and I continued becoming more and more unhappy. Life followed its habitual course... part of me thought, *"This is life, deal with it."* Though deep down I knew there HAD TO BE MORE.

When my daughter was 3-years-old, one Sunday morning while attending this "big box church," singing praises to Yahweh {God}, I was sitting near the back looking over the sea of familiar heads. I heard Yahweh {God} speak.

> If you are not accustomed to hearing about modern day "hearing Yahweh {God} speak," you are not alone. I was not aware of this phenomenon. I was possibly JUST as surprised as you! I was taught in the Lutheran Church, from birth to age 15, that Yahweh {God} **no longer** speaks to people!

Now, He did not speak out loud. Others around me did not hear it. He spoke into my mind, into my spirit.

He said: ***"Everyone here is dead."***

I was saddened at the realization of the lifeless hearts of EVERYONE in that gathering.

Deep in my spirit it resonated with me. I KNEW it was true.

It sent my mind into a SPIN. I felt LOST. *"So, where do I go? What do I do? HOW DO I WORSHIP YOU then, Father?"*

The following week, on Resurrection Sunday (Easter) in 2010, at sunrise, I drove to the ocean (about a twenty minute drive) and sought Yahweh {God} there. All alone. Worshipping. I had begun my own "church" (though I did not realize it at the time).

I felt uncomfortable by myself, away from "a gathering." It felt wrong. I was SO confused. This was going against EVERYTHING I HAD BEEN TAUGHT *in religion*. The Scripture came to me:

> **And we may be considering one another to incite to love and ideal acts, not forsaking the assembling of ourselves, according as the custom of some is, but entreating, and so much rather as you are observing the day drawing near.**
>
> *Hebrews 10:24-25*

Scriptures that come to mind today, that I believe would have helped me that day include…

> **And, approaching, one scribe said to Him, "Teacher, I will be following Thee wheresoever Thou mayest come away."**
>
> **And Jesus is saying to him, "The jackals have burrows, and the flying creatures of heaven roosts, yet the Son of Mankind has no where that He may be reclining His head."**
>
> **Now a different one of the disciples said to Him, "Lord, permit me first to come away and entomb my father." Yet Jesus is saying to him, "Be following Me, and leave the dead to entomb their own dead."**
>
> *Matthew 8:19-22*

Do not be mindful of the former things,
And do not consider those preceding.
Behold, I am doing a new thing; Now it is sprouting;
Do you not know it?
Indeed, I am placing a way in the wilderness,
Tracks in the desolation.
The animals of the field shall glorify Me,
Wild jackals and ostriches;
For I provide water in the wilderness,
Streams in the desolation;
To give drink to My people, My chosen.
This people I have formed for Myself,
And they shall recount My praise.

Isaiah 43:18-21

... and now I pray these will help you, dear reader, if you desire a deeper connection with Yahweh {God}, and you question rules and regulations of religion that may be "boxing" you in.

Today, writing this, I now compare most "big box churches" to the Pharisees in Yeshua's {Jesus'} day, when He walked on earth. Yeshua {Jesus} was constantly rebuking the Pharisees for many things, including: making others obey rules, rules that they were not keeping themselves...

All, then, whatever they should be saying to you, do and keep it. Yet according to their acts do not be doing, for they are saying and not doing.

Matthew 23:3

...caring about pomp and stature (when, in stark contrast, Yeshua {Jesus} cared only about the heart):

> **"But woe to you, Pharisees! for you are taking tithes from mint and rue and all greens, and you are passing by judging and the love of God. Now these it was binding for you to do and not to be devoid of those. Woe to you, Pharisees! seeing that you are loving the front seat in the synagogues and the salutations in the markets."**
>
> *Luke 11:42-43*

...focusing on the law, while neglecting the matters of the heart:

> **"Stiff-necked and uncircumcised in your hearts and ears, you are ever clashing with the holy spirit! As your fathers, you also! Which of the prophets do not your fathers persecute? And they kill those who announce before concerning the coming of the Just One, of Whom now you became the traitors and murderers -- who got the law for a mandate of messengers and do not maintain it!"**
>
> *Acts 7:51-53*

(Read also Matthew 15:7-12 and Matthew 23:23-39.)

In the "big box church" I had attended, everyone was pressured to "share their faith." Literally. *ALL the time.* And to bring as many people (or visitors) to church as possible. I heard many stories about small group leaders being REBUKED by the church leaders when their "numbers" were too low! There was an article in the paper (of the state's capital city) that this very church was a CULT! The entire church service was more for "entertainment" than for the true worship of Yahweh {God}, completely contrary to the Scripture:

> **"But coming is the hour, and now is, when the true worshipers will be worshiping the Father in spirit and truth, for the Father also is seeking such to be worshiping Him. God is spirit, and those who are worshiping Him must be worshiping in spirit and truth."**
>
> *John 4:23-24*

In his **Light Up the Scriptures** study titled *"104 - Don't look behind when God is re-determining your life,"* Dr. Tom Taylor reads from **Luke** and then makes a point regarding *the dead*:

> **Luke 9:57-62**
>
> **And at their going in the road, someone said to Him, "I will be following Thee wheresoever Thou mayest be coming away, Lord!" And Jesus said to him, "The jackals have burrows and the flying creatures of heaven roosts, yet the Son of Mankind has no where that He may be reclining His head."**
>
> **Now He said to a different one, "Follow Me!" Yet he said, "Lord, permit me first to come away to entomb my father." Yet He said to him, "Let the dead entomb their own dead. Yet you, coming away, publish the kingdom of God."**
>
> **Now a different one also said, "I shall be following Thee, Lord! Yet first permit me to take leave of those in my home." Yet Jesus said to him, "No one, putting forth his hand on a plow and looking behind, is fit in the kingdom of God."**
>
> …

As far as the Lord is concerned, people not following after Him are dead. Literally, all human beings are dying from the moment of conception; and figuratively, all human beings are dead spiritually if He isn't their source of life, despite what some may think who are busy right now meditating or worshiping some other god.

Light Up the Scriptures study "*104 - Don't look behind when God is re-determining your life,*" by Dr. Tom Taylor. (Time: 1:49 – 2:53 and 4:35 - 5:00)

May I encourage you to listen to this entire study, which you will find together with all 183 Scripture study recordings at LightUpTheScriptures.com. (This is also listed in the resources section at the end of the book as well as on my website.)

Sat on the rocks above the ocean, gazing at the waves, each crashing over another, like my tears, I just sat there. Lost. Convinced in my *mind* that I was doing the wrong thing.

YET, deep in my ***spirit***, I KNEW what Yahweh {God} had spoken was true!

Now (today) I know that my spirit was then warring with my mind and the spirit of religion INSIDE me. At the time, I had no idea this was what was happening.

For the disposition of the flesh is death, yet the disposition of the spirit is life and peace...

Romans 8:6

For I am gratified with the law of God as to the man within, yet I am observing a different law in my members, warring with the law of my mind, and leading me into captivity to the law of sin which is in my members.

A wretched man am I! What will rescue me out of this body of death? Grace! I thank God, through Jesus Christ, our Lord. Consequently, then, I myself, with the mind, indeed, am slaving for God's law, yet with the flesh for Sin's law.

Romans 7:22-25

For the flesh is lusting against the spirit, yet the spirit against the flesh. Now these are opposing one another...

Galatians 5:17

Yeshua {Jesus} did not belong to a church, He did not even endorse "church." And these Scriptures also came to my mind:

"… lo! the kingdom of God is inside of you."

Luke 17:21

And He taught and said to them, "Is it not written that 'My house a house of prayer shall be called, for all nations'? Yet you make it a burglars' cave."

Mark 11:17

And, passing along, He [Jesus] perceived a man, blind from birth. ...

Jesus hears that they cast him out (of the church), and, finding him, said to him, "Are you believing in the Son of Mankind?"

He answered and said, "And Who is He, Lord, that I should be believing in Him?"

Now Jesus said to him, "You have also seen Him, and He Who is speaking with you is He."

Now he averred, "I am believing, Lord!" And he worships Him.

And Jesus said, "For judgment came I into this world, that those who are not observing may be observing, and those observing may be becoming blind." And those of the Pharisees who are with Him hear these things, and they said to Him, "Not we also are blind?" Jesus said to them, "If you were blind, you would have had no sin. Yet now you are saying that 'We are observing.' Your sin, then, is remaining."

John 9:1 and 35-41

As I said, Yeshua {Jesus} was often rebuking the Pharisees and religious leaders of His day, as they were missing the point, focusing on the law and not looking at the heart. Yet Yahweh {God}... He looks at the heart:

... You must not look at his appearance and at the loftiness of his stature, for I have rejected him. For not as a human sees, does the One, Elohim, see. A human sees the visible appearance, yet Yahweh sees into the heart...

1 Samuel 16:7

I was encouraged by Deborah to read the book **The Shack.** Oh… what an incredibly moving book, and what revelations opened up to me! (Though a few of the chapters I could barely read through, entailing the graphic details of the main character's life.) However, my eyes were opened to how loving and kind Yahweh {God} is… **as loving and kind as a sweet southern grandma!** In stark contrast to the "wrathful condemner" character that I had been taught about. So, in this book, Mack, the main character, is struggling to come to terms with an unimaginably horrific event in his life. He is learning who Yahweh {God} *really* is… compared to the lies he had previously learned in religion (emphasis mine):

> Mack: "I really do want to understand. I mean, I find You so different from all the well-intentioned religious stuff I'm familiar with."
>
> Jesus: "As well-intentioned it might be, you know that religious machinery can chew up people!" Jesus said with a bite of his own. "An awful lot of what is done in My name has nothing to do with me and is often, even if unintentional, very contrary to My purposes."
>
> Mack: "You're not too fond of religion and institutions?" Mack said, not sure if he was asking a question or making an observation.
>
> Jesus: "I don't create institutions - never have, never will."
> …
>
> Jesus: "I don't create institutions; that's an occupation for those who want to play God. So no, I'm not too big on religion, and not very fond of politics or economics either… And why should I be? They are the man-created trinity of errors that ravages the earth and deceived those I care about. What mental turmoil and anxiety does any human face that is not related to one of those three?"
> …

Jesus: "Put simply, these terrors are tools that many use to prop up their illusions of security and control. People are afraid of uncertainty, afraid of the future. These institutions, these structures and ideologies, are full of vain effort to create some sense of certainty when there isn't any. It's all false! Systems cannot provide you with security, only I can."

(The holy spirit): "Religion must use law to empower itself and control the people needed in order to survive."

The Shack by William P. Young,
Kindle pages 215-216 and 247 of 351.

I went home from the beach that morning... still lost, pondering on all the Scriptures and barely keeping up with the thoughts racing through my mind.

I did NOT share what Yahweh {God} had spoken to me with ANYONE until I started "broaching the subject" with Red, but being steeped in religion, with so many friends in that church, he thought I was crazy. Nevertheless, I told Red that I was no longer going to attend that church. He continued attending that same church, in and about which Yahweh {God} spoke to me.

The marriage was a wreck even prior to this. *(I will be the first to admit I was not perfect, not even close.)* Back then, aside my other faults I did not have a "gentle and quiet spirit" *(read 1 Peter 3:2-4)*. I will not write a list of all of Red's faults. I am not writing this to seek vengeance. The sin lists, for all mankind, all humans, are quite clear in *1 Thessalonians 4:3-5, Galatians 5:19-21, Mark 7:20-23, Proverbs 4:24-25, Colossians 3:5-6, Exodus 20:1-17, 1 John 1:7-9 and James 4:17 (to list but a few)* and there are more... However, for you, the reader, IF you are stuck in an untenable, miserable marriage as I was, I encourage you, IF the reason it is miserable is because your heart is to follow Yeshua {Jesus} more closely, more radically, and your spouse is not so led, THEN press on! Go! Follow Yeshua {Jesus}. Walk on… follow the spirit in you.

A few things I will say for you to understand my situation a little… Red was a very charming man (on the outside), unfortunately not just with me. He also spent almost all of his "free time" playing soccer with his brothers and friends, watching television and movies, and playing Nintendo. His culture was to not spend much time with "the spouse," nor help raise children *at all*, (that was the woman's job). I would beg him to watch my daughter for even half-an-hour a week so I could go enjoy a cup of coffee with a girlfriend, (parents out there will understand what I mean). He refused.

Leaders in the church would meet with Red and myself attempting to "help the marriage," and they would strongly quote and requote the same piece of *one* Scripture:

Let the wives be subject to their own husbands...

Ephesians 5:22

Period. Almost as if to say, literally: End of discussion.

I could NOT SPEAK NOR ASK, not dare even challenge this because it was so engrained in me, the broken record playing in my mind, *"Tamra be quiet, it does not matter what you think or say, it is wrong."* And that, *"wives are to SUBMIT."* But still I would wonder, *"What about him? Does he not have to change his ways too? Is it ONLY me? What about the VERY NEXT few verses of that SAME chapter in Ephesians that declares,"* (emphasis mine):

Let the wives be subject to their own husbands, as to the Lord, for the husband is head of the wife even as Christ is Head of the ecclesia, and He is the Saviour of the body. Nevertheless, as the ecclesia is subject to Christ, thus are the wives also to their husbands in everything.

Husbands, be loving your wives according as Christ also loves the ecclesia, and gives Himself up for its sake, that He should be hallowing it, cleansing it in the bath of the water (with His declaration), that He should be presenting to Himself a glorious ecclesia, not having spot or wrinkle or any such things, but that it may be holy and flawless. Thus, the husbands also ought to be loving their own wives as their own bodies. He who is loving his own wife is loving himself.

Ephesians 5:22-28

When you read the entire Scripture above (as opposed to only the piece of verse 22 regarding the wife being subject, which is taught and quoted in Christianity, as you yourself may well know), you see an example of where the Scriptures have been misinterpreted, misunderstood and misapplied. This is where the word of the truth needs to be correctly cut, WHEN the husband is loving the wife AS Christ {the Messiah} loved the church... (example: Christ {the Messiah} DIED for the church, gave up His own life, so... the husband must give up his own life for his wife) THEN the wife must be subject to the husband. **Then and ONLY then** the wife must be subject to the husband.

What does that look like? What does "the husband must give up his own life for his wife" look like in real life? Now that is a thought to ponder (especially if you have ever been a part of "organized religion" or, as I call it, "big box religion").

I later learned much more about what the **Bible** TRULY TEACHES regarding marriage, again from Dr. Tom Taylor's "**correctly cutting the word of truth" Bible** study series **Light Up the Scriptures**, in the study titled "50 - *Christ Sets the Standard.*" He states (emphasis mine):

> *Now, notice the relationship of the wife to the husband is defined AS TO the Lord. And it is further defined, in verse 24 [of Ephesians 5], in comparison with the ecclesia, as it is subject to Christ. THUS are the wives also subject to… The standard set here, again, is Christ.* ***If that standard is not being met, all bets are off and we are in deep trouble.*** *This is NOT a license for men to put their wives into bondage, some kind of bondage of submission. ON THE CONTRARY,* ***Paul is about to lay out the highest standard for husbands to come up to… they better be rightly and completely subject to Christ IF they expect right order in their relationships to their wives!*** *It is all well and good to expect wives to be subject to their husbands, and for husbands to be the heads of their wives. BUT… as I said earlier, we must be living according to the standard of Christ Himself IN HIS RELATIONSHIP to His ecclesia. And, lest we forget, in the fear of Christ, which is up above in this chapter.*
>
> *Verse 25 [of Ephesians 5], this is the one to me that just… lowers the boom here.* ***This is a direct instruction to husbands.*** *Once again the standard is Christ, loving the ecclesia to the point of giving Himself up for it!* ***SO, HUSBANDS, are we loving our wives like that? Like it or not, if THAT standard is not being met, we have nothing to say about dis-harmony, or strife in our marriage.*** *In fact, I believe, this is me talking, that failing to live by this standard is what WILL produce dis-harmony and strife.*
>
> **Light Up the Scriptures** study "50 - *Christ Sets the Standard*"
> by Dr. Tom Taylor. (Time: 37:04 - 38:55)

May I encourage you, dear reader, to listen to this entire study, as well as his other studies speaking on what Yahweh {God} truly directs about marriage and divorce. You will find all of these at LightUpTheScriptures.com:

"*49 - Neither Male nor Female*"
"*50 - Christ Sets the Standard*"
"*60 - Blood and flesh, Fight the Right Giants*"
"*63 - Marriage and Divorce*"
"*115 - What God Joins, We Must Protect*"

Barbara Brown includes two fantastic chapters in her book, *"Chapter 17 – Holiness Will Prevail"* and *"Chapter 18 – Marriage… Battleground or Blessings?"* I encourage you to read them! Here she boils down the Scripture discussed above as follows:

Wives are instructed to ***"be subject,"*** but being subject doesn't mean being a doormat. The scripture assumes that husbands are already acting toward the wives with ***"love"*** and ***"honor."***

GOD *is* GOD *and* We Are Not
by Barbara Brown, MSE, page 187.

On that Resurrection Sunday (Easter), that very afternoon that I stopped attending the "big box church," I received a call from the Ministry Leader's wife. The wife of the leader of the entire church called *me*! This was a first. And of course, I knew why. I was TERRIFIED inside… however I somehow found the guts to tell her that I had left the church. She replied to me, *"You know you are going to hell, since you have decided to stop going to church, this church, don't you?"* I stood strong, held my ground and graciously ended the call.

I stopped answering my phone. I knew others would call. And they did.

Persecution led to more intense fear. I felt lost. I was so confused. My spirit KNEW that I was walking the right path… however, this is one of the FIRST TIMES that I had ever LISTENED to and OBEYED my spirit.

I knew very little about the spirit.

As I write today remembering this, my legs are tense and my muscles are tightening... oh that I knew THEN what I know NOW about bioenergetics, about religion… (Pointless thought, yes, I know. I describe more about bioenergetics in the next chapter.) Well! Praise YAHWEH {GOD} for all He has revealed to me throughout this journey! Bless His Holy Name!

In these last few months I see myself as if I am walking in a wheat field… No set path. And I do NOT KNOW THE WAY!!! Ahhhhh!! Now, today, I am more calm about it (compared to back in 2010), though there are times when I can still feel a little unnerved. I thought there was a PATH to life! THE PATH to Yahweh {God}. ONE PATH. The SAME path for all His children. An encouraging word was spoken to me the other day when I shared this vision, "Good! I am glad you do not know the way. That means Yahweh {God} is guiding. This is how He guides."

Yahweh said to Abram: <u>Go by yourself from your land</u>, from your kindred and from your father's house <u>to the land</u> <u>that I shall show you</u>.

Genesis 12:1

Interesting… I had closed the door to the false, and now the next step on my way to the truth opened. When Yahweh {God} closes a door (or when He guides you to close a door), He *always* opens another!

Chapter 3

LEAVE THE DOCTOR'S OFFICE! GO FIND TRUE HEALING!

Yahweh created us perfectly!

And Elohim said: Since I have given you all seed-yielding herbage that is on the face of the entire earth, and every tree on which there is the fruit of a seed-yielding tree, it shall be yours for food.

Genesis 1:29

To have described life as miserable, in the last chapter, is a bit of an understatement.

I am not sure words can adequately describe the crippling fear, the anxiety attacks, the depression, the excruciating migraine head-aches, the insufferable back pains, (due to a depleted disk in my sacrum), and more. Maybe you have experienced some of these too.

Growing up, I was led to understand that doctors were practically gods, meaning: They KNEW everything, and they were NOT to be questioned. (Though, *laughing inside as I write this*, in my house you really ONLY went to the doctor if your condition was so SERIOUS you were *"almost dead."*) I had adopted my family's lower-middle class American view, that you were not to bother "important" doctors with trifles, nor were you to bother parents with the excessive time wasting and bills (as it took TIME to wait what seems like "forever" in doctors' offices, even WITH an appointment, and of course, it costs MONEY)!

Jumping ahead... to when I was 29-years-young and pregnant with my daughter, in 2006 through to May 2007. My best friend in the whole world, Tina, was also a *kindred spirit*. I had met Tina in the "big box church" over seven years prior. (We remained close friends... even after my leaving the church.) Tina opened my eyes to some shocking truths in "the medical model" world. She was my guide, though she would not have wanted me to call her that. She always encouraged me to carry out my own due diligence. She was VERY INSISTENT and CAREFUL to tell me often, *"This is how I do things, but it does not mean you have to do it this way.*" She had done extensive research on health and wellness versus what "the medical model" provides and prescribes; she had dug deep into many books, and fine tooth-combed *both scientific and medical* papers and journals. I sifted through her books, some of which I then read, and subsequently we would discuss. I began learning (or shall I say "wise'ning up to") the TRUTH about doctors and "the medical model."

Medical Model Myths

These are some of the myths I had previously learned and believed, (fell for hook, line and sinker), and subsequently the truths I have since learned that bust them. Buckle up and hang on, you might be in for some belief busting too…

MYTH 1 ~ Placebos Can't Do What Drugs Do!

I learned at an early age about placebos… A sugar pill with the "ability" to cure THE SAME as drugs! Amazing!

However… I also remember the casual way in which placebos were spoken about in News Papers, on the News, and taught of in Science classes. "Not that big of a deal." WHAT!?!

Don't just take my word for it … Bruce Lipton Ph.D., (as I previously shared), is a world-renowned scientist (including pioneering stem cell research in 1967), speaker, epigenetics specialist and author of his best-selling book **The Biology of Belief**, which amongst many things shares proven findings on the placebo pill, nature and nurture, mind and matter, and science and spirituality. He writes in his book, (emphasis mine):

> Every medical student learns, at least in passing that the mind can affect the body… The placebo effect is quickly glossed over in

> medical schools so that students can get to the real tools of modern medicine and surgery. This is a giant mistake.
>
> **If the power of your mind can heal your sick body, why should you go to the doctor and, more importantly, why would you need to buy drugs?** In fact, I was recently chagrined to learn that drug companies are studying patients who respond to sugar pills [the placebo] with the goal of eliminating them from early clinical trials. It inevitably disturbs pharmaceutical manufacturers that **in most of their clinical trials the placebos, the "fake" drugs, prove to be as effective as their engineered chemical cocktails.** (Greenberg 2003)
>
> The Biology of Belief, Unleashing the Power of Consciousness, Matter & Miracles (10th Anniversary Edition) by Bruce Lipton, Ph.D., Kindle page 247-248 and 249 of 533.

He also shared in his interview (emphasis mine):

> *And we have to wake up now. And the wake up is this:* ***"I want to be healthy!" Yeah but that hasn't been a mission.*** *When you go to the doctor, he doesn't say, "Listen, before I give you the pill, I want you to do all these exercise things and eat this way and I want you to stay healthy and THEN I'll give you the pill." No, no, no. "Here's the pill... and maybe you should take care of yourself."*
>
> *What do you mean? Firstly, take care of yourself, take a pill LATER. And the reality is, that is not the mission statement. A doctor doesn't really emphasize... "If I give you a prescription for the pill, I want you to follow this prescription to get healthy. I can't help you if you're not healthy. And the pills not going to help you either."* ***And yet the idea, are they selling health first? No. First they are selling the pill, then health will come later. I go, "Backwards. Totally backwards." We have to take care of ourselves: eat healthy, eat organic, do***

exercises, move... you gotta use this machine, use it or lose it! It applies to EVERY part of our human body, from mind to toes, use it or lose it. And we're not being encouraged with the idea of this. We're not in harmony. We're not in health.

Quote from a podcast with Bruce Lipton Ph.D. at
BruceLipton.com/the-frontier-sciences-evidence-based-practises-principles-guiding-you-to-transform

Yeshua {Jesus} Himself said:

"...the truth will be making you free."

John 8:32

I was **shocked**, even in **disbelief** for a time, *(and deeply saddened)* to **learn** that medical universities focus PRIMARILY on drugs for cures!

Which led into busting the next myth I had believed...

MYTH 2 ~ Doctor's Teach (and Prescribe) Health!

Do you know who funds medical universities? DRUG COMPANIES! In many cases, unbeknownst to them in their passion to save lives, doctors are barely taught about wellness: sleep, food intake, stress, etc.; they are taught that drugs are the solution to anything and everything. PERIOD.

Again, Bruce Lipton Ph.D. stated in an interview (emphasis mine):

So, the medical industry is led by this pharmaceutical industry, which has got its hands in the FDA (which is the Federal Drug

Administration in the United States). It is still run by these pharmaceuticals. ***The medical schools teach by funding, and funding comes from big organizations like the pharmaceutical industry, so you teach what is in their interest.***

So, medical schools do not fully go into this new area of healing and ***all*** *that is, fundamentally, the direction we need. Why? Corporate interest.*

Quote from a podcast with Bruce Lipton Ph.D. at:
BruceLipton.com/the-frontier-sciences-evidence-based-practises-principles-guiding-you-to-transform

It took me YEARS to see the truth in this… I had been so brainwashed into "normal society" by watching television, seeing hundreds and thousands of adverts on *"this drug will cure your ________"* and *"if you are feeling this, take this new drug __________!"*

I do know a doctor whom Yahweh {God} placed in my path, Praise Yahweh {God}, who had recently begun learning about the UTMOST IMPORTANCE of health, food intake, etc. and had already decided to STOP EXCLUSIVELY SELLING (or prescribing) DRUGS! *What a miracle!*

It reminds me of the **Old Testament Bible** account of the precise MOMENT when Gehazi was recalling to the king the miracles of Elisha, and during the telling of the story of a widow's son whom Elisha had revived from the dead, this very woman and her son WALKED IN TO see the king! (As Deborah says, *"God is into the details!"*)

Now the king was speaking to Gehazi the lad of the man of Elohim, saying, Oh do recount to me all the great things that Elisha has done. And it came to pass <u>while he was recounting to</u>

> **the king how he had revived the dead, that, behold, the woman whose son Elisha had revived was crying out to the king for her house and for her fields. Now Gehazi said, My lord the king, this is the woman, and this is her son whom Elisha revived.**
>
> *2 Kings 8:4-5*

(Read the whole account in 2 Kings 8:1-6.)

Yahweh {God} lines ALL THINGS UP, according to HIS purpose.

> **Now we are aware that God is working all together for the good of those who are loving God...**
>
> *Romans 8:28*

I am so grateful for learning the truth about the "ONLY drugs cure" myth (or lie), and the in-humane effect drugs have on our bodies. While they DO WORK as a band-aid for a pain or symptom of dis-ease... they do NOT seek to find the REASON of the dis-ease in the first place.

Couple this with the incredible power of our minds (which is how Yahweh {God} created us), and our own natural ability to heal ourselves, proven by the *placebo effect*! Mind over matter. I personally know full well how the mind can, and does, affect the body.

When I was already a week overdue (soon to birth my baby girl), my contractions finally began Sunday evening around 2 or 3 pm. I told Red. He had a singing gig an hour's drive away and was about to leave. I was petrified and on asking him for his reconsideration, he simply said, "*I have to go sing.*" He left. I was completely mortified of being alone and unable to drive myself to the Birth Center. (I was HUGE, overdue, and way beyond miserable.) Now terror-stricken, fear clamped down on my entire body. The stress, panic, and monumental fear STOPPED the contractions for hours... My body's launch into survival mode changed the priority of its functions, including a very overdue birth. Around 11 pm the contractions began again... I called Red and begged him to come to the house. He did. Though he was over a one-hour drive away. (Ugh.) This relaxed me... a little.

I gave birth in a Birth Center (not in a hospital) with NO assistance from drugs. None. No epidural. Nothing. I would not submit to drugs. I could not because I knew that any drugs given to me WOULD AFFECT my baby. I was prepared to bear the pain, whatever it took, to give her a most healthy and happy body and life, from her very first breath (and before). Which brings us to...

MYTH 3 ~ Epidurals DON'T Affect The Baby!

Chris Kresser, M.S., L.Ac., is a renowned expert, leading clinician, and top educator in the fields of Functional Medicine and ancestral health, as well as the New York Times bestselling author of **The Paleo Cure**. He wrote the article *"Natural Childbirth V: Epidural Side Effects and Risks,"* and in the section titled "*Epidural also have side effects for babies*" he states the following:

> It's important to understand that drugs administered by epidural enter the baby's bloodstream at **equal and sometimes even higher levels** than those present in the mother's bloodstream.
>
> Some studies have found **deficits in newborn abilities** that are consistent with the known toxicity of drugs used in epidurals.

> Other studies have found that local anesthetics used in epidurals may **adversely effect the newborn immune system**, possibly by activating the stress response.
>
> There is evidence that epidurals can **compromise fetal blood and oxygen supply**, probably via the **decrease in maternal blood pressure** that epidurals are known to cause.
>
> *"Natural Childbirth V: Epidural Side Effects and Risk"*
> by Chris Kresser, M.S., L.Ac. (gathered on June 9 2021) at:
> ChrisKresser.com/natural-childbirth-v-epidural-side-effects-and-risks/#Epidural_also_have_side_effects_for_babies

The pain was UNBEARABLE ... and the labor and contractions lasted for HOURS and HOURS... And, I do admit, after hours of beyond horrifically painful contractions, I desperately cried to the midwife that I had changed my mind, *"Give me the epidural. NOW!"* It was too late though, the contractions were too close together. And, obviously, I lived through it!

In the end, I was **grateful** that I could not receive drugs... as that kept my baby safe. 100%.

A few days after, I told my sister Christina, when she asked what giving birth was like, *"It hurt SO MUCH... it felt like pushing an* ***elephant*** *out of my... you know, down there."*

As Yahweh {God} said to Eve, after she and Adam sinned:

> **And to the woman He said:**
> **I shall increase, yea increase your grief**
> **And the groanings of your pregnancy**
> **In grief shall you bear children...**
>
> *Genesis 3:16*

I distinctly recall, (after finally *giving birth* at 7 am the next morning, utterly exhausted, my teeny tiny, purple-skinned newborn baby lying on me…), my thought being, *"Am I going to push out a manual for her too? I sure hope so!"* Sadly, it did not happen. NEITHER did I push out a bag of syringes and vaccines for her, I might add!

Yahweh {God} created us perfectly!

So Elohim created humanity in His image; in the image of Elohim He created it: male and female He created them.

Elohim blessed them, and Elohim said to them: Be fruitful and increase; fill the earth and subdue it…

…

And Elohim saw all that He had made; and behold, it was very good.

And evening came to be, and morning came to be: the sixth day.

Genesis 1:27-28a and 31

MYTH 4 ~ Milk is Milk!

Babies **gain immunity** from mother's milk. THUS if a *one hour old baby* is given a vaccination, they have NOT HAD much mother's milk (if any at all) to gain immunity; not to mention the overwhelming sensory experience that your baby has just lived through coming into the world. Yahweh {God} created us perfectly from day one, "in His image"! *(Read Genesis 1:27)*

Bruce Lipton, Ph.D., discusses artificial formulas and mother's milk in his book **The Biology of Belief** (emphasis mine):

... despite attempts to convince the public that milk is milk, be it human breast milk, cow's milk, or formula, nothing could be further from the truth. **Artificial formulas do not contain the powerful energy resources or immune protection found in mother's milk.** In fact, a nutritional imbalance in synthetic formula feeding is associated with deaths from diarrhea in infants in both developing and developed countries. (Victoria, et al, 1989)

Nature has evolved a chemical composition for breast milk that is specifically formulated to support the growth and health of human babies that has yet to be replicated. Breast milk contains antibodies that immunologically protect the baby until its own immune system becomes functional; **to compensate for a baby's immature and non-functioning immune system,** human milk contains vitally important immunoglobulin A (IgA) antibodies. These antibodies, which defend against infections in the infant's respiratory, digestive, and urogenital systems, provide passive immunity until the infant's own immune system can actively produce antibodies. Mother's milk is also a significant source of the bacteria that are proving to be crucial not only for a healthy digestive tract but also **for a healthy immune system.** Breast milk provides the highest energy and most concentrated source of lipids that are required to build the brain's structure---there is simply no substitute that can match complex maternal lipids as a readily assimilable, "high-octane" energy source.

You might think it's easy for me as a man to tout the maternal investment hypothesis and natural childbirth because I've never experienced the pain of childbirth!... I'm not presenting this research to induce guilt and to dictate women's decisions, but instead to stress that we should look at the modern medical industry's "improvements" with extreme skepticism. Whether it's messing with evolution in the form of decreasing the diversity of our microbiome, **creating formula that doesn't hold a candle to mother's milk, promoting unnecessary C-sections, over-**

prescribing antibiotics, or substituting parent-child interaction with a babysitting television screen, I think it's clear that we've gone astray by tampering with evolutionary mechanisms we don't fully understand.

The Biology of Belief, Unleashing the Power of Consciousness, Matter & Miracles (10th Anniversary Edition) by Bruce Lipton, Ph.D., Kindle page 350-351 of 533.

Oh that this pure and wonderful wisdom could be taught in health class in grade schools and high schools!

I continued raising my daughter as healthy as possible. I nursed her *exclusively* until 9-months of age. I flat out REFUSED to give her any formula. Even when I was **beyond tired**, exhausted and could scarcely think straight, evidenced once by the placing of a dirty diaper in the fridge! (Oops…) Even during migraines and feelings of deep depression, I continuously nursed my daughter. I wanted ONLY **the best** for her!

Dr. Mercola, founder of Mercola.com the world's most visited natural-health site, whose goal is "to empower you to Take Control of Your Health® by providing trustworthy natural health information and advocating for your right to make informed health choices," wrote an article titled *"The Amazing Benefits of Breastfeeding"* on January 2, 2016, including the following:

- Infant formula cannot replace breast milk when it comes to protecting your baby's health and promoting healthy long-term development. (And benefits for the mother as well.)
- Babies have been successfully raised on breast milk since the beginning of mankind, breast milk is a perfect food in every way.

- He later states: As noted in the featured article, "*Not nearly enough people know about this mind-blowing characteristic of breast milk: It changes daily based on signals from the baby.*" Indeed, it's not just vitamins, minerals, proteins, and fats that make breast milk far superior to formula.
- Breast milk provides the baby with natural immunity to illnesses that the mother is immune to. (So breastfed babies tend to have far fewer colds.)
- Breastfed babies also have fewer ear, respiratory, stomach, and intestinal infections than their formula-fed counterparts. Perhaps even more remarkable, when a newborn is exposed to a germ, he or she will transfer it back to the mother while nursing.
- The mother will then make antibodies to that particular germ and transfer them back to the baby at the next feeding, thereby speeding up the recovery process and promoting future immunity toward the organism, should it be encountered again.
- Breast milk also contains growth factors that significantly enhance your baby's gut and brain development, and even helps augment emotional perception and social development.

Mercola.com article "*The Amazing Benefits of Breastfeeding*" (gathered on June 7, 2021) at: Articles.Mercola.com/sites/articles/archive/2016/01/02/amazing-benefits-breastfeeding.aspx

At the age of 9-months, my daughter's FIRST EVER food was fresh avocado! I almost always fed her *fresh* vegetables...

And Elohim said: Since I have given you all seed-yielding herbage that is on the face of the entire earth, and every tree on which there is the fruit of a seed-yielding tree, it shall be yours for food.

Genesis 1:29

...and continued giving my baby the best nutrients possible, *mine*, until around 1½ years of age, (which in fact, nursing was looked down upon by many people period, much more to a 1½ year old child). She did not eat one BITE of sugar until her 1st birthday... and even then I regretted giving it to her. (Peer pressure teaming up with the people-pleaser in me, sadly.) But that is what you do, right? You give a child CAKE on their 1st birthday! Ugh.

MYTH 5 ~ Top Food Brands Contain ONLY the Good Stuff!

I fed my daughter fresh vegetables and fruits, steaming and mashing them myself into baby-food, (with NO preservatives nor additives, *I might add*). I believe, ONLY a handful of times, out of pure desperation, did I ever feed my daughter store-bought baby food, being RIFE with preservatives and toxins, a shocking discovery that is still true. Just two years ago, in an article titled *"Arsenic, toxic metals found in baby food including Walmart, Gerber, Beech-Nut brands,"* in the USA Today, they reveal that the U.S. House Subcommittee requested data from a number of baby foods manufacturers after a non-profit organization's test results on baby foods found arsenic, lead and other toxic metals... including in *organic* foods! What!?!

Toxins do NOT belong in our bodies! This would seem a simple, LOGICAL statement... Right?

MYTH 6 ~ Toxins should be put INTO our bodies! (This is health!)

When my daughter was around 9-months-old, her doctor (and everyone in the entire office for that matter) was pressuring me to give her far more vaccinations than I wanted in her teeny-tiny body, and EVERY TIME I went to the doctor it was a **battlefield.** I was sick and tired of it. So, I began searching for a new-age doctor, well-versed in the truth and opposed to biased teachings, with whom I would not have to argue about the ever-increasing number of mandatory vaccinations, ever, anytime I brought my daughter in for a check-up or anything else. Finding one was MUCH more difficult than I realized. I must have called fifteen to twenty doctor offices.

I had included in this book, in the first draft, a list of the ingredients in vaccinations. Now, I understand some may throw their arms up in disagreement here... (because this is what I was taught to do from a young age also)! However, once I began doing my own research, investigating what IS actually included in the list of "advised vaccines" - oh man, talk about throwing my arms up in disagreement... with what the medical model claims does belong in a person's body! I was shocked. SHOCKED that such toxins were "mandatory" for people... not to mention YOUNG children! (Anyway, IF you would like to read this information, please feel free to request it on my "Contact Form" on my website WhereTheSpiritOfTheLordis.com!)

Now, most of the United States seem very much indoctrinated similarly to how I was raised, "DOCTORS ARE GODS" and "DRUGS HEAL"! (And, thus, sadly also still seem blind to the fact that drug companies ONLY want to do ONE THING, make money! And let's not forget, as discussed previously in this chapter, *who funds medical universities?* Drug companies! Who profits from vaccines? Drug companies!)

> **Now, those intending to be rich are falling into a trial and a trap and the many foolish and harmful desires which are swamping men in extermination and destruction.**
>
> **For a root of all of the evils is the fondness for money...**
>
> *1 Timothy 6:9-10a*

Bruce Lipton Ph.D., again stated such in an interview (emphasis mine),

> *...if it's not the top, the second top income producing corporation is* ***the pharmaceutical industry... They sell drugs...*** *The pharmaceutical industry is a corporation. Its job is to make money...*
>
> *Well, it makes money by what? Having you* ***believe*** *that* ***the only way*** *to heal yourself is through the chemistry, called drugs, they sell at exorbitant prices...*
>
> Quote from a podcast with Bruce Lipton Ph.D. at: BruceLipton.com/the-frontier-sciences-evidence-based-practises-principles-guiding-you-to-transform

After "doctor hopping" for months, Yahweh {God} led me to another angel... a doctor just over the state border, in New Hampshire, who was open-minded to the truth, and agreed to be my daughter's doctor and apply NO pressure what-so-ever, including nursing, solid foods and even regarding vaccinations. (It was only a forty minute drive from home. New England states are small... compared to Texas!)

MYTH 7 ~ Energy Healing Is Just For "Quacks!"

Migraine head-aches had been plaguing me for years, and to add to it, I was now becoming incredibly depressed. Because I held so much respect for my daughter's doctor, a family practitioner, I asked if she would be my doctor also. She agreed. Bless her Father! Unable to bring myself up to joy and happiness, and knowing by this stage of my daughter's life that medication would affect only me and my own body, I sought help. ANY and all help. I was prescribed an anti-depressant, and MORE IMPORTANTLY was referred to an alternative medicine specialist who worked with bio-energetics. (The doctor went to this specialist also, and said the treatments are LIFE-CHANGING.)

What is Bio-Energetics, you may ask?

I myself wondered… though I was SO miserable, I did not really care at the time. I ONLY wanted to feel better and I had heard that this natural method actually works… without medicinal drugs!

Bruce Lipton, Ph.D. describes energy medicine (also known as bio-energetics) in an interview as the following (emphasis mine):

> *…energy medicine reveals you don't need pharmaceuticals to heal yourself, you just need to change your energy fields, which is* ***quantum physics.*** *I go, "So why is it relevant?" I said, "If you could put energy into a capsule, the pharmaceutical companies would be selling that energy drug at this very minute. But you cannot put it into a unit and sell it. And therefore, it is competition for drug companies. The more you buy energy healing, the less you buy drugs."*
>
> *…the new physics,* ***quantum physics is about 100 years old…*** *So… it shouldn't be the* ***new*** *physics. And* ***it should be the most understood science of the entire public…***
>
> Quotes from a podcast with Bruce Lipton Ph.D. at:
> BruceLipton.com/the-frontier-sciences-evidence-based-practises-principles-guiding-you-to-transform

Woah! When I heard *quantum physics*, I balked with thoughts of nuclear fusion and rocket science stuff. Surely I would need a degree from MIT to understand this. How wrong was I!

What a blessing to be one of the relatively few to hear about this *"out of the box"* science.

Astonishingly, while quantum physics is a part of rocket science, it is way, way more simple as I discovered from Bruce Lipton Ph.D. who declares that biology, "LIFE", cannot exist *without* it:

> I realized that quantum physics is relevant to biology and that biologists are committing a glaring, scientific error by ignoring its laws...
>
> In fact, most biological dysfunctions (except injuries caused by physical trauma) start at the level of a cell's molecules and ions. Hence the need for a biology that integrates both quantum and Newtonian mechanics...
>
> ...the journal *Nature* revealed that the laws of quantum physics, not Newtonian, control a molecule's life-generating movements...
>
> Frontier research on the mechanisms that cause proteins (the most important single component for living organisms) to change shape reveals the primacy of quantum properties in producing the movements that result in life.

The Biology of Belief, Unleashing the Power of Consciousness, Matter & Miracles (10th Anniversary Edition) by Bruce Lipton, Ph.D., Kindle pages 174, 192 and 194 of 533.

Barbara Brown, MSE and Dr. Tom Taylor are, as I have shared, bio-energetic experts, authors and speakers. Barbara Brown was miraculously healed from "incurable" muscular dystrophy (she is currently walking and hiking when doctors said she should be in a wheelchair by now). She had believed doctors her whole life who said that basically DNA is in charge, period. And since her father had died of muscular dystrophy, the doctors told her and her siblings that 2 of the 4 of them would also inherit muscular dystrophy. Well, Barbara finally chose to stop listening to those lies, and believe Yeshua {Jesus} Himself, who had appeared to her and said, *"When are you going to trust me?"* And He then said to her, *"Start walking."* So, she chose to obey Yeshua {Jesus}, and within 30 days she was healed! From flat on her back to running again! Praise Yahweh {God}!

She was also healed from nearly dying of gangrene in her body. Barbara Brown's learnings led her to create her own line of natural whole body cleansing products (compared to "the medical model" toxins prescribed for human bodies that do nothing helpful for the body and do not belong anywhere near them, frankly). Dr. Tom Taylor is also recognized internationally as an expert in pH, practical nutrition, and Bio-Energy Balancing.

> Other doctors called him, came to him for help, or sent him their "hopeless cases."
>
> **Rescuing God From the Rubble of Religion**
> by Dr. Tom Taylor and Barbara Brown, MSE, page 1.

He has trained health care practitioners from around the world, written dozens of professional articles, and led numerous seminars for the public around the United States; Yahweh {God} has granted him a wealth of knowledge that is unsurpassed, from Biblical revelations to how energy works to pH in the body. In one of their books, they describe the mind-body-spirit connection (bio-energetics, also known as energy healing) in the following way:

The relatively new science of epigenetics demonstrates what we observe throughout the wellness field: No matter who you are, where you're from, or the condition you're in, your state of health and well-being is more directly tied to your spiritual, mental, emotional, and nutritional environment than your family history or so-called genetic predisposition.

...The fact is that what you think, feel and believe is one of eight keys that can unlock your total health and well-being. Whether you acknowledge it or not, health and healing is intimately woven together with your thoughts, feelings and beliefs about yourself, your life, and, yes, even your relationship with God (or the absence of one).

Scientists, and other experts in human energy fields and quantum physics, recognize the presence of your spirit. They use terms like "energy field," "information field," or "innate intelligence," but behind the words is the inescapable, intangible spirit of wisdom.

Your Personal Roadmap to Whole Body Cleansing
by Barbara Brown, MSE and Dr. Tom Taylor,
pages 67 and 108-109.

I would like to highlight... what MANY people have said, including Bruce Lipton, Ph.D., Barbara Brown, MSE and Dr. Tom Taylor... the very same thing Henry Ford said, (and then applying it to quantum physics):

If you think you can or if you think you can't, YOU ARE RIGHT.

In other words...

IF you believe something will work… IT WILL!

IF you believe SOMETHING will NOT WORK… IT WILL NOT!

The ONE EXCEPTION to this saying… that Dr. Tom Taylor pointed out is that: BIO-ENERGETICS works. Period. It works whether you believe it or not! It is truth. It works from truth. Period (again).

This is PRECICELY why the placebo pill works for some… and NOT for others! The placebo pill is PROOF of quantum physics… *mind over matter!* Actually, this is ALSO why prescription drugs work for some, and not for others. So many things are dependent on BELIEF!

Let that soak in for a moment!

In fact, Bruce Lipton, Ph.D., further reveals in his book (emphasis mine):

> When patients get better by ingesting the sugar pill, medicine defines it as the *placebo effect*… I call it the *belief effect* to **stress that our perceptions, whether they are accurate or inaccurate, equally impact our behavior and our bodies.**
>
> I celebrate the *belief effect*, which is an amazing testament to the healing ability of the body/mind…
>
> Doctors should not dismiss the **power of the mind** as something inferior to the power of chemicals and the scalpel.
>
> The Biology of Belief, Unleashing the Power of Consciousness, Matter & Miracles (10th Anniversary Edition) by Bruce Lipton, Ph.D., Kindle page 248 of 533.

Dr. Mercola, mentioned earlier, wrote the following testimony of Bruce Lipton's book, **The Biology of Belief** (emphasis mine):

> Finally, a compelling and easy-to-understand explanation of how your emotions regulate your genetic expression! You need to read this book to truly appreciate that **you are not a victim of your genes but instead have unlimited capacity to live a life overflowing with peace, happiness, and love.**
>
> The Biology of Belief, Unleashing the Power of Consciousness, Matter & Miracles (10th Anniversary Edition) by Bruce Lipton, Ph.D., Kindle page 6 of 533.

As Yeshua {Jesus} Himself said many times, according to your faith you are healed:

> **And Jesus said to the centurion, "Go! As you believe let it come to be with you!" And healed was the boy in that hour. And the centurion, returning into his house in the same hour, found the boy sound.**
>
> *Matthew 8:13*

> **…Jesus said to her, "O woman, great is your faith! Let it come to be with you as you are wanting." And healed was her daughter from that hour.**
>
> *Matthew 15:28*

As did the Apostle Paul:

> **And a certain man in Lystra, impotent in the feet, sat there, lame from his mother's womb, who never walks. This one hears Paul speaking, who, looking intently at him, and perceiving that he has faith to be saved, said with a loud voice, "Rise upright on your feet!" And he leaps, and walked.**
>
> *Acts 14:8-10*

(Read further examples of people saved through their faith in Matthew 9:20-22, Matthew 9:28-31, Mark 10:51-52, Luke 17:12-19, John 9:1-38 and Acts 3:1-16.)

I was SO discontented and desperate to feel alive again, that I decided to go ahead with the bio-energetics treatment. (I was, honestly, petrified inside though, because it was completely *"out of Tamra's box."* It almost felt like going to a medium or fortune-teller, a sin to Yahweh {God}.) However, as Yahweh {God} plans EVERYTHING perfectly and is "into the detail," *(read Exodus 25-31 regarding how to build Yahweh's {God's} tabernacle, and Leviticus 1-7 detailing the Old Testament laws for the priests when sacrificing to Yahweh {God}, etc.)*, it is by no other means than by His sovereignty that BOTH my doctor and the bio-energetics specialist had attended the same denominational church as myself. This helped me feel calmer about the "new" treatment and about the specialist, knowing this person was not a fortune-teller nor demonic.

Now understanding bio-energetics, I recognize why it was SO HARD for me to do something "against the grain" or *"out of the box"* and do something so very DIFFERENT than that which I was raised to believe (from birth to age 7).

Bruce Lipton Ph.D., states in an interview (emphasis mine):

> *Do you want to change the subconscious? You have to teach it in a different way that that subconscious learns. It doesn't learn from creative "read a book." No. It learns in three different ways. Number one, first seven years of your life, the brain is operating at a vibration lower than consciousness... Theta is the first seven years that's just below consciousness. And it's also hypnosis.* ***So for seven years, a child is unconsciously downloading behaviors from all those around them.*** *So what? That's the behaviors that create culture. That's behaviors that create family. How do I learn them? I watch, download them. Now I've already learned how to be a member of the family and the community. I didn't even read a book!*
>
> Quotes from a podcast with Bruce Lipton Ph.D. at: BruceLipton.com/the-frontier-sciences-evidence-based-practises-principles-guiding-you-to-transform

I am so grateful I walked through the "wall of fear" feeling to go to the appointment! Unbeknownst to me, it was about to change my life!

This brings to mind the incredible book called **The Dream Giver - Following Your God-Given Destiny**... a simple, short, very well-written description of the journey of following Yahweh {God}! Here Ordinary, the main character, is going through a "Wall of Fear" on his journey out of his normal, habitual, every-day life and into true life and adventure. Ordinary's mind chatter was whirling. He wondered how he could be courageous, when he had no courage? "Ordinary decided. If his fear wasn't going to leave, he would have to go forward in spite of it. Still trembling, he picked up his suitcase, turned his back on Familiar, and walked to the sign. **And even though his fear kept growing, Ordinary shut his eyes and took a big step forward—right through the invisible Wall of Fear.** And there he made a surprising discovery. On the other side of that single step—the exact one Ordinary didn't think he could take—he found that he had broken through his Comfort Zone. Now the Wall of

Fear was behind him. He was free, and his Dream was ahead. He began to whistle again as he walked on, his Big Dream beating brightly in his chest." (The Dream Giver - Following Your God-Given Destiny by Bruce Wilkinson and David and Heather Kopp, Kindle page 26 of 179.)

The specialist, another beloved and kind angel (I will call her Elena), sent from Yahweh {God} to walk with me on my journey, worked on me energetically... and spoke to me about healthy eating as well. She also helped guide me spiritually, as she was further along the path of her own journey from "big box church" to following the TRUE YAHWEH {GOD}. She helped me and my daughter so much! Bless her Father! I was SUCH an unhealthy eater that when I was encouraged to *"eat one raw vegetable each day"* I was completely overwhelmed. Knowing what I now know, I am truly embarrassed to share this. I was encouraged to drink **only** water (as I drank much Dr. Pepper at the time), and was also introduced to **Juice Plus+**®, as described in their own publications:

> "Inspiring Healthy Living Around The World."
>
> Juice Plus+ is more than just the next best thing to fruit and vegetables: Juice Plus+ is the way to a new life in which you will feel better and more at ease with yourself.

They further state:

> It has been proven in various studies that phytonutrients, vitamins and minerals contained in fruit and vegetables, are important for a healthy life. Experts recommend five portions of fruit and vegetables a day. However, it's not always easy to manage that everyday. We know how important a balanced diet is for our lives. So that is what we want to offer you. We have developed Juice Plus+ so that the ingredients processed are of the highest quality possible, that you get the best of 30 different fruit, vegetable and berry

varieties, so you can get through the day with renewed energy and vigour…

Juice Plus+ helps you take control of your life and keeps your diet balanced and healthy!

Juice Plus+® (gathered on December 16, 2021) at:
JuicePlus.com/es/en/franchise/about-the-juice-plus-company/juiceplus-company

It sounds so simple… and I do not even want to write about simple nutrition here, as there are SO MANY BOOKS on it. However, the analogy comes to mind, *"Why not fill up your car with water? It is cheaper than gas, right?"* Well, yes, as we ALL KNOW, it may be cheaper, but it will NOT DRIVE well! You MUST put into a car what is designed specifically for it! Well… same as our bodies… How did Yahweh {God} create our bodies? What did HE intend for us to eat to be our utmost?

And Elohim said: Since I have given you all seed-yielding herbage that is on the face of the entire earth, and every tree on which there is the fruit of a seed-yielding tree, it shall be yours for food.

Genesis 1:29

Me personally? I must unlearn the "what do you feel like eating" and simply give my body what it will utilize most! (Please know, I am talking to myself, first and foremost here.)

I learned that the same people who taught bio-energetics were holding a seminar, and I was encouraged to attend. Still a bit scared (at doing something new and *"out of Tamra's box"*), I decided to go! So, at the *"Live the Victory"* seminar, I met the aforementioned Barbara Brown, MSE and

Dr. Tom Taylor. Putting into practice their knowledge and teachings changed my life completely!

THANK YOU FATHER IN HEAVEN!!!
MY LIFE DESPERATELY
NEEDED *ME* TO CHANGE!

I learned so much from them. More than words can ever describe in one book. Some lessons were exciting, some beyond blissful, some painful… but all for my good in the end. Life is a journey!

Now we are aware that God is working all together for the good of those who are loving God, who are called according to the purpose…

Romans 8:28

Yet not only so, but we may be glorying also in afflictions, having perceived that affliction is producing endurance, yet endurance testedness (tried and tested and proved worthy ~ *Thayer*) **yet testedness expectation.**

Romans 5:3-4

Just as Deborah always says,

"God never said it'd be easy.
He said He'd be with us."

I was immediately drawn to both Barbara Brown and Dr. Tom Taylor. (I now know it was the "spirit of Yahweh {God}" IN them that drew me.) I was so **inspired** and **filled with life** ***simply*** by *being around them… their spirits*, as well as learning more profoundly about the spirit-mind-body connection, about energy, about health (just to name a few things).

I would ***love to say*** that I steadily became happier and filled with joy, that my life got easier, that "I lived happily ever after!"

However, like the course many things in life follow, my life got worse BEFORE it got better. At least I was on the PATH to "better," actually I was on the path to "My Utmost for His HIGHEST"! (Which is, by the way, a truly inspired book by the late, dedicated follower of the Messiah, Oswald Chambers.) The Biblical principle that I experienced that comes to mind is when Moses went to set Yahweh's {God's} people free… their lives became harder, BEFORE they were set free.

> **Hence Pharaoh instructed… You shall not continue to give crushed straw to the people to mold the bricks as heretofore. They themselves shall go, and they will rake together crushed straw for themselves. You shall place on them the regular number of bricks which they were making heretofore.**
>
> *Exodus 5:6-8a*

So… if I may ENCOURAGE you… WHEN your life seems to be harder, or getting worse, as Deborah would encourage me, HOLD ON, KEEP GOING, IT GETS BETTER! PRAISE YAH {GOD}! And if you're feeling the pangs of change, Yahweh {God} is working on you, in you and through you. (I admit, when she would say this to me, I would think to myself, *"Where am I 'going'? I do not even know which way is up? Or which path is the correct one?"* I did not see or feel Yahweh {God} showing nor pointing me in His direction. ALL I did know was, whatever the direction, whatever the hardship, I was NOT going BACK.)

Months after meeting Barbara Brown and Dr. Tom Taylor, I remember calling Barbara on the phone late one night, during one of my debilitating anxiety attacks. I could barely breath and thought I was going to die... Bless her, she answered her phone and coached me calm. The alarm bells stopped ringing.

In the evening, lamentation may lodge,
But in the morning there is jubilant song.

Psalm 30:5b

Rejoicing comes to a man in the apt response of his mouth,
And a word in its season, how good!

Proverbs 15:23

As the months went by, I was eating more and more healthily, regularly receiving bio-energetics treatments, embedding new programs, and hearing inspired wisdom through Dr. Tom Taylor's weekly **Light Up the Scriptures** studies. In some areas of life I was becoming increasingly happier, even to the point of my doctor beginning to ween me off anti-depressants. Actually, I weened myself off them QUICKER than prescribed! I KNEW MY BODY did not need them. So, "I took over!" Possibly **for the first time** I was taking control in my life. Miraculous!

I began learning how powerful the mind is! Just as Yeshua {Jesus} teaches, to disregard others' opinions and words... and focus and believe on Yahweh {God} and HIS words alone:

While He is still speaking, they are coming from the chief of the synagogue, saying that "Your daughter died. Why are you still bothering the Teacher?" Yet Jesus immediately, disregarding the word spoken, is saying to the chief of the synagogue, "Do not fear! Only believe!"

Mark 5:35-36

(Read the whole story… Mark 5:22-24 and 35-43.)

I learned that I can do anything!… and I learned what you feed yourself *does* affect you! (This seems *obvious* to me **now**.) If you eat "garbage" you feel like garbage. (Garbage meaning: anything called "fast food," anything that is sold boxed, bagged, processed, preservatives added, and yes, non-organic and GMO!) As Bruce Lipton Ph.D. states in an interview:

The food we eat is industrialized garbage!

Quote from a podcast with Bruce Lipton Ph.D. at:
BruceLipton.com/the-frontier-sciences-evidence-based-practises-principles-guiding-you-to-transform

And as Dr. Tom Taylor would so often say, *"You control what you put in your mouth, but once the fork **leaves** your mouth you have no control over what your body does with it."*

Barbara Brown includes in her own daily routine what she calls her *"Non-Negotiable 5."* She knows exactly how the body works… and more importantly what the body needs in order to be in "tip-top" shape… spirit, soul, mind and body! She is a natural health advocate! One item on her *"Non-Negotiable 5"* is **Juice Plus+**®, and one I readily advise others to check out for themselves. **Juice Plus+**® assists in keeping the body healthy. (You can find links to all of this information in the resources section at the back of the book as well as on my website.)

I admit, when I had migraines and was depressed… I was NOT taking care of myself. NOT as Yahweh {God} intended. So, I blame no one. When I began eating as He intended, (food from the ground, not "industrialized garbage"), and paying attention to and following the leading of my spirit, THEN I felt better! (What a journey it was for me to learn that!) I pray you, dear reader, know this already, or learn it the easy way… from my mistakes, instead of your own!

Are you not aware that you are a temple of God and the spirit of God is making its home in you?

1 Corinthians 3:16

And Elohim said: Since I have given you all seed-yielding herbage that is on the face of the entire earth, and every tree on which there is the fruit of a seed-yielding tree, it shall be yours for food.

Genesis 1:29

Now profane and old womanish myths refuse, yet exercise yourself in devoutness, for bodily exercise is beneficial for a few things, yet devoutness is beneficial for all, having promise for the life which now is, and that which is impending.

1 Timothy 4:7-8

I also admit, today, while writing this I do not eat as perfectly as I had learned to and trained myself for years and years… However, I do currently eat over 50% vegetables (and yes, mostly raw). I do not eat pasta. None. No cheese. No yogurt. No dairy. (Frankly: human milk is for human babies, cow's milk is for calves.) Yahweh {God} created our bodies for vegetation.

I must say this now also (as the emphasis of this chapter is health...), the excruciating lower back pains that I mentioned I had been suffering with for years beginning in 2001, doctors had diagnosed as a depleted disk in my sacrum. I had no idea what they meant. "*It's like a jelly donut but the jelly has gone,*" they described it, "*the natural cushion has diminished to nothing so your bones are literally rubbing against each other.*" They also told me there currently was no cure. That possibly in five to ten years there **might** be one. That there was nothing they could do. Nothing. It was almost like, "*End of conversation. There's the door.*" I am thinking, "*WHAT! I can't wait five to ten years for a 'possibly,' living with pain like a knife in my back whether sitting, standing, or lying down!*"

Well...

Thank Yahweh {God} doctors are NOT gods!

To be totally transparent with the truth, the "patterns" of old, the "*what I say does not matter*" and other similar false beliefs still sometimes play their tune. From a feeling of fear while writing this chapter, (well, this book really), sharing my truth, I find myself eating bio rice cakes and chocolate granola cereal! Knowing what I know now about bio-energetics... I do believe *(laughing out loud actually)* that I still have some work to do on deleting this "old pattern" and creating a-new, a more healthy pattern!

I feel similar to Gideon when Yahweh {God} told him that He (Yahweh) had chosen Gideon to go and do, now, "just as he is" and in the strength he had at the time:

Then Yahweh turned toward him and said, Go in this vigor of yours and save Israel from the clutches of Midian! Have I not sent you? Yet he replied to Him, O! Yahweh, With what shall I save Israel? Behold, my contingent is the weakest in Manasseh, and I am the most inferior in my father's house.

Yahweh answered to him, But I shall come to be with you, and you will smite Midian as one man.

Judges 6: 14-16

This example continues to help me "walk through" what Yahweh {God} has for me on my path... I do not have to be perfect, nor do I have to possess what I would consider to be all the tools and talents. Instead, to simply obey and trust Yahweh {God}! Amen!

During this season of my life, Deborah also encouraged me to read **The Practice of the Presence of God** by Brother Lawrence. I read it… however I must tell you when I read it again in 2021 I felt a gushing of Yahweh's {God's} love through the open floodgates of heaven, with such grace and no anger nor condemnation, in a way that I had never before seen nor known in religion, nor anything I had heard or read in the past. Brother Lawrence's belief and countenance is so calm, overflowing with grace, love, kindness and patience! He holds the most gracious view of life, one lived entirely *in* Yahweh {God} Who created him, that I have ever seen or heard in my entire life! My muscles relax when I read it, (which I do almost every day, due to its encouraging nature)!

The following piece from Brother Lawrence comes to mind (emphasis mine):

He remarked that **thinking often spoils everything**; that **evil usually begins with our thoughts.** In Brother Lawrence's opinion,

> <u>we should reject any thoughts which distract us from serving the Lord</u> or which undermine our salvation. Freeing the mind of such thoughts will permit a comfortable conversation with God. But **Brother Lawrence added that this isn't always easy.** When he was first saved, he had often spent his entire prayer time rejecting distractions and then falling immediately into them again.
>
> The Brother Lawrence Collection – An Christian Classic – Practice and Presence of God, Spiritual Maxims, The Life of Brother Lawrence by Brother Lawrence, Kindle page 75 of 139.

It feels strange… the intensity of muscle gripping fear while, at the same time, receiving Yahweh's {God's} all conquering peace as I write. I choose to focus on His peace. It is as if He is saying to me, *"Finally daughter of Mine, you are sharing your experience. You are doing good! Courage, do not fear. You are using your life through 'trials and tribulations'… to help My other children on their same path to My freedom and My peace! Just as I sent 'angels' (as you call them) to help you, now I am calling on you to be an 'angel' to others."*

> **"<u>Peace</u> I am leaving with you. <u>My peace</u> I am giving to you. Not according as the world is giving to you, am I giving to you. Let not your heart be disturbed, neither let it be timid."**
>
> *John 14:27*

> **"Gratuitously you got; gratuitously be giving."**
>
> *Matthew 10:8b*

Now the Lord is the spirit; yet where the spirit of the Lord is, there is freedom.

2 Corinthians 3:17

Blessed is the God and Father of our Lord Jesus Christ, the Father of pities and God of all consolation, Who is consoling us in our every affliction to enable us to be consoling those in every affliction, through the consolation with which we ourselves are being consoled by God...

2 Corinthians 1:3-4

Blessed be the God and Father of our Lord Jesus Christ, Who blesses us with every spiritual blessing among the celestials, in Christ, according as He chooses us in Him before the disruption of the world, we to be holy and flawless in His sight, in love designating us beforehand for the place of a son for Him through Christ Jesus; in accord with the delight of His will, for the laud of the glory of His grace, which graces us in the Beloved...

Ephesians 1:3-6

Chapter 4

THE LITTLE LUTHERAN CHURCH

Growing up in religion (the truth and the lies)!

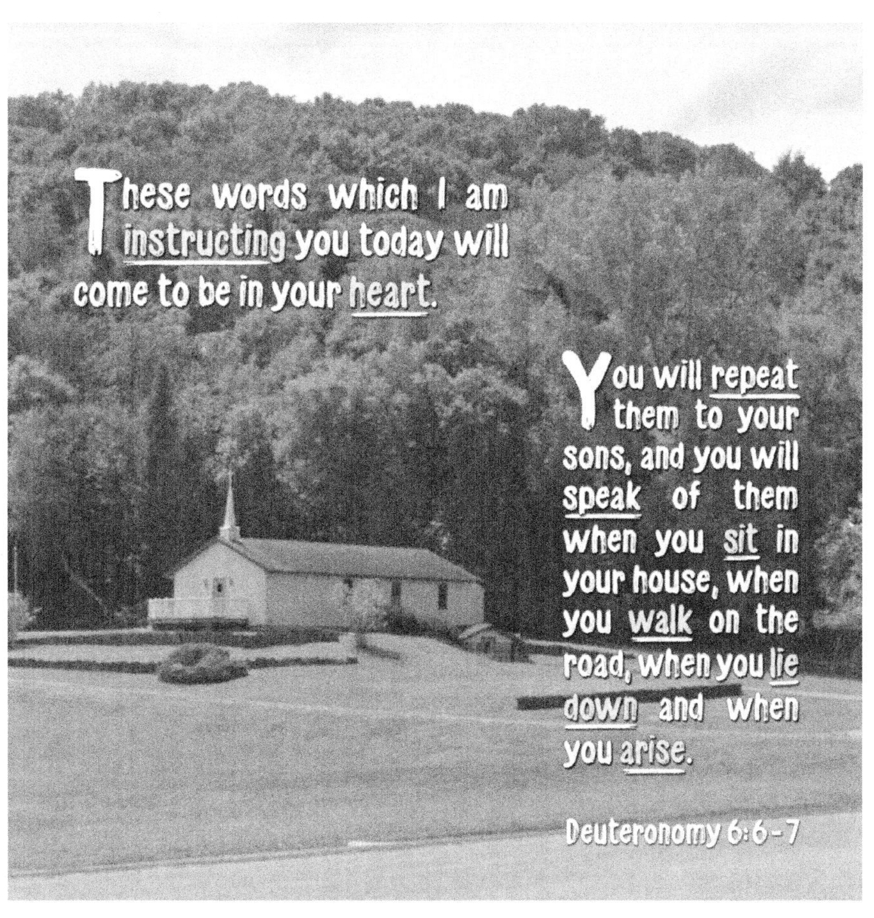

> **Hear, Israel! Yahweh is our Elohim; Yahweh the only One. So you will love Yahweh your Elohim with all your heart and with all your soul and with all your intensity. These words which I am instructing you today will come to be in your heart.**
>
> **You will repeat them to your sons, and you will speak of them when you sit in your house, when you walk on the road, when you lie down and when you arise. You will tie them for a sign on your hand, and they will come to be for the brow bands between your eyes; you will write them on the jambs of your house and on your gates.**
>
> *Deuteronomy 6:4-9*

I am going to take a brief moment and bring you back in time…

Have you ever seen (or heard of) the famous **Little House on the Prairie** books or television series?

This is almost exactly how I was raised. **Truly!**

Let me paint you a picture. Growing up, I (and my entire family) attended a small, strict Lutheran Church consisting of approximately forty members in total. We built a small, stereotypical white church on a large plot of land in the country. A photograph of which I used for the chapter title Scripture on the previous page! It was a one-roomed, combined church and school house. We would set up folding chairs for church on Sundays, pushing the children's desks to one side of the room. And, after church, we all would help fold the chairs up, and arrange the children's desks ready for school again. Twelve desks. Twelve children.

My brothers and sisters, the five of us, made up almost half of the school… for years! (Yes, this is 1982, not 1892.) There were two, (yes, two), people in my entire grade, from Kindergarten (age 5 or 6) to 8th grade (age 13 or 14). My mother was one of the two full-time teachers there. (I could not *"get away"* with ANYTHING growing up… my mother was with me 24/7. Literally.)

When I moved on to high school, (at age 14), a very different picture of school emerged. There were more than three hundred and fifty students in my grade *alone*, and around thirty students in each classroom throughout the day. I quickly learned how blessed I was to have received almost one-on-one, personal education for SO many years. As a result of our fast-paced learning, all of my sisters and brothers, (me being the youngest of the five), took the *advanced* classes of English, Math, etc. … such that the "regular classes" in 9th and 10th grades were covering lesson material we had covered years previously. (The exception being science class, which the one-roomed school house lacked the technology and all the lab equipment to satisfy that level of curriculum.)

I LOVED the one-roomed school house! I LOVED the school, I LOVED THE CHURCH, I LOVED the **Bible** classes we had every day, from Kindergarten through 8th grade! I LOVED *all* my classes… well *alright*, not history class so much. Not one bit.

My absolute favorite time of the year was celebrating Yeshua's {Jesus'} birth! (While at the same time most of the world would celebrate Christmas.) For months before Yeshua's {Jesus'} birthday, all the kids would memorize and prepare for the Celebration Service, where we (the kids) would sit up at the front of the church house, preaching and reciting **Old Testament** prophesies and singing songs, *heralding the story of Yeshua's {Jesus'} birth!* I cannot tell you enough, how much I THOROUGHLY ENJOYED this time… every single year! (Of course at that time, I **was yet to learn** that Yeshua {Jesus} was not even born in the month of December.)

I would sing the songs AS LOUD AS I POSSIBLY COULD! I did not understand why everyone else did not? Baffled as to why the other kids were not as excited about heralding the story of Yeshua's {Jesus'} birth as I was, I was told to "*quiet down*" while I belted out the songs! "*Not so loud, Tamra. We want to hear the other kids too.*" Well, even when I did, you could NOT hear the other kids… they were lacking any zeal, some barely whispering! I felt I was "making up" for them!

My favorite of ALL favorite Scriptures… (and I have over 1,000 *favorite Scriptures!*), is one I had memorized and heralded repeatedly as a child:

> **And shepherds were in the same district in the field fold, and maintaining watches at night over their flock. And lo! a messenger of the Lord stood by them, and the glory of God shines about them, and they were afraid with a great fear. And the messenger said to them, "Fear not, for lo! I am bringing you an evangel of great joy which will be for the entire people, for today was brought forth to you a Saviour, Who is Christ, the Lord, in the city of David. And this is the sign to you: you will be finding a Babe, swaddled and lying in a manger.**
>
> **And suddenly with the messenger there came to be a multitude of the heavenly host, praising God and saying,**
>
> > **"Glory to God among the Highest!**
> > **And on earth peace,**
> > **Among men, delight!"**
>
> **And it occurred, as the messengers came away from them into heaven, that the shepherds spoke to one another, saying, "By all means we may be passing through to Bethlehem, and we may be perceiving this declaration which has come to pass, which the Lord makes known to us." And they came hurrying, and they found both Miriam and Joseph, and the Babe lying in the manger.**

> **Now, perceiving it, they make known concerning the declaration that is spoken to them concerning this little Boy. And all who hear marvel concerning that which is being spoken to them by the shepherds. Now Miriam preserved all these declarations, parleying them in her heart. And the shepherds return, glorifying and praising God for all that which they hear and perceived, according as it was spoken to them.**
>
> *Luke 2:8-20*

Later in my life, as you'll read in another chapter, I was given a most gracious gift of actually going to Jerusalem. While sitting on a hillside in Bethlehem, this same Scripture heralded loud in my mind...

I *loved* going to this little church to worship, the songs we would sing in Praise to Yahweh {God}, the same hymns sung over and over. I *loved* them ALL!

I *loved* the **Bible** accounts spoken of during the sermons. I must admit, I would sometimes fall asleep during the sermons when I was very young. It would get quite warm (even hot) during the summer, and there was no air conditioning in the building.

I *loved* the prayers the pastor would pray, the exact same prayers every Sunday, literally, but still there is little me embracing EVERY WORD!

And the prayers did not stop at the church doors. Even at home we prayed before and after every meal. After supper, (at 5:30 pm sharp every single evening), we would read a short devotional and then discuss it. I loved reading and discussing the devotionals after supper.

(Now, please do not get me wrong... I was not a perfect child. Far from it. I sinned. I got angry. I disobeyed my parents, and was spanked... **often** it seemed.)

Yet, when I was about 7 or 8-years-old, one Sunday in church with the entire congregation, I was sitting on the brown metal folding chair, praying the Lord's Prayer. I recall praying earnestly to Yahweh {God}, thinking that since He was "dead," that maybe I must shout loudly (in my mind at least) for Him to hear me praying (speaking) to Him.

"Thus, then, you be praying: 'Our Father Who art in the heavens, hallowed be Thy name. Thy kingdom come. Thy will be done, as in heaven, on earth also. Our bread, our dole, be giving us today. And remit to us our debts, as we also remit those of our debtors. And mayest Thou not be bringing us into trial, but rescue us from the wicked one.'"

Matthew 6:9-13

I was doing what I would do EVERY Sunday, and during EVERY prayer, personally and earnestly **speaking to Yahweh** {God} with all of my heart. And it was then, at that early age, that I heard a voice inside me saying, *"You are the **only one** here who means every word you say."* I remember thinking to myself, *"What?!? Doesn't EVERYONE here do the same thing? Doesn't EVERYONE here love You in this way?"*

I held these encouraging words close to my heart. I did not tell anyone, especially as the youngest of five children, often being told to *"be quiet"* and *"better seen and not heard."* Feelings and conversations were a rare occurrence, if at all, with my parents, family or even friends, and while I was best friends with my brother, only a year older than me... he did not seem to *"love"* Yahweh {God} in the same way I did. So, thinking myself a little crazy, I kept this to myself. I did not realize until YEARS LATER, that that still small voice I heard was the spirit of Yahweh {God} Himself *speaking to me.*

Father in Heaven,
Thank You!
Thank You for walking
with me throughout my life!
I did not feel You much, or know it was You
at the time… however You were there,
with me, always!
Thank You for persevering with me, until
I did come to realize it was You speaking!
Thank You! Bless You! Praise You!
Amen.

As a Lutheran, **I was taught** that yes, Yahweh {God} performed miracles with the Israelites, thousands of years ago, and Yeshua {Jesus} performed miracles while walking with the disciples on earth… and, even, some of the disciples performed miracles *because* they had walked with Yeshua {Jesus}. However, NO LONGER. (It was almost as if GOD WAS DEAD. Sure, He was up in heaven, watching us down here on earth, but He would not help us. Nope. Not anymore. He and His miracles "died" along with the 12 Apostles of the **Bible.**) And like so many, I followed every wind of teaching, not the Word (the **Bible**) itself.

One of MANY Scriptures in the **Bible** clearly states that "**the word of God is living and operative**…" The word "*living*" is PRESENT TENSE! The Word *is living* and *operative* (contrary to all those teachings!). The Word is not dead. Therefore, Yahweh {God} is not dead. Yahweh {God} is the Word.

For the word of God is living and operative, and keen above any two-edged sword, and penetrating up to the parting of soul and spirit, both of the articulations and marrow, and is a judge of the sentiments and thoughts of the heart.

Hebrews 4:12

Now to Him Who is able to do superexcessively above all that we are requesting or apprehending, according to the power that is operating in us, to Him be glory in the ecclesia and in Christ Jesus for all the generations of the eon of the eons! Amen!

Ephesians 3:20-21

Now there are apportionments of graces, yet the same spirit, and there are apportionments of services, and the same Lord, and there are apportionments of operations, yet the same God Who is operating all in all.

Now to each one is being given the manifestation of the spirit, with a view to expedience.

1 Corinthians 12:4-7

Additionally, Lutheran teachings dictated that the holy spirit, "**the consoler that will be coming... and guiding you into all the truth**" also DIED at the same time as the 12 Apostles died. Dead. *"It (the spirit) no longer does that anymore."* NO ONE speaks in tongues as the Apostles did during Yeshua's {Jesus'} life and, through Him, were anointed with tongues of fire.

And at the fulfillment of the day of Pentecost they were all alike in the same place. And suddenly there came out of heaven a blare, even as of a violent, carrying blast, and it fills the whole house where they were sitting. And seen by them were dividing tongues as if of fire, and one is seated on each one of them. And they are all filled with holy spirit, and they begin to speak in different languages, according as the spirit gave them to declaim.

Now there were dwelling in Jerusalem, Jews, pious men from every nation under heaven. Now when this sound occurs, the multitude came together and was confused, for each one hears them speaking in his own vernacular (native tongue). Now they are all amazed, and marveled, saying, "Lo! are not all these who are speaking, Galileans? And how are we hearing, each in our own vernacular in which we were born? Parthians and Medes and Elamites and those dwelling in Mesopotamia, Judea, as well as Cappadocia, Pontus, and the province of Asia, Phrygia, Pamphylia, Egypt, and the parts of Libya about Cyrene, and the repatriated Romans, both Jews and proselytes, Cretans and Arabs -- we are hearing them speaking in these languages of ours of the great things of God!"

Now, amazed are they all, and they were bewildered, saying one to another, "What is this wanting to be?"

Acts 2:1-12

I was taught, *"Speaking in tongues is crazy, wicked and pure evil."*

This reminds me of the Scripture where it speaks of the different beliefs of the Sadducees and the Pharisees:

For Sadducees, indeed, are saying there is no resurrection, nor messenger, nor spirit; yet Pharisees are avowing both.

Acts 23:8

And this is precisely what Paul meant when describing how the religious "deny Yahweh's {God's} power":

...having a form of devoutness, yet denying its power. These, also, shun.

2 Timothy 3:5-6a

Ohhh... so many lies taught and preached within religion. I do believe it is our responsibility, our *accountability* to Yahweh {God}, to seek out the truth from the Source, letting go of any sentimental memories, traditions or ties.

I personally believe, possibly naively, that all people and their ideas begin with good intentions... let's use the example of Lutherans, who did not set out to become religious... or MAKE GOD DEAD! No. Actually, Martin Luther wrote his 95 Theses NOT to begin his own church... BUT to stop the outrageous corruption of the Roman Catholic Church. After he was excommunicated from the church, he translated the first German translation of the Bible. In 1597, (51 years after Martin Luther died of natural causes), people began to distinguish themselves as "Lutheran" referring to their "true" church. Many people followed him and his beliefs and called themselves after his name, which I do NOT believe was Luther's original intention. It just became that way... over time. I am also NOT excusing people from choices and consequences... I am simply stating that I like to believe that intentions begin from a "*good heart*," as many often do.

Another lie unquestioned, unchecked and, to some degree unknown, to many followers of the **Bible**…

You may want to sit down for this one.
I was UTTERLY SHOCKED
and frankly in disbelief for a while when I first learned it.

During his Scripture studies called **Light Up the Scriptures**, (which Yahweh {God} graciously led me to be a part of), when at all possible Dr. Tom Taylor would read *ONLY* the **Concordant Literal** versions, the most accurate Biblical translation of the original Hebrew and Greek texts *in the world*. He revealed why he read *ONLY* this translation, and pointed to the book **God's Eonian Purpose**, by Adlai Loudy, giving credit to the source where he (Dr. Tom Taylor) himself learned of the misinterpretation, mistranslation, and misapplication of the many "**Bible**" versions throughout the world today.

In the book **God's Eonian Purpose** the author, Adlai Loudy, writes that A. E. Knoch, an Ancient Greek scholar, researcher and author, desiring to understand the word of Yahweh {God}, found that within all versions of the **Bible** there were numerous errors in translation and some blatant additions and omissions that were edited after the inspired word was created in its completion. He deemed it important to start anew, rather than revise incorrect versions already published, in order to "*do it right to be worth doing at all.*" Hence, the **Concordant Literal Versions of the Old and New Testaments** were born.

As Adlai Loudy states in his book (emphasis mine below) when referring to one of many versions of the **Bible**, it:

> …contained many passages wrongly translated, and some even which had no right to a place in it at all. But our faith should be founded on the divine verities. It is no discouragement if we discover that infallible men in studying and translating these

words, have sometimes made mistakes, and it is certainly no honor to the words which we profess to reverence, if we knowingly allow mistakes to remain uncorrected.

Truth lovers desire that the old Hebrew and Greek writings should speak to them as they spoke to their first readers in the days of the apostles, freed from the human traditions imposed upon them by later eras, and from unconscious errors of imperfect scholarship. Regardless of sacrifice, we should ever seek for the version that will give the *clearest and purest expression of the original.* A version that fails to meet this demand may serve the needs of a few for sentimental purposes, but it will fail to fill the hearts of a wider humanity who love the truth so deeply they will be satisfied only with a version that expresses exactly what God has really spoken.

… A concordance of every form of every Greek word was made and systematized and turned into English. The whole Greek vocabulary was analyzed and translated, using a STANDARD English equivalent for each Greek element. The Greek grammar was entirely revised in accord with the findings made in this task of transcribing into English precisely what God has really revealed in the sacred original. The result of this arduous and exhaustive work is the Concordant Version of the Sacred Scriptures, which is at once scientific, systematic, uniform and consistent – a standard by which all other translations may be tested – truly the most valuable work ever printed. **Never before has such earnest endeavor been made to give the people the revelation of God with the unvarying uniformity, consistency, and purity found in the Concordant Version, enabling the reader to establish his faith on divine verities rather than human authority.**

Only by *comparison* can one appreciate the Concordant Version, so we propose a few examples with brief comments for consideration.

How can anyone believe Hebrews 11:1?

Now faith is the substance of things hoped for, the evidence of things not seen.

"Faith" is neither "substance" nor "evidence", as it is rendered in this passage. Faith is intangible, the very opposite of substance. It cannot become "substance" without being transmuted into sight, and is no longer faith. Later versions changed "substance" to "confidence", yet this is not at all suitable for some of the other contexts where the other word occurs. The Concordant Version renders it uniformly:

Now faith is an assumption of what is being expected, a conviction concerning matters which are not being observed.

The word "assumption" fits every passage in which the word occurs, and opens up a marvelous vista of truth. Faith assumes that to be truth which it expects to become fact in the future.

God's Eonian Purpose by Adlai Loudy,
Pages 37, 53, 39, 42 and 50.

My first realization of an entire MISSING WORD from many popular translations was in Dr. Tom Taylor's spirit-led **Bible** studies, as well as included in his book **Rescuing God From the Rubble of Religion**:

The following passages from three different Bible versions illustrate instances in which whole words are missing. The first is from *Romans 7:24*:

Who will set me free from the body of this death? (NASB)

Who shall deliver me from the body of this death? (KJV)

Who will rescue me from this body that is subject to death? (NIV)

All three above begin with, "*Who,*" and end in a *question.* Now look what happens when the Greek manuscript is translated properly:

What will rescue me out of this body of death? Grace! (CLNT)

Asking "*What,*" not "*Who,*" leads to a different understanding of the subject: The Apostle is referring to some*thing*, not some*one.* Furthermore, Paul answered his own question, and an important answer it is, too: "**Grace!**"

We can only speculate about why the translators acted more like *interpreters* of Scripture, changed *What* to *Who*, and leave a question hanging, which the Apostle answered!

Rescuing God From the Rubble of Religion
by Dr. Tom Taylor and Barbara Brown, MSE, page 22-23.

Did you see that? An ENITRE WORD was left out… in addition, the word "what" was changed to "who" in other versions. *WHAT?!?* The word, and thus the entire concept of GRACE here was entirely left out. "Grace," (through which we are justified, forgiven and set free, in this current eon), was omitted!

(In fact, in my own experience, the concept of Grace was largely left out of religions… ones I partook of anyway. Let me be clear, grace *was* taught and spoken of regarding Yeshua {Jesus} dying on the cross and giving us the forgiveness of sins; yet grace and the vast love of the Father in Heaven, *read Zephaniah 3:17, Psalm 36:5-9, Ephesians 2:4, etc.,* was far from a "popular topic," and rarely ever taught at all!

My impression of Yahweh {God} in Heaven was that yes, our sins are forgiven, but He is angry with us... literally all the time.)

I am now completely on board with Dr. Tom Taylor's decision to read **ONLY** the **Concordant Literal Versions** of the New and Old Testaments! I am entirely grateful for A.E. Knock meticulously translating the Scriptures directly from original manuscripts... NOW I know in the depths of my heart that what I am reading is the WHOLE TRUTH and nothing BUT the truth! (Well, the closest we have in the world today, translated from the original Greek and Hebrew.) Bless him Father!

I want to "share all" here and let you know that when I first heard this I did not receive the revelation with open arms and a believing heart! I had memorized Scriptures in the **Bible** I grew up with since childhood, and "loved" the precious wording of those recited Scriptures that would scroll through my mind and were written on my heart. So, dear reader, I understand IF this is the first time you have heard this shocking news regarding **Biblical** translations being incorrect, and if you do not LEAP UP and receive this truth with open arms. However, I do want to bridge the gap, and share my journey of truth-seeking with you, openly expressing my initial fears and blocks to this news as well. I myself was taught at a young age that the definition of faith was to NOT QUESTION ANYTHING taught by ANYONE other than those few forty in the small Lutheran Church community. Thus, if you can imagine, my willingness to even LOOK at this fact as a possibility was similar to the world believing Christopher Columbus when he proved that "the world was ROUND!" It took YEARS for people to accept this proven fact... since it had been *"scientifically stated"* that the world was FLAT!

However, after the initial emotions played their course... I looked, I searched deep into my heart with a magnifying glass for where I may have "tightly gripped" words spoken to me at a young age, "facts" that were not facts at all... simply traditions and beliefs innocently handed down from one generation to the next. I realized that not only were mistranslations possible due to human error.... IT WAS PROVEN! No other **Bible** interpretation has been so meticulously translated from the original languages as the **Concordant Literal Versions of the New and Old Testaments** have been.

> **Now these** [the Bereans] **were more noble than those in Thessalonica, who receive the word with all eagerness, examining the scriptures day by day, to see if these have it thus.**
>
> *Acts 17:11*

May I humbly encourage you, dear reader, to seek the entire truth yourself also! Do your own research! Look into the **Bible** version you may yourself "love dearly." One way would be to follow Adlai Loudy's unbiased research of example instances of this documented in his book, **God's Eonian Purpose**, comparing your **Bible** to the **Concordant Literal Versions**. (The whole New Testament in webpage format and a downloadable pdf of the Old Testament are graciously provided FOR FREE at Concordant.org.)

And the lies do not stop there... for instance, the truth of, and surrounding, Yeshua's {Jesus'} birth, which I share later.

Religion. Oh man! Talk about "**having a form of devoutness, yet denying its power**" and "**invalidating the word of God by your traditions...**" which is making the word of Yahweh {God} of no effect!

Now this know, that in the last days perilous periods will be present, for men will be selfish, fond of money, ostentatious, proud, calumniators, stubborn to parents, ungrateful, malign, without natural affection, implacable, adversaries, uncontrollable, fierce, averse to the good, traitors, rash, conceited, fond of their own gratification rather than fond of God; having a form of devoutness, yet denying its power. These, also, shun.

2 Timothy 3:1-6a

Yeshua says to the Pharisees and some of the scribes from Jerusalem: you are "…invalidating the word of God by your tradition which you give over. And many such like things you are doing."

Mark 7:1 and 13

And, I had believed the religious lies as well as the incorrectly translated "**Bible**." I had believed ALL OF IT, "hook line and sinker":

- Yahweh {God} was dead.
- Miracles do not happen anymore.
- Speaking in tongues is wickedness.
- All translations of the **Bible** are exact and correct.
- Grace ONLY refers to Yeshua's {Jesus'} dying for our sins; and does NOT include kindness at all from our Father in Heaven.

The list goes on and on…

No WONDER I had such a hard time leaving religion. I was steeped in it, *in* religion.

Praise Yah {God} for HIS grace and patience with me, His daughter... as I (sometimes slowly) climbed OUT of "big (and small) boxed religion!" The spirit was and still is "**guiding me into all the truth.**" Praise His Holy Name!

> **"Yet whenever that may be coming -- the spirit of truth -- it will be guiding you into all the truth..."**
>
> *John 16:13*

> **...having this same confidence, that He Who undertakes a good work among you, will be performing** (to bring to an end, accomplish, perfect, execute, complete ~ *Thayer*) **it until the day of Jesus Christ...**
>
> *Philippians 1:6*

> **Now, seeing that you are sons, God delegates the spirit of His Son into our hearts, crying "Abba! Father!" So that you are no longer a slave, but a son. Now if a son, an enjoyer also of an allotment from God, through Christ.**
>
> *Galatians 4:6-7*

However, I admit... *at the time* I did not FEEL like I was being guided into all the truth. I FELT lost and stuck.

This is precisely what Bruce Lipton Ph.D. states in an interview, which now, today, makes complete sense to me… (emphasis mine):

> *…the only way you really see the change is to look back. In the process of change, you don't see it because it's live action. It's only when you look back, and go, "Well, how were those actions?" Now you have review you can see;* ***in the midst… it's process, you do NOT see the changes happening now… until you look back.***
>
> Quotes from a podcast with Bruce Lipton Ph.D. at: BruceLipton.com/the-frontier-sciences-evidence-based-practises-principles-guiding-you-to-transform

All of this religion, embedded into me from birth to age 7, and indeed, through my choice, that which I continued to believe in for much of my adult life, I finally left behind me, and began attending and participating in the **Light Up the Scriptures Bible** study conference calls… where the truth was taught! No religion. No traditions. Simple FREEDOM!

> **Jesus, then, said… "If ever you should be remaining in My word, you are truly My disciples, and you will know the truth, and the truth will be making you free."**
>
> *John 8:31-32*

> **Now the Lord is the spirit; yet where the spirit of the Lord is, there is freedom.**
>
> *2 Corinthians 3:17*

All that said, through the memories surfacing during the process of writing this, I cherish being raised in a Lutheran Church and on the Word of Yahweh {God}. Yes, there are pieces of religion that are wrong, and some missing… which all amount to lies. However, there was MUCH good to my upbringing also. I was raised on the Word of Yahweh {God}, the unmovable bedrock on which to now restructure my knowledge of the truth.

Hear, Israel! Yahweh is our Elohim; Yahweh the only One. So you will love Yahweh your Elohim with all your heart and with all your soul and with all your intensity. These words which I am instructing you today will come to be in your heart. <u>You will repeat them to your sons</u>, <u>and you will speak of them when you sit in your house</u>, <u>when you walk on the road</u>, <u>when you lie down and when you arise</u>. You will tie them for a sign on your hand, and they will come to be for the brow bands between your eyes; you will write them on the jambs of your house and on your gates.

Deuteronomy 6:4-9

(Also read Deuteronomy 11:18-21.)

He who keeps back his club hates his son,
Yet he who loves him is early to discipline him.

Proverbs 13:24

(My modern-day take on this Proverb, for the love of their future refined character… which is exactly how I was raised, as well as how I brought up my own daughter, is: Discipline your kids, including spanking, or end up raising whiny and spoiled children.)

Let not this scroll of the law ever remove from your mouth, but soliloquize (speaking your thoughts out loud) on it by day and by night, so that you may observe to obey according to all that is written in it; for only then shall you prosper in your way, and then proceed intelligently.

Joshua 1:8

I believed in Yeshua {Jesus}.

"Do not work for the food which is perishing, but for the food which is remaining for life eonian, which the Son of Mankind will be giving to you, for this One God, the Father, seals." They said, then, to Him, "What may we be doing that we may be working the works of God?" Jesus answered and said to them, "This is the work of God, that you may be believing in that One Whom He commissions."

John 6:27-29

I always have believed, (though I have not always lived my life in harmony with Him). Praise Yahweh {God} for His forgiveness!

For thus God loves the world, so that He gives His only-begotten Son, that everyone who is believing in Him should not be perishing, but may be having life eonian.

John 3:16

I have seen others who were not raised as I was, and thus they had to learn to believe, to struggle to have faith. I am *so grateful* to Yahweh {God} to have given me the *gift of faith* as a little girl… to have been raised in a believing home and school as well!

I am convinced that my own journey "**out** of the *religious* box" and the journey of others to even believe in Yahweh {God} are similar though… similar hurdles, similar emotions, a similar web of lies to cut away from, similar opposition to breakthrough and, similarly, the truth to embrace!

"... and the truth will be making you free."

John 8:32b

Chapter 5

THE SPIRIT…

and speaking in tongues.

Now we obtained…
the spirit which is of
Yahweh, that we may be
perceiving that which is
being graciously given to
us by Yahweh, which we
are speaking also, not with
words taught by human
wisdom, but with those
taught by the spirit,
matching spiritual blessings
with spiritual words.

1 Corinthians 2:12-13

Now we obtained, not the spirit of the world, but the spirit which is of God, that we may be perceiving that which is being graciously given to us by God, which we are speaking also, not with words taught by human wisdom, but with those taught by the spirit, matching spiritual blessings with spiritual words.

Now the soulish man is not receiving those things which are of the spirit of God, for they are stupidity to him, and he is not able to know them, seeing that they are spiritually examined.

...

For who knew the mind of the Lord? Who will be deducing from Him? Yet we have the mind of Christ.

1 Corinthians 2:12-14 and 16

Beyond the little white church house, and now jumping ahead to having left the "big box church," I was learning to hear Yahweh {God}, to follow His lead, to find the truth!

Just the other day I said to my friend, talking about the direction of my journey, my path, *"I feel like I am walking through the middle of a wheat field... no 'set path or road'... simply walking with my Father, one step at a time, one day at a time! Serving Him with all my heart, soul, mind and spirit. Hearing and heeding His voice."* (My humble living abode is surrounded by breath-taking BEAUTY in the country... surrounded by mountains, olive groves, wheat fields, oh yes, and a pig farm. I have actually gotten used to the smell! LOL.)

Let me say here: While I am not yet an expert on the spirit and **speaking in languages** (tongues), simply sharing my story, my journey, may help you on yours... Even today I continually progress with speaking in tongues. My relationship with my Father in Heaven deepens the more often I speak in tongues to Him. So, dear reader, regarding this subject,

I also point you to Scriptures, as well as giving reference to the lives, testimonies, and teachings of others.

Now… on to the spirit and speaking in tongues!

One day, some ten years ago, Deborah asked if I spoke in tongues. "*No…*" I replied hesitantly.

I was encouraged to read the Scriptures on the spirit, pray and ask Yahweh {God} for the spirit, and just *begin* to speak in tongues! (It sounded so simple! One. Two. Three. Done!)

I do not recall which Scriptures I read in my "spirit study" upon this advice years ago… However, I currently have a "spirit study" in progress. Extracted from that study, I pray the few Scriptures that I have added here are helpful to you:

Now we obtained, not the spirit of the world, but the spirit which is of God, that we may be perceiving that which is being graciously given to us by God, which we are speaking also, not with words taught by human wisdom, but with those taught by the spirit, matching spiritual blessings with spiritual words.

Now the soulish man is not receiving those things which are of the spirit of God, for they are stupidity to him, and he is not able to know them, seeing that they are spiritually examined.

…

For who knew the mind of the Lord? Who will be deducing from Him? Yet we have the mind of Christ.

1 Corinthians 2:12-14 and 16

"And I to you am saying, Request, and it shall be given to you. Seek, and you shall find. Knock, and it shall be opened to you. For everyone who is requesting is obtaining and who is seeking is finding, and to the one knocking it shall be opened.

Now of some father of you a son will be requesting bread. No stone will he be handing him!... If you, then, being inherently wicked, are aware how to give good gifts to your children, how much rather will the Father Who is out of heaven, be giving holy spirit to those requesting Him!"

Luke 11:9-13

And at the placing of Paul's hands on them, the holy spirit came on them. Besides, they spoke languages and prophesied.

Acts 19:6

"But coming is the hour, and now is, when the true worshipers will be worshiping the Father in spirit and truth, for the Father also is seeking such to be worshiping Him. God is spirit, and those who are worshiping Him must be worshiping in spirit and truth."

John 4:23-24

For if I should be praying in a language, my spirit is praying, yet my mind is unfruitful.

1 Corinthians 14:14

Now, similarly, the spirit also is aiding our infirmity (weakness ~ *CLKC*), for what we should be praying for, to accord with what must be, we are not aware, but the spirit itself is pleading for us with inarticulate groanings. Now He Who is searching the hearts is aware what is the disposition of the spirit, for in accord with God is it pleading for the saints.

Romans 8:26-27

Let the word of Christ be making its home in you richly, in all wisdom, teaching and admonishing yourselves; in psalms, in hymns, in spiritual songs, singing, with grace in your hearts to God.

Colossians 3:16

Now you, beloved, building yourselves up in your most holy faith, praying in holy spirit, keep yourselves in the love of God, anticipating the mercy of our Lord Jesus Christ for life eonian.

Jude 1:20-21

My "religious mind" was at war with my spirit, my *growing spirit.* Old religious traditions, embedded in me so early on, were telling me that what I was doing was WRONG and, further still, *evil*! The spirit in me, (which I was desperately trying to learn to hear) was nudging me on... telling me to keep going on this unknown and "scary" path, (scary because, firstly, it was **new** and **different**, *"out of the box"* to me, and secondly, the path to the truth was and is often hindered by those entrenched in the lies that create their comfort zone).

The <u>spirit indeed is eager</u>, yet the flesh is infirm (weak ~ *CLKC*).

Mark 14:38b

I *finally* drummed up the courage and, having prayed for the spirit, went outside and began walking up and down along the row of hedges in the front yard, embarking on the process of speaking in tongues. At first, babbling and babbling, I felt completely stupid… RIDICULOUS. I did not really *believe* in what I was doing… nor believe in what I was asking for! **PRAISE YAH** {GOD} **for His patience with me!!!**

As far as the east is from the west,
So He removes our transgressions far from us.
As a father shows compassion over his sons,
So Yahweh shows compassion over those fearing Him.
<u>For He knows our formation,</u>
<u>Remembering that we are soil</u>.

Psalm 103:12-14

"…if we are disbelieving, <u>He is remaining faithful</u> -- He cannot disown Himself."

2 Timothy 2:13

I was told to *"listen for a word."* Listen for something that sounds "*different.*" I had NO IDEA what that meant… however, day after day I kept walking up and down, still babbling and babbling. (Now, an important realization was that "*listen*" meant listen *in the spirit* as well as *in the physical.*) However, nothing was happening.

Deborah suggested a few of the "Sold-Out-Seekers" (the women) meet with me, pray over me, and walk me through breaking any curses either spoken over me or that I had made myself (both known and unknown). So, one night three of us met and followed all of the above instructions. (I felt STRANGE and SCARED. It was so new to me, breaking curses and praying to receive the spirit. I am sure that my feelings of fear and unbelief stopped anything that could have happened that night. I thank Yahweh {God} for His continual patience with me...) I drove home late that night feeling many things, glad of the help from other followers, yet scared of the new things I had just done. *Breaking curses?!?*

I continued walking up and down outside. And, days later it finally happened! I "heard" a word that sounded (or felt) different than babble. I wrote it down. (Well, I wrote it down phonetically!) I raced to the phone in my excitement to tell Deborah! *"Good!"* she replied! *"Now, just say that word, over and over."* I thought: *"Really? Ok..."* I still did not have a CLUE what I was doing!

Deborah, on the other hand, spoke in tongues **often**. She would begin praying in English, and most often seamlessly flow into praying in tongues. It had become so natural to her... as Daniel likes to share, *"She sings in tongues around the house and does not even realize it!"*

I knew that following past strict traditions WAS NOT WORKING... however, while a little scared of "the new" and reluctant to embrace it, I forged on. I kept walking.

Walking back and forth in the front yard, (praying the neighbors could not hear me), I repeated my cherished *one word* over and over... Finally, I heard what sounded like four words, and I quickly wrote them down. Then I repeated the new collection of four words, over and over. (The words sounded sort-of like Aramaic, and while I clung to them, my mind chatter told me I was doing it all wrong.) Looking back, I desperately needed to tell my mind to SHUT-UP!

<u>All be doing without murmurings and reasonings</u>…

Philippians 2:14

As I said I am not yet an expert on speaking in tongues. However, this I know… I will be! Praise Yahweh {God}! So, I echo Daniel's so often stated wisdom: learn to hear the spirit, study the word, *spirit-check* and *fact-check* **everything yourself**, (be like the Bereans who were of noble character, *read Acts 17:10-11*). Do not just take my word for it… or anyone else's for that matter. Not one human on this earth is perfect. (Not breathing today, at least.) So… let us be led by the spirit. Let us learn to listen to that *"still small voice."* Unlearn what the world has taught, and learn about Yahweh {God} and His ways! (I did not always do this… and sometimes ended up following others, well-meaning as they may have been, **straight** INTO A HOLE. Oops. Then I had to climb OUT of the hole! Ugh.)

Barbara Brown writes in her book that it took months and months for her to begin speaking in languages. She explains *why* as follows:

> The church I had grown up in taught that the "gifts of the Spirit" ended in the first century and were not for us today…
>
> Clearly, my church had been wrong. My "religious head" was keeping me from getting the gift that Jesus paid a big price to send.
>
> *GOD is* GOD *and* We Are Not
> by Barbara Brown, MSE, page 23.

Now, I would like to point out here that, while Barbara Brown did not speak in tongues right away when she prayed for the spirit… she does share in her book how Yahweh {God} had given her the gift of healing and the working of miracles! (Utterly miraculous!) Yahweh {God} would instruct her to pray for people, and they would be healed! She writes in her book:

> **Cathy's doctors said she only had weeks to live.** By the time she arrived at the store, she had given up hope. After I shared with Cathy about Jesus, and how much He loved her, I asked her if she wanted to live. She said, "Yes," and we prayed. God began restoring Cathy's life and, in the weeks that followed, He healed her body and gave her new vision and purpose.
>
> Miracles like that started happening all the time. Thank God that His anointing breaks the yokes and sets His children free.
>
> *GOD is* GOD *and* We Are Not
> by Barbara Brown, MSE, page 19-20.

Now, my personal opinion here, is that while Barbara Brown was not speaking in tongues, the evidence that Yahweh {God} was using her and her prayers for miraculous healings proves to me that she DID have the spirit of Yahweh {God} living in her. As I said, as evidenced by the working of miracles:

> **Now to each one is being given <u>the manifestation of the spirit</u>, with a view to expedience. For to one, indeed, through the spirit, is being given the word of wisdom, yet to another the word of knowledge, according to the same spirit yet to another faith, by the same spirit, yet to another <u>the graces of healing</u>, <u>by the one spirit</u>, yet to another operations of powerful deeds, yet to another prophecy, yet to another discrimination of spirits, yet to another species of languages, yet to another translation of languages.**
>
> *1 Corinthians 12:7-10*

Now, back to speaking in tongues again... Barbara Brown shares that she was prayed over by others, asking Yahweh {God}, seeking the spirit's gift of speaking in tongues:

> The women at the retreat prayed for me to receive the Holy Spirit. I felt like their "guinea pig," but I didn't get a single word. They said, "You'll speak in tongues yet." I was still asking God for His Spirit months later.
>
> *GOD is* GOD *and* We Are Not
> by Barbara Brown, MSE, page 22.

Yahweh {God} works in His own ways, in His own timing... with everything! Barbara Brown shares her own life experience of this, of His timing in her life of finally gifting her with speaking in tongues:

> Months later, while driving and singing along with worship music, a word came out of my mouth that I'd never heard before. I wrote it down and called a friend. "I got a word," I said, "ONE word! What should I do now?"
>
> "Keep saying it," my friend replied.
>
> *GOD is* GOD *and* We Are Not
> by Barbara Brown, MSE, page 24.

Now, on the other hand, Dr. Tom Taylor shares his experience of first speaking in tongues, saying it was like the gush of a water hydrant (literally 1.2.3. Done.) in his case:

> ...a friend... said, "I think you're ready for the baptism of the Holy Spirit." I agreed and we set a date to drive to the mountains. When he pulled up to my apartment, it was already snowing hard and

going into the mountains was out of the question. "We can do this right here," he said when I got into the car. "I'll pray and then I'll start praying in the Spirit. You ask God to fill you with His Spirit and then start speaking in tongues."

"That's it?" I thought. I expected that God would make my mouth speak in tongues; I was NOT expecting to have to speak on my own!

My friend began praying and soon began praying in tongues. I wavered and hesitated. I felt foolish and almost panicky, as if I had been asked to read for the first time in front of my elementary school class and I had no idea how to start. I was certain that I would make a fool of myself.

I finally asked God to fill me with His spirit; then I waited ... nothing. I knew I was going to have to utter the first sound, but every part of me with an ounce of dignity recoiled at the idea. I was frozen ... until I made myself just blurt out a sound ... just one; but then I blurted out another, then another and another. Pretty soon, I was uttering a string of sounds that had no meaning to my rational brain, but something welled up inside me and began gushing out like a water hydrant in a farm yard. I was aware for the first time of my own spirit... truly aware. Suddenly, I felt a direct communication with God that I never wanted to shut off ... ever. God had suddenly become real and I was talking to Him. I couldn't understand a word, but I didn't care.

Rescuing God From the Rubble of Religion,
by Dr. Tom Taylor and Barbara Brown, MSE, pages 6-7.

What a blessing! It seems he received an ENTIRE language from Yahweh {God} within just a few moments of asking!

My personal initial experience was similar to that of Barbara Brown's, described previously, (which was in stark contrast to that of Dr. Tom Taylor's immediate gushing hydrant of language with the Father). Years and years after I received my one word, and then four words of speaking in tongues, I still was not flowing (or speaking fluently like others I knew) in my prayer language. While I had a few paragraphs of tongues... it did not seem the same to me, compared to others around me. I still felt embarrassed, guilty and like I was "doing it wrong." Deborah graciously shared her heart with me one day:

> *Don't get into striving about praying in tongues freely. But share your heart with the Father...*
>
> > *"Father, I really want... I want my language with YOU! That is just for US!"*
>
> *And it would be, not entreating, but almost:*
>
> > *"Father, you will not withhold this from me, I just want to talk to You freely."*
>
> *But as you got into your heart TOWARD GOD, and NOT trying to work something up so you would be like everybody else...*
>
> *And it is THAT kind of heart that the little girl can come trusting her Father that:*
>
> > *"You want to talk to me, probably as much as I... I just want it to FLOW."*
>
> *Anyway, it is a RELIGIOUS box that you are breaking through.*

Praise Yahweh {God} for His patience with me and His faithfulness!

I was listening to **Light Up the Scriptures** study "*182 - Experience versus belief*" just yesterday, and something spiritually caught my attention, when Dr. Tom Taylor said...

> *... they become like curious little children. And there is, seems to me, Scripture about little children! Those who remain suspicious, now, (and there are those), they are the ones simply deciding to carry their wounds around, rather than experience healing!*
>
> Light Up the Scriptures study "*182 - Experience versus belief*"
> by Dr. Tom Taylor. (Time: 52:04 - 52:24)

I knew the Scripture well that he was referring to:

> **"Let the little children be coming to Me, and do not forbid them, for of such is the kingdom of God. Verily, I am saying to you, Whosoever should not be receiving the kingdom of God as a little child, may under no circumstances be entering into it."**
>
> *Mark 10:14-15*

My heart was pierced. It seemed both Deborah and Dr. Tom Taylor had the same message: "***What if*** *one of the reasons that I do not yet speak an entire 'language of tongues,' like I hear others speaking, is because I have not 'come as a child'* ***completely****, purely and humbly before Yahweh {God}? Could there still be a lingering piece of a 'spirit of religion' in me, taught from a young age that 'speaking in tongues is wickedness or evil'?*" This concurs with Barbara Brown's statement above, a "spirit of religion" stopping the gift from Yahweh {God}. So, I immediately canceled any agreements I had made, known and unknown, with any spirit of religion. I cast them off in Yeshua's {Jesus'} Name. (Again, breaking curses spoken over me, or that I had spoken myself. THIS time though, in absolute confidence, I completely understood AND thus wholeheartedly meant what I was saying and breaking.)

My personal view, regarding Yeshua's {Jesus'} instruction to "just believe" explains why Dr. Tom Taylor received tongues SO QUICKLY… it seems he completely and utterly believed it would happen right away, and thus it did! Compared to my own experience, and that of Barbara Brown, it took time because of a lingering "spirit of religion" still in my belief system, (embedded in my subconscious), which I needed to reject first, before being able to RECEIVE this gift from Yahweh {God} within myself truly. This shows to me, again, the simple direction (and blessing when it is obeyed) to ***come as a child.***

A fellow truth-seeker, (I will call her Pamela), shared with me something that she remembered from years and years ago when she was beginning to speak in tongues:

> *I remember questioning if I really was speaking in tongues.*
>
> *A friend told me not to question the gift.*

This has helped and encouraged me greatly… sounding similar to when I knew I desperately needed to tell my mind to shut up! When Pamela shared this with me something happened, chains broke off of me, I found it much easier to "keep going." I saw myself as a little child, gleefully holding hands with my Father in Heaven as we walked down a bright and glorious path… speaking and singing to Him joyfully, in my own special language, just mine and His.

Now, another child of Yahweh's {God's} came to my mind here… Kathryn Kuhlman. Later on in my walk of faith, Deborah encouraged me to read about her, His instrument whom He opened the floodgates of heaven over and flowed His signs and wonders through miraculously. Kathryn Kuhlman was known world-wide for bringing the presence of the spirit, and miraculous healings occurring by Yahweh {God} through her... for the last 10 years of her life!

During her teaching on *"Knowing the Holy Spirit"* and speaking in languages, at Oral Roberts University in 1972, she says that it is not something you can learn, it is not something that can be taught. She shares of witnessing the spirit coming upon people, people who had NEVER been taught the mechanics nor told to "babble until you speak in tongues." She shares that she believes in the baptism of the holy spirit, but that it is not from being taught by a person. (View Kathryn Kuhlman teaching at Oral Roberts University in 1972, *"Knowing the Holy Spirit"* on a YouTube video found at https://www.youtube.com/watch?v=q3hfHeGZyfg.)

Another fellow follower of Yahweh {God}, (I will call her Olivia), shared with me her experience of the gifting of the spirit with speaking in tongues. She said she was "exposed" to it in church from a very young age. She had always wanted to do it.

> *...for me, it just came over me one evening at a house church meeting. I was around 14-15. I wasn't specifically trying to do it at that moment, I was just laying my hands on someone else, praying for them about sickness, and it just kind of flowed out of me. I had tried many times before that evening though, but I always felt like I didn't want to force it. I asked Him to give it to me when He wished. So for me... the Spirit just filled me with it at that moment. Cannot really explain it or put reason to it.*

Now, on the other hand, Dr. Tom Taylor adamantly teaches that speaking in tongues occurs smoothly (and instantly) when praying for the holy spirit. He teaches that speaking in tongues IS THE PROOF that one has the spirit of Yahweh {God}. In his **Light Up the Scriptures** studies he more than once points to the Apostle Paul, highlighting that the FIRST question Paul asks believers is: *"Did you get the spirit?"*

Now it occurred while Apollos is in Corinth, Paul, passing through the upper parts, comes down to Ephesus and, finding some disciples, said to them, "Did you obtain holy spirit on believing?" Yet they to him, "Nay, neither hear we if there is holy spirit." Yet he said, "Into what, then, are you baptized?" Yet they say "Into John's baptism." Yet Paul said, "John baptizes with the baptism of repentance, telling the people that in the One coming after him they should be believing, that is, in Jesus." Now, hearing this, they are baptized in the name of the Lord Jesus. And at the placing of Paul's hands on them, the holy spirit came on them. Besides, they spoke languages and prophesied. Now there were, in all, about twelve men.

Acts 19:1-7

Also, in his study *"32 – The Absolute Necessity of Being Filled With The Holy Spirit"* he reads *Acts 2:38* and explains about the spirit as follows (emphasis mine):

Acts 2:38

Now Peter is averring to them [or "saying, declaring, verifying"], "Repent and be baptized each of you in the name of Jesus Christ or the pardon of your sins, and you shall be obtaining [you shall be getting] the gratuity of the holy spirit."

Now, listen. You repent, you get baptized here, and then what happens next? It is not an "if" and it's not a "maybe" - ***you shall be obtaining the gratuity of the holy spirit – "obtaining,"*** *is getting, passively, as opposed to taking actively.*

Do you see the difference? If you're obtaining, you're getting it. ***And you don't have to do anything to get it, other than repenting and***

***being baptized, according to Peter here at that time.** You don't have to take it actively. You get it passively.*

*But listen, remember what it says above - the spirit gave them language "**to declaim,**" (or speak in a lofty style). [Tom is referring to Acts 2:4.] <u>They had to speak</u>. <u>The spirit gave them the language but they spoke</u>. <u>They begin to speak</u>. Do you see what I'm saying here? This is not a passive act. It is passive infilling. The infilling is given. It is granted.*

Light Up the Scriptures study "32 - *The Absolute Necessity of Being Filled With The Holy Spirit"* by Dr. Tom Taylor. (Time: 17:22 - 18:52)

People share different experiences of beginning to speak in tongues... there seems to be no "one size or set timing fits all," as you can see for yourself from the few examples shared above in these pages alone!

Please do note that I am very spiritually cautious of any and every teaching or preaching that I listen to and follow (as Yeshua {Jesus} Himself said, this is a "cramped gate and narrowed way... and few are those who are finding it" and there will be many false teachers or prophets, read *Matthew 7:14* and *Matthew 24:24*). I do not follow every teaching of any human being on this earth; I do follow every teaching of Yeshua {Jesus}, and Yahweh {God} alone. Sadly, many out there with a microphone (or a video camera on their phone) share information that is not led by the spirit, especially in this day and age with the world-wide-web! So, with much prayer and petitioning of Yahweh {God}, I share these teachings and experiences of myself and others with you.

Do remember, dear reader, as I shared previously in the introduction to this book, for you (and I) to put on our panoply, ***spirit-testing*** and ***Scripture-checking*** what ***all*** others say and do, and that includes myself and this book! While I point to others' teachings... I personally do not agree with *everything* that others believe and teach. I keep watch in the spirit when I hear (or read) others, seeing what the spirit shows... I do also humble myself, remembering that sometimes if I do not agree with others it may NOT be "the spirit," it may be my flesh, not wanting to see something new or different than I am used to. I give room for Yahweh {God} to show that I may simply not understand something that someone else knows... and I may have to remove "old stuff" and "old beliefs" before I can open myself up to clearly see His truth and wisdom through others. As Deborah says, *"We are all a work-in-progress for sure."*

I do have this whole subject of *speaking in tongues* before the Lord... seeking what is His view on speaking in tongues and HOW He gives this gift to His children:

- Is speaking in tongues the one and only evidence of His spirit in us?
- Can or should everyone be able to receive it in the same manner?
- Is it supposed to happen in mere seconds (how Dr. Tom Taylor shares in his experience above)?
- Can everyone practice babbling to learn tongues (how I myself and others learned)?
- Does speaking in tongues only just suddenly come upon you, waiting without babbling, (like with Barbara Brown, Olivia and others)?
- Is it different for each person? Is that His way?
- How did it specifically occur with the Apostle Paul and others in the New Testament?
- What can block the gift of speaking in tongues?
- Is it ALL about *belief*?

Father,
I fall on my knees, seeking the truth.
Open our eyes and grant us Your wisdom,
I pray, in Yeshua's {Jesus'} holy name.
Amen.

What comes to mind, again, is "come as a child" and "according to **your belief**, let it be." So, as Barbara Brown shared, the religious beliefs she chose to hold onto in her mind were **stopping** the gift of speaking in tongues. The same is what happened to me.

It seems to be about your belief… or unbelief (doubt).

As Yeshua {Jesus} Himself said so many times, "Only believe!"

"And all, whatsoever you should be requesting in prayer, believing, you shall be getting."

Matthew 21:22

(Also read Mark 5:36, Luke 8:50, Mark 11:24, Mark 9:23-24, John 14:1, Mark 5:36, Luke 1:45, and John 11:40.)

So, fellow truth-seeker, let us come as a child to Yahweh {God}, with all pure innocence, trust and faith that ALL is possible WITH Him! As well as to continually rely on the faithfulness of our Father in Heaven, knowing that His spirit WILL guide us into all the truth! Amen!

"Yet whenever that may be coming -- the spirit of truth -- it will be guiding you into all the truth, for it will not be speaking from itself, but whatsoever it should be hearing will it be speaking, and of what is coming will it be informing you."

John 16:13

Endeavor to present yourself to God qualified, an unashamed worker, correctly cutting the word of truth.

2 Timothy 2:15

"Request and it shall be given you. Seek and you shall find. Knock and it shall be opened to you. For everyone who is requesting is obtaining, and who is seeking is finding, and to him who is knocking it shall be opened."

Matthew 7:7-8

"Verily, I am saying to you, If you should not be turning and becoming as little children, you may by no means be entering into the kingdom of the heavens. Who, then, will be humbling himself as this little child, he is the greatest in the kingdom of the heavens."

Matthew 18:3-4

"With men this is impossible, yet with God all is possible."

Matthew 19:26

Chapter 6

LIGHT CANNOT WALK WITH DARKNESS

Choices and Consequences!

Do not become diversely yoked with unbelievers. For what partnership have righteousness and lawlessness? Or what communion has light with darkness?

…

For you are the temple of the living God, according as God said, that I will be making My home and will be walking in them, and I will be their God, and they shall be My people. Wherefore, Come out of their midst and be severed, the Lord is saying. And touch not the unclean, and I will admit you, and I will be a Father to you, and you shall be sons and daughters to Me, says the Lord Almighty.

2 Corinthians 6:14 and 16b-18

As I continued following the spirit of Yahweh {God}, (though I honestly did not realize that I *was* learning to hear and obey Yahweh's {God's} spirit at the time), turning away from man-made religion, and as I stopped pleasing people, stopped doing "what I had always done," and began surrendering more and more of my life to Yahweh {God}, by living more radically (or seriously) for Him, *my life changed.* (Obviously stated, yes! But still, in ways beyond any I could have imagined.)

I had previously shared with Red some of the new religion-free, truly spirit-filled revelations that I was learning about the **Bible** and Yahweh {God}. He listened and even seemed interested… for a day or two. Then, he stopped, abruptly. Instantly, in fact. And did not want to hear any more of what I was learning. I guessed that he had spoken with others including his family. Red's sister and brothers attended the same religious "sister Spanish church," and he was very close to them. He also had many, many friends in the church he attended. Plus, as a somewhat locally well-known singer, making good money singing in bars as well as restaurants, he also sang at weddings and parties, including those of church members.

He would also sing at church services once in a while. And so it was, his choice was made: *religion.*

A ravine was developing and ever broadening between Red and I. As I shared previously, I covered the television with a tablecloth, and Red thought I was completely crazy, thinking I had "lost my rocker" because TV (entertainment) was his life. Yet I wanted no more negativity nor distractions of the world interfering with my walk with Yahweh {God}. I was learning all about bio-energetics and energy, and Red wanted nothing to do with any of it. The list goes on and on... instead of opening his mind, he chose to remain in his comfort zone, the "boxes of *lies.*"

A few times... I attended a very small church in New Hampshire, and would again go up for prayer at any alter call. One day, the pastor (who did not know much if anything about me at all) spoke a word from Yahweh {God} over me... he prayed, *"You are the head, and not the tail." (Read Deuteronomy 28:13)* I said *"Amen,"* and walked out of the church. That word stuck in me... I mulled it over and over in my mind. I asked Yahweh {God} what it meant in my life? Of what was I *"the head and not the tail?"*

So Yahweh will make you to be the head and not the tail, and you will surely be above, and you shall not be below, in case you should hearken to the instructions of Yahweh your Elohim that I am enjoining on you today, to observe and to obey.

Deuteronomy 28:13

He then revealed to me that, *"I am the head and not the tail,"* of the marriage with Red first and foremost. It also pertained to my actions toward all others. Yahweh {God} was instilling in me a right relationship to Him, as His beloved daughter, (one amongst many of His beloved children), and thus I was to walk confidently IN Him. To always be in spiritual authority in all communications and relationships with others in the world, those not truly following Him. While it also included my speech and actions towards others who were following Him, I was to remember and submit to His chosen leaders in His ecclesia, as and when they were hearing and heeding His voice.

I fumbled around like a 2-year-old learning to walk… as I was learning what "spiritual authority" meant and looked like in my life! (One time I even said out loud to someone, *"I am in spiritual authority."* Feel free to laugh with me. *I am as I share this!* IF you say it to someone… you are NOT, in fact, in spiritual authority! Oh the lessons I had to learn…)

As the days went by, my spirit was growing, and thus becoming more and more estranged in the marriage; I moved to the living room, and slept on the couch.

My Father in Heaven knew I was still stuck in my mind, stuck in old beliefs… Looking back, Yahweh {God} knew I would need His help to completely break free, His help to overcome my deep, deep (beyond imagination) rooted belief, and its accompanying broken record playing in my mind that *"divorce is worse than murder,"* learned from man-made rules of religion during the first thirty plus years of my life.

O Yahweh, You have investigated me and are knowing me;
You Yourself know my sitting down and my rising up;
You understand my thought from afar;
My path and my pallet You have measured off,
And for all my ways You have made provision.
For though there be no declaration on my tongue,
Behold, O Yahweh, You know it all.

Psalm 139:1-4

And so He graciously gave me a gift, the loving Father that He is, *(read Matthew 7:11 and Luke 11:13).*

He spoke to me.

Yes. He *spoke* to me. It was not an audible voice that anyone else could have heard, but it was sounded out CLEAR AS DAY **in my spirit**. A loud, unmistakable declaration. It was similar to when He spoke in my spirit as a child, and again at church only a year prior when He said, ***"Everyone here is dead."*** HOWEVER, this was a MUCH LOUDER voice inside me, He said:

"Light cannot live with darkness."

At first, I was shocked. Shocked that He spoke to me... again! I eagerly wrote it down.

I remember this profound, divine moment vividly when my Father in Heaven spoke to me. I remember the exact place I was standing, the room in which I was standing, every discernible detail, even the direction I was facing, the sun streaming in the windows. Everything.

I was confused again though, sadly, because I had never had (or very little at most) self-esteem to draw from. I even wondered if I was the "darkness" to which Yahweh {God} was referring. My mind, again, was warring against my spirit.

My **mind** said: *"Me? Little old me? Youngest of five children, the OTHERS all much more talented and wiser than myself? Me? I have accomplished nothing in this world. I am a sinner. I have committed horrendous sins, actions deserving of death (if I had lived during* ***Old Testament*** *times). Me? Yahweh {God} is speaking to me? And telling me that I, Tamra, was 'light'?"*

In contrast, my **spirit** was at peace, knowing Yahweh {God} meant that I was "walking in the light."

What was Yahweh {God} saying? What was He asking me to do with His spoken word to me?

Do not become diversely yoked with unbelievers. For what partnership have righteousness and lawlessness? Or what communion has light with darkness? Now what agreement has Christ with Belial? Or what part a believer with an unbeliever? Now what concurrence has a temple of God with idols? For you are the temple of the living God, according as God said, that I will be making My home and will be walking in them, and I will be their God, and they shall be My people. Wherefore, Come out of their midst and be severed, the Lord is saying. And touch not the unclean, and I will admit you, and I will be a Father to you, and you shall be sons and daughters to Me, says the Lord Almighty.

2 Corinthians 6:14-18

And I saw there is more advantage for wisdom than for frivolity Just as there is more advantage for light than for darkness;

Ecclesiastes 2:13

"Come out of their midst and be severed, the Lord is saying." *(2 Corinthians 6:17)* Is Yahweh {God} telling *me to "be severed" and to get a divorce?* Oh, that did not *"fit in my box of religious upbringing."* Correct, it did not. Yahweh {God} was busting me OUT of religion (or at least trying to anyway).

Confused still as I was in my mind, the only correct answer to my Father in Heaven was, *"Yes, I will obey You, Yahweh {God}."*

I Praise the Lord's Holy Name for speaking to me, for HIS leading and guiding of what HE wanted me to do, His next step for me.

With a price are you bought. Do not become the slaves of men.

1 Corinthians 7:23

You are My friends, if you should be doing whatever I am directing you.

John 15:14

But Samuel said,
Does Yahweh have as much delight in
ascent offerings and sacrifices
As in hearkening to the voice of Yahweh?
Behold, to hearken is better than sacrifice,
To pay attention than the fat of rams.
For rebellion is like the sin of divination,
Insubordination, like the lawlessness of teraphim.
Because you rejected the command of Yahweh,
He has also rejected you from being king over Israel.

1 Samuel 15:22-23

So Abraham rose early in the morning, saddled his donkey and took his two lads and his son Isaac with him. When he had split the wood for the ascent offering, he set out and went to the place which the One, Elohim, had indicated to him.

Genesis 22:3

What also comes to mind is the opposite of obedience… disobedience. I did NOT want to reject Yahweh's {God's} word, for look what happened to King Saul when HE REJECTED the word of Yahweh {God}, a distinct act of disobedience. He chose to please the people, blaming his actions on others, "**because I feared the people**" he said. And Yahweh {God} rejected him as king. (Dr. Tom Taylor teaches on this also in **Light Up the Scriptures** study "*142 - From Revelation to Obedience, from hearing to heeding, in 7 steps.*")

Behold, to hearken is better than sacrifice,
To pay attention than the fat of rams.
For rebellion is like the sin of divination,

1 Samuel 15:22b-23a

Again, my mind was warring with my spirit.

I feared Red, and what he would do if I told him I wanted a divorce, but I was DETERMINED to walk with and obey Yahweh {God}.

Now… as I painstakingly slogged through and **out of** old religious beliefs (Praise Yahweh {God}), to seek the truth, deliberating over the Word, I was directed to read the Scriptures plainly describing where **Yahweh** {God} **commanded** divorce. Yes, you read that right. Yahweh {God} *commanded* divorce!

"Why did Yahweh {God} command divorce?" you may ask...

Because His previous instruction to His people was very clear:

When Yahweh your Elohim brings you into the land where you are about to enter in order to tenant it, and He eases many nations out before your face... seven nations more numerous and substantial than you, when Yahweh your Elohim gives them up before you, and you smite them, then you shall doom, yea doom them. You shall neither contract a covenant with them nor be gracious to them, nor shall you intermarry with them. You shall not give your daughter to his son, and you shall not take his daughter for your son. For it might take away your son from following after Me, and they might serve other elohim, and the anger of Yahweh would grow hot against you, and He would exterminate you quickly.

Deuteronomy 7:1-4

Do you know what happened next? Some, in fact, many of the Israelites disobeyed.

Thus... in the book of Ezra, there were over one hundred people **commanded to divorce** and send away the foreigners whom they had abhorrently intermarried with, as they had disobeyed His previous command to NOT intermarry with those not following and obeying Yahweh {God}, and Him alone:

Then Ezra the priest arose and said to them: You yourselves have offended and located in your houses foreign women, thus adding to the guilt of Israel. So now make confession to Yahweh Elohim of your fathers and get His approval, and separate yourselves from the peoples of the land and from the foreign women.

The entire assembly responded and avowed with a loud voice: Just so; it is on us to act according to your word.

Ezra 10:10-12

(I encourage you to read chapter 8:31 through chapter 10 of Ezra for all the details, to understand the background and the entire story! In fact, feel free to read the whole book of Ezra... it is only ten chapters long and reveals the whole-hearted devotion of many Israelites returning to Elohim, Yahweh {God}.)

Again, in the book of Nehemiah, the children of Yahweh {God} were **commanded to divorce** the foreigners they had abhorrently married. Yes, Yahweh {God} commanded them also (through Nehemiah), since they had disobeyed His command to NOT intermarry with those not following and obeying Yahweh {God}, and Him alone:

Moreover, in those days I saw Judeans who had located in their houses foreign women, Ashdodite, Ammonite and Moabite.

...

So I contended with and maledicted them, I smote some men of them and plucked out their hair. I made them swear by Elohim: You ought not to give your daughters to their sons or take up some of their daughters for your sons or for yourselves. Was it not on account of such women as these that Solomon king of Israel sinned? Among the many nations there was no king like him; he

was loved by his Elohim, and Elohim made him king over all Israel. Yet foreign women caused even him to sin. As for you, should we acquiesce in your doing all this great evil and in offending our Elohim by locating in your houses foreign women?

Nehemiah 13:23 and 25-27

(I encourage you to read all of chapter 13, for the whole context of Yahweh's {God's} command of divorce.)

I do not recall focusing on *these* stories in children's **Bible** class… However, as an adult my responsibility is: to increase my own knowledge and understanding, *as well as* for me to be accountable for my own actions, through the process of "correctly cutting" the word of truth in the Scriptures and obeying them.

Endeavor to present yourself to God qualified, an unashamed worker, correctly cutting the word of truth.

2 Timothy 2:15

Yet be testing all, retaining the ideal.

1 Thessalonians 5:21

Today, while writing this, I was led by the Spirit to read this Scripture in *Mark 10* again (below) and when I did *two words* **leapt out** to me like never before:

Jesus averred to him, "Verily, I am saying to you that there is no one who leaves a house, or brothers, or sisters, or father, or mother, or wife [or husband], or children, or fields, on My account and on account of the evangel, who should not be getting back a hundredfold now, in this era, houses and brothers and sisters and mother and father and children and fields, with persecutions, and in the coming eon, life eonian. Yet many of the first shall be last, and the last first."

Mark 10:29-31

Yahweh {God} has just opened my eyes to another declaration, spoken through Yeshua {Jesus}, confirming my obedience to His word:

Yeshua {Jesus} averred (which means, declare forcefully and confidently ~ *CLKC*) that people WILL LEAVE family... INCLUDING "**wife** [husband]." Meaning, He knew people would be separated, severed (and thus divorced) on account of His name and on account of His evangel!

Yeshua {Jesus} did NOT *only* say, "... a house, or brothers, or sisters, or father, or mother, or children, or fields..." NO! In His list, Yeshua {Jesus} **INCLUDED** leaving a "**wife** [husband]" **on account of His name.** Contrary to what I was taught in religion, *"divorce is worse than murder,"* Yeshua {Jesus} here, in His list of what and whom you leave on His account, includes ... "**wife** [husband]." Thus, when correctly cutting the word of the truth, this means Yeshua {Jesus} is OK with... in fact, it is His *requirement* that, each of His true followers (whose wife/husband is **not** devoutly following Yeshua {Jesus}) "**leaves... a wife** [husband]..." on account of His name. (To my recollection, I had NEVER seen this in all the times I had read this Scripture, for over forty-four years!)

I pray I am explaining this clearly. My point above in Mark 10 is... Yeshua {Jesus} Himself SPOKE (and thus is in no doubt **in agreement with the fact** that), people WILL LEAVE THEIR WIFE [HUSBAND] on account of following Him!

Let THAT soak in for a moment or two...!

Praise Yah {God} for his spirit leading us into ALL the truth:

> **"Yet whenever that may be coming -- the spirit of truth -- it will be guiding you into all the truth..."**
>
> *John 16:13a*

Please note: In my personal opinion, in accord with the Apostle Paul and many others, when the **Bible** states "wife" here, it can also be substituted "husband;" just as in most of the Scriptures where it says "son" or "he," I have come to know and understand that "daughter" is to be added in almost every place where it says "son," and "she" to be added in most cases where it says "he."

As the Apostle Paul writes: **For whoever are baptized into Christ, put on Christ, in Whom there is no Jew nor yet Greek, there is no slave nor yet free, there is no male and female, for you all are one in Christ Jesus.** *(Galatians 3:27-28)* "There is no male and female..." here Paul means it does NOT MATTER if you are one OR the other, we are all "one in Christ Jesus." It is as if he were saying, "*We are all on the same level, or the same 'playing field'.*"

For example, in **Luke 14:27** it states: "**And anyone who is not bearing his** [her] **cross and coming after Me, can not be My disciple.**" Here, "his" can also be exchanged for "her." Women also were followers and thus disciples of Yeshua {Jesus}. *(Read Mark 15:40-41, Luke 8:1-3, and Luke 23:49 and 55, etc.)*

Also, in *2 Timothy 3:16-17* it states: **"All scripture is inspired by God, and is beneficial for teaching, for exposure, for correction, for discipline in righteousness, that the man** [woman] **of God may be equipped, fitted out for every good act."** Here "man of God" can also be exchanged for "woman of God." Women were also instruments of Yahweh's {God's} plan throughout the Scriptures. *(Read about Deborah the Prophetess, who was married yet she was a judge of Israel not her husband, in Judges 4:1-5; Miriam the Prophetess in Exodus 15:20a; Huldah the prophetess in 2 Kings 22:14; the "first evangelist" in the New Testament was a woman, in John 4:28-30 and 38-42; also listen to* **Light Up The Scriptures** *"49 - Neither Male nor Female" where Dr. Tom Taylor discusses this topic as well.)*

Again in *Romans 8:14* it states: **"For whoever are being led by God's spirit, these are sons** [daughters] **of God."** Same conclusion here... and, indeed, throughout the Scriptures!

In July 2011, every member of my family was "best friends" to me, kind and caring as they were. I loved chatting on the phone with my parents and all my brothers and sisters (and I would... often)!

During this time, still learning to hear and heed the spirit, the constant warring in my mind continued over what Yahweh {God} had spoken to me versus old religious beliefs, marriage a wreck, body in a "physical state" as well, (which I now completely understand why), terrible migraines, debilitating anxiety, depression, depleted disk in my sacrum, to list a few...

One day my sister, Christina, encouraged me to "*get away for a week as I did not seem myself.*" She even paid for my flight to Central America to stay with a friend and "clear my head." Bless her! She was so loving, kind and generous! (She also offered to completely pay for my daughter to go to a pre-school two to three days per week so I could enjoy some "me time" as I was a stay-at-home mom! She had completely spoiled both me and my daughter... she bought me the most INCREDIBLE five-layer chocolate cake, costing $50, for my baby-shower which she and Stacey completely planned and organized. Christina would often take me shopping during my pregnancy as I got bigger and bigger, and she constantly bought my daughter toys and lovely outfits all too often also.)

So, leaving where I was stuck to find some open thinking space, I gladly sought clarity for a week. (This was the first time I had EVER left the country by myself. I was scared... but also RELIEVED to "get away"!) My friend in Central America said I could stay with her for a week. Bless her!

Yahweh {God} worked it out that my friend had to work much that week, which gave me ALL the time in the world to seek Him, to seek His will for my life, and to "cleanse my mind." I was in turmoil inside, and I needed this time to FIGURE THINGS OUT. (Well, looking back, all I needed to do was to DECIDE to obey what Yahweh {God} had spoken, and to STOP listening to "the voices" of the world! Simple.)

My friend continued her life as usual, working during the day and going out with her friends at night. I was not interested in going to bars and restaurants with her and her friends, and she was not interested in reading the **Bible** with me. So, we did not see each other nor even speak much. This gave me space to SEEK YAHWEH {GOD} and continue to LEARN to hear and follow Him, and HIM ALONE!

"...**seek first** the kingdom and its righteousness..."

Matthew 6:33a

I prayed MUCH. I read the **Bible** MOST OF THE DAY, every day! My journal filled with my feelings as they pendulumed. My (worldly and religious) mind and my spirit were BATTLING against each other. In my lost*ness* I did not know which way was up. I cried a lot. I was in SUCH upheaval, with chaos and utter confusion running rife within. I was still so confused about what Yahweh {God} had said to me, His word being opposed by religion's *"divorce is worse than murder"* mantra repeatedly playing in my head. Yahweh {God} Himself had DECLARED that I ***not*** "walk with darkness," however I was having a very hard time believing that He was DIRECTING ME to get a divorce. I wanted SOMEONE, (someone tangible), to tell me what to do, what the right answer was. Argh! However, the wanting for someone else to make decisions for my life... is one of the EXACT REASONS why I was so miserable *in* life. I had still not learned to follow Yahweh {God} and, instead, I had followed what OTHERS thought I should do in and with my life. (**That** is NOT life and certainly not one surrendered to Him.)

For I am gratified with the law of God as to the man within, yet I am observing a different law in my members, warring with the law of my mind, and leading me into captivity to the law of sin which is in my members.

A wretched man am I! What will rescue me out of this body of death? Grace! I thank God, through Jesus Christ, our Lord. Consequently, then, I myself, with the mind, indeed, am slaving for God's law, yet with the flesh for Sin's law.

Romans 7:22-25

Along with Paul, I thank Yahweh {God} for the gift of Grace!

> **For the flesh is lusting against the spirit, yet the spirit against the flesh...**
>
> *Galatians 5:17a*

I would go outside and walk around the little town, by myself. Just a few blocks from the house I discovered a little smoothie shop with FRESH fruit and veg! Miraculous! Yahweh {God}, of course, knew what would help "clear" my mind of gunk. It would cost the equivalent of \$1 (*one* dollar!) to blend fresh spinach, cucumber, carrot and fresh fruit into a "smoothie!" (In New England, that same smoothie cost eight bucks!) WHAT A BLESSING! It became my EVERY morning delight!

One of the books Barbara Brown and Dr. Tom Taylor wrote focuses on healthy and natural ways to cleanse our bodies, where they state (emphasis mine):

> When you decide to clean the gunk out of your insides, you begin a liberating adventure to unload the "gunk" you've accumulated, and discover how good your body, <u>mind</u> and <u>spirit</u> can feel!
>
> **Your Personal Roadmap to Whole Body Cleansing**
> by Barbara Brown, MSE and Dr. Tom Taylor, page 5.

Clearing out the gunk helped me clear out my mind. All by simply eating what Yahweh {God} always intended.

And Elohim said: Since I have given you all seed-yielding herbage that is on the face of the entire earth, and every tree on which there is the fruit of a seed-yielding tree, it shall be yours for food.

Genesis 1:29

So Daniel said to the steward whom the chief of the eunuchs had assigned over Daniel, Hananiah, Mishael and Azariah, I pray, try out your servants for ten days. Let them give us of the seed-foods of the land that we may eat, and water that we may drink. Let our appearance be seen before you, and the appearance of the boys who are eating the king's dainties. According to what you shall see, do with your servants.

Now he hearkened to them in this matter and tried them out for ten days. And at the end of the ten days their appearance was seen to be better and plumper in flesh than any of the boys who were eating the king's dainties. So the steward kept on carrying their dainties away and the wine of their drink, and was giving them seed-foods.

Daniel 1:11-15

The town I stayed in is at the bottom of a small mountain. Every day I KEPT FEELING my spirit calling me to the top of the mountain. I kept hearing a small, gentle voice calling, beckoning, *"Come up here."* For a few days I ignored the voice inside me, (again, the spirit of Yahweh {God}). *WHEN would I learn?!?*

The voice said, Go forth, and you will stand on the mount before Yahweh. And behold, Yahweh was passing by, and a great and steadfast wind was ripping apart the mountains and was breaking up the crags before Yahweh; yet Yahweh was not in the wind.

After the wind was an earthquake; yet Yahweh was not in the earthquake. After the earthquake was a fire; yet Yahweh was not in the fire. After the fire was the sound of a gentle stillness.

It came to pass as Elijah heard it, he wrapped his face in his mantle and went forth and stood at the opening of the cave. And behold, a voice came to him and said, What have you to do here, Elijah?

1 Kings 19:11-13

A few times I even thought I was crazy for thinking such a thing... *"Me? Climbing a mountain? I am no Moses nor Elijah?"* But then I thought, *"Can't we all be?"*

I FINALLY LISTENED one day. I came out of *"my box of ridged and habitual normal"* and CLIMBED THE MOUNTAIN! By myself! It was an amazing experience. I walked through tiny villages. I walked through fields. I became utterly exhausted about three-quarters of the way up. Every time I thought I had reached the top... I hadn't. So, I stopped at a small store and had some ice-cream and asked the owner where the top was. I headed off in that direction and I kept on going. Four hours of perseverance finally got me to the top. It was exhilarating! Mostly because I had *made* it to the top and there was no further to go! I had conquered it! Even with *debilitating back pains*... I broke through the pain barrier. The calling to follow the spirit was ***greater***. I had moved a mountain to climb one.

For all am I <u>strong in Him</u> Who is invigorating me -- Christ!

Philippians 4:13

Jesus said to them, "With men this is impossible, yet <u>with God</u> <u>all is possible</u>."

Matthew 19:26

And, as Deborah says, *"What happens in the physical, happens in the spiritual."* I had physically succeeded in conquering an earthly mountain… in mere hours I would succeed in conquering the mountain blocking my spiritual freedom as well!

While in Central America "clearing my head," (including during the ascent and descent of the mountain), after MUCH prayer, MUCH **Bible** study and seeking Yahweh {God}… and STILL MUCH warring between my worldly mind and my spirit, I might add… on July 26th (my 34th birthday) I **finally made the decision** to get a divorce.

One of the thousands of things that came to my mind was: when I was around 20-years-young (before I was married), while nannying for a lovely family who were vacationing in the State of Maine for the summer in the most glorious house, I spotted a "random" book, amidst a whole library full of them, about a woman who was MISERABLE in her marriage. (I say "random" because I KNOW that EVERYTHING is led by Yahweh {God}. There is NO SUCH THING as coincidence. Not one.) The woman in the book had two very young daughters, and because of them she decided not to get a divorce. When the children were young adults and the mother unfolded the whole story to them, the two girls said they WISHED she had FOLLOWED HER HEART and gotten a divorce years ago, instead of living in misery (and beyond) just for their so-called "stability." The message in this VERY BOOK that Yahweh {God} led me to read, helped convince me to NOT stay in a miserable marriage. (This was another "belief system" of the time throughout much of the United States… to "stay in a marriage for the stability of the children," and when the kids are age 18 and adults, *then* get a divorce. I had known people in situations who believed and lived out JUST THAT.) Not me, I decided. No. I am going to follow Yahweh {God} today, NOW, *as He guides me.*

It is so comforting, KNOWING that Yahweh {God} led me to read THAT book. He had prepared the way for me, for this very day of my life. HE KNEW, fourteen years prior… that THAT VERY BOOK would help me to make this vital decision years later! He truly is an AWEsome Yahweh {God}! He plans EVERYTHING perfectly!

Thus says Yahweh your Redeemer, the Holy One of Israel: I am Yahweh your Elohim, Who is teaching you to benefit, Positioning you in the way you shall go.

Isaiah 48:17

Now, let me tell you: My life shifted… completely changed more than I ever would have imagined, the day **I** finally **decided to get a divorce.**

As you may understand, this was no easy decision to say the least. It was ENGRAINED in me from a young age that: *"Divorce is worse than murder!"*

Etched in stone into me, you could say.

Well, Praise Yahweh {God} I finally "unetched" it OUT of me!

So, it now makes sense to me WHY it was SO HARD for me to **even consider** getting a divorce, to even consider that Yahweh {God} *ordered* me to get a divorce, knowing all I now know about bio-energetics and programming from birth to age 7. (Not to mention then ACTUALLY GOING THROUGH WITH IT.) I now understand more fully the quote from Winston Churchill:

"If you are going through hell KEEP GOING!"

Let us always remember:

Jesus said to them, "With men this is impossible, yet with God all is possible."

Matthew 19:26

Chapter 7

THE IMPORTANCE OF FAMILY IN YESHUA'S EYES

...compared to the world's view!

> **"If anyone is coming to Me and is not hating his father and mother and wife [and husband] and children and brothers and sisters, and still more his soul besides, he can not be My disciple. And anyone who is not bearing his cross and coming after Me, can not be My disciple."**
>
> *Luke 14:26-27*

Recently a worship song was playing, *"Dear Younger Me,"* by MercyMe, and it got me to thinking, *"Had you told 'the younger me' what would happen in my life, I would never, NEVER have believed you. Nope. Not a chance."* (I think this is the case for everyone called by Yahweh {God}, since His ways are not our ways, *read Isaiah 55:8*, evidenced in my case as you have read, and will continue to read in this book, consisting of events that I would not have wished for nor would I have architected and directed myself, as Daniel himself so often states.)

As I have said, I thank and Praise Yah {God} for my faith, for being raised by believing parents, believing in His Word. Yahweh {God} stands by me through everything, just as He did with the Apostle Paul *(read 2 Timothy 4:16-17)*. Though at the time, rarely if ever did I actually *feel Him* standing there with me. However, I am jumping ahead… Let's go back a bit.

To set the stage: In less than a year, most members of my family not only turned *away* from me… they completely turned *against* me.

Why?

Because I was choosing to more devoutly follow Yeshua {Jesus}, and thus, my new choices and actions did not fit into their own "comfort zone box" nor did they fit the patterns of the *old Tamra* they were used to.

Yahweh {God} bless everyone.

Sadly, right now, today, I confess I again feel a little like Gideon, a tentative fear of others, as he felt, as I speak out and share the truth.

> **It came to be in that night that Yahweh said to him, Take the young bull, the bull that belongs to your father, that is, the second-born young bull of seven years; demolish the altar of Baal that belongs to your father, and cut down the Asherah pole beside it. Then build an altar to Yahweh your Elohim on the summit of this stronghold in the proper arrangement. Take the second-born young bull and offer it up as an ascent offering with the wood of the Asherah pole that you shall cut down.**
>
> **So Gideon took ten men of his servants and did just as Yahweh had told him; that is, he worked at night because he feared his father's household and the people of the city too much to do it by day.**
>
> *Judges 6:25-27*

However, **helping** Yahweh's {God's} children who are seeking strength and encouragement to climb "out of the box" they might feel "imprisoned" by is of **far greater importance** to me! I choose to follow my Lord wholeheartedly, no matter the cost. Today, and every day! And if my life events can help any of His kids, (my *true* brothers and sisters) on their path, then I confidently and gladly choose to help **you**, dear reader, *as Yahweh {God} directs me*, with all my strength. For He Alone is my Yahweh {God}, and with my every breath I serve Him, in my heart, mind, body, soul and spirit.

In Elohim I trust;
I shall not fear;
What can flesh do to me?

Psalm 56:4

Blessed is the God and Father of our Lord Jesus Christ, the Father of pities and God of all consolation, Who is consoling us in our every affliction to enable us to be consoling those in every affliction, through the consolation with which we ourselves are being consoled by God…

2 Corinthians 1:3-4

Now He averred to him, "You shall be loving the Lord your God with your whole heart, and with your whole soul, and with your whole comprehension."

Matthew 22:37

(Read also Joshua 22:5-6.)

For whoever are being led by God's spirit, these are sons of God.

For you did not get slavery's spirit to fear again, but you got the spirit of sonship, in which we are crying, "Abba, Father!" The spirit itself is testifying together with our spirit that we are children of God.

Romans 8:14-16

Brother Lawrence's devoted view of doing all things for Yahweh {God} alone is refreshing (emphasis mine):

> You must know his (that is, Brother Lawrence's) continual care has been... to be always with GOD, and **to do nothing, say nothing,** and **think nothing which may displease Him**; and this without any other view than purely for the love of Him, and because He deserves infinitely more.
>
> **The Brother Lawrence Collection – An Christian Classic – Practice and Presence of God, Spiritual Maxims, The Life of Brother Lawrence**
> by Brother Lawrence, Kindle page 39 of 139.

I hold out my hand to all of you, my sisters and brothers, on your path to Yahweh {God}, seeking and finding the "**cramped gate and narrow** way..."*(Matthew 7: 14)*, which may well cost everything, as Yeshua {Jesus} said... including "**a house, or brothers, or sisters, or father, or mother, or wife** [or husband], **or children, or fields...**" *(Read Matthew 19:29, Mark 10:29 and Luke 14:26.)*

> **"Enter through the cramped gate, for broad is the gate and spacious is the way which is leading away into destruction, and many are those entering through it. Yet what a cramped gate and narrowed way is the one leading away into life, and few are those who are finding it."**
>
> *Matthew 7:13-14*

> **"But coming is the hour, and now is, when the true worshipers will be worshiping the Father in spirit and truth, for the Father also is seeking such to be worshiping Him. God is spirit, and those who are worshiping Him must be worshiping in spirit and truth."**
>
> *John 4:23-24*

Even in "big box churches," and in Christian religion generally, I was taught (along with millions of others) to *"pray for your spouse and family to get saved."* **Did Yeshua** {Jesus} ***ever*** **do this?** No. There is no Scripture that states this. Quite the opposite, frankly. Yeshua {Jesus} **did** say:

> **And Jesus said to them that "A prophet is not dishonored, except in his own country and among his relatives and in his home." And He could not do any powerful deed there except, placing hands on a few who are ailing, He cures them. And He marvels because of their unbelief.**
>
> **And Jesus went about the villages around, teaching.**
>
> *Mark 6:4-6*

For years and years (back when I was in "big box religion") I felt so **blessed** that all my family members were either believers of Yeshua {Jesus} or knew of Him, and that I personally did not experience harsh persecution or resistance from them regarding my faith.

Little did I know what would happen
when I *left* religion,
and followed the *true* Yeshua {Jesus}.

I have seen and heard leaders and experts across The United States, (and this probably applies to most of the entire human race across the globe), follow and endorse **deep rooted "family blood systems."** What do I mean? The strong and deep rooted belief that FAMILY (blood relatives, including those adopted) means MORE THAN ANYTHING. Anything! Meaning, no matter what, "come hell or high water," you stay with and/or you help your family, NO MATTER how they treat you. NO MATTER how abusive they are or become. NO MATTER WHAT. Period. The end. (End of discussion.)

The moment you realize, as I did, that your life is more important than ANYONE else's belief or opinion, you take back control of your own life.

Just as Dr. Tom Taylor teaches in his study titled "*174 - The reward and price of total surrender, utter vulnerability, and unequivocal obedience*" (emphasis mine):

> *Home is where family is, where everyone you knew since you were "this tall." And they all think they know you, and that's where the spirit you're full of and walk in the power of is* ***not appreciated.***
>
> *We ought never to think that anyone we used to know will grasp who we are today, assuming we walk as sons and daughters of YaHoVeH, as Yeshua did.*
>
> ***We also ought never to change who we are to suit them...***
>
> ***Listen to me! We ought never to change who we are to suit anyone,*** *other than the Father Himself...*
>
> Light Up the Scriptures study "*174 - The reward and price of total surrender, utter vulnerability, and unequivocal obedience*" by Dr. Tom Taylor. (Time: 7:57 - 8:43)

Notice Dr. Tom Taylor spoke the same words twice, one almost right after the other. Practicing what he teaches when highlighting that Yahweh {God} does this in the **Bible**. Let us PAY ATTENTION... with words when spoken twice.

Some of the more difficult Scriptures for me to even imagine would ever apply, let alone be required to obey *in my own life* with my own **family members**, were:

Now someone of His disciples said, "Lo! Thy mother and Thy brothers stand outside. They are seeking to speak to Thee." Yet He, answering, said to the one saying it to Him, "Who is My mother, and who are My brothers?" And stretching out His hand over His disciples, He said, "Lo! My mother and My brothers! For anyone whoever should be doing the will of My Father Who is in the heavens, he is My brother and sister and mother!"

Matthew 12:47-50

"Are you supposing that I came along to give peace to the earth? No, I am saying to you, but rather division. For from now on there will be five in one home divided, three against two, and two against three will be divided, father against son and son against father, and mother against daughter and daughter against mother, mother-in-law against her daughter-in-law and daughter-in-law against her mother-in-law."

Luke 12:51-53

> **"If anyone is coming to Me and is not hating his father and mother and wife [and husband] and children and brothers and sisters, and still more his soul besides, he can not be My disciple. And anyone who is not bearing his cross and coming after Me, can not be My disciple."**
>
> *Luke 14:26-27*

Back in Central America... having finally made the decision to get a divorce (after ten years of marriage), the first person I called was my brother and, as his wife answered the call, I told her. I was incredibly close to them both at the time. My brother, (I shall refer to him as Zack), having overheard the conversation, refused to even speak to me that day on the phone, and has *not since.* Not once.

I had adored, almost idolized my brother Zack, all my life. I even "became" left-handed in some things (which he had taught me as a child how to do) just because *he* was left-handed! He was my best friend growing up. He was my best friend until he started dating the girl he eventually married. I later became close to them both (he and his wife), very close... **until** the day I decided to get a divorce.

I also called my parents to tell them I was getting a divorce, (scared witless because I knew FULL WELL they believed, as Lutherans are taught, again, that literally, *"divorce is worse than murder"*). However, I was finally learning to stop people-pleasing... and was now *only* God-pleasing! Yes. Yah-pleasing, by ***getting*** a divorce!

> **"...seeing that I speak not from Myself, but the Father Who sends Me, He has given Me the precept, what I may be saying and what I should be speaking."**
>
> *John 12:49*

For whoever are being led by God's spirit, these are sons of God.

For you did not get slavery's spirit to fear again, but you got the spirit of sonship, in which we are crying, "Abba, Father!" The spirit itself is testifying together with our spirit that we are children of God.

Romans 8:14-16

The very next day, on the flight back to New England, my insufferable back pain disappeared. COMPLETELY! (The flight to Central America had been excruciating, even with a "tush cush," a special cushion to help sooth pain from the depleted disk in my sacrum.)

I was healed!

100% healed from that day on!

The "jelly" came back into my "donut!"

From the day I decided and then spoke the words, *"I am getting a divorce."* My body changed. My body *healed*!

What the doctors, the medical world and the pharmaceuticals failed to heal, was healed by my decision to obey Yahweh {God} and get a divorce.

For the disposition of the flesh is death, yet the disposition of the spirit is life and peace…

Romans 8:6

Bless Yahweh, my soul,
And all within me, bless His holy Name!
Bless Yahweh, my soul,
And do not forget any of His well-dealings,
Who is pardoning all your depravity,
<u>Who is healing all your ailments,</u>
Who is redeeming your life from ruin,
Who is crowning you with benignity (mercifulness, kindness and bountifulness ~ *CLKC*) **and compassion,**
Who is satisfying your future with good,
<u>So your youth is renewed</u>...

Psalm 103:1-5

He [Yahweh] said to me: Son of humanity, shall these bones live?
And I answered, My Lord Yahweh, You know.
...
When I prophesied as He had instructed me, the spirit came into them, and they lived...

Ezekiel 37:3 and 10a

(Read the entire life-giving, inspiring account of Ezekiel 37:1-14.)

Wow!

I myself was LIVING PROOF of **quantum physics**... Me!?! I was living out *"mind over matter"* WITHOUT COMPLETELY UNDERSTANDING what was happening!

I am MOST amazed... even to this day! I pray this discovery, this realization, is as exciting to you as it was to me.

THIS healing BLEW my mind! It helped COMPLETELY launch me OUT of "the medical model box" of lies!

What comes to mind is a little kid who puts on a cape, climbs onto a high wall and JUMPS... believing that he or she will fly! Only to be taught a QUICK and painful lesson about gravity.

Now, in my case quite the opposite outcome... pain gone, I FLEW out of the "the medical model box" into the celestial sphere!

I LEPT INTO THE FIELD of quantum physics... and I DID FLY! (Instead of believing both the lies that most of the world believes and the doctors' claims to me of: *"There is no cure,"* I BEGAN SOARING!)

Bruce Lipton Ph.D. himself, describing this very phenomenon, states the following (emphasis mine):

> ***Heaven on earth can be EVERY DAY of your life.*** *Because when you have your wishes and desires as programs, the 95% of the day, they're automatically... Manifesting your program, without you even thinking about it! Because that's what you're doing right now!*
>
> Quotes from a podcast with Bruce Lipton Ph.D. at: BruceLipton.com/the-frontier-sciences-evidence-based-practises-principles-guiding-you-to-transform

Even though I was unaware that my very own words healed me... even though my MIND was not aware that healing was taking place in my body... this did NOT change the fact that my body healed!

This is precisely what Dr. Tom Taylor and Barbara Brown write in their book **Your Personal Roadmap to Whole Body Cleansing** (emphasis mine):

> **You determine how sick or healthy you are** – not genes, not family history – **YOU do it and you can also undo it.** Your thoughts, feelings, beliefs, and the habits they produce, determine your well-being in every area of life.
>
> **Your Personal Roadmap to Whole Body Cleansing**
> by Barbara Brown, MSE and Dr. Tom Taylor, page 106.

Identically, they write about this same proven principle again in their book, **It Happened, It's Over, It's OK Now! How to Let Go of the Past and Heal Your Mind, Memory and Emotions.** Knowing it well from their own lives, as well as witnessing it in the lives of countless others, they share:

> Researchers now know that emotions, such as loneliness, worry, and anxiety produce chemicals that lower the efficiency of your immune system. They not only make you susceptible to illness, but they allow latent viruses like Epstein-Barr to reactivate, systemic inflammation to run amuck, cause tissue damage, and increase your risk of chronic diseases such as atherosclerosis (hardening and narrowing of the arteries), cancer and diabetes.
>
> The good news is that emotions like happiness also produce chemicals that reinforce your immune system and reverse the damage that negative emotions cause. The more delighted you feel about every aspect of your life, the greater the benefit to your physical health and your sense of well-being.
>
> **It Happened, It's Over, It's OK Now! How to Let Go of the Past and Heal Your Mind, Memory and Emotions**
> by Barbara Brown, MSE and Dr. Tom Taylor, page 11.

Louise Hay, the bestselling author of **You Can Heal Your Life** (of which over fifty million copies have been sold throughout the world), speaker, soulful teacher, healer and artist, explains in her book, **HEAL YOUR BODY – The Mental Causes for Physical Illness and the Metaphysical Way to Overcome Them**, (emphasis mine):

> Both the good in our lives and the dis-ease are the results of mental thought patterns that form our experiences. We all have many thought patterns that produce good, positive experiences, and these we enjoy. It's the negative thought patterns that produce uncomfortable, unrewarding experiences with which we're concerned. It's our desire to change our dis-ease in life into perfect health.
>
> We've learned that for every effect in our lives, there's a thought pattern that precedes and maintains it. Our consistent thinking patterns create our experiences. Therefore, by changing our thinking patterns, we can change our experiences.
>
> What a joy it was when I first discovered the words metaphysical causations. This describes the power in the words and thoughts that create experiences. This new awareness brought me an understanding of the connection between thoughts and the different parts of the body and physical problems. **I learned how I had unknowingly created dis-ease in myself**, and this made a great difference in my life. Now I could stop blaming life and other people for what was wrong in my life and my body. I could now take full responsibility for my own health. Without either reproaching myself or feeling guilty, I began to see how to avoid creating thought patterns of dis-ease in the future.
>
> HEAL YOUR BODY The Mental Causes for Physical Illness and the Metaphysical Way to Overcome Them by Louise L. Hay, page 5.

Louise Hay healed herself of cancer by doing deep mental work of releasing and forgiving, (see the Introduction in her book, **HEAL YOUR**

BODY)! She explains simply how to free yourself from doctor labels of "incurable" anything... she writes:

> Now when I hear about someone's illness, no matter what dire their predicament seems to be, I know that if they're willing to do the mental work of releasing and forgiving, almost anything can be healed. The word incurable, which is so frightening to so many people, really only means that the particular condition cannot be cured by "outer" methods and that we must go within to effect the healing. The condition came from nothing and will go back to nothing.
>
> **HEAL YOUR BODY – The Mental Causes for Physical Illness and the Metaphysical Way to Overcome Them by Louise Hay, page 2.**

I have learned that "incurable" is a conclusion by means of man's wisdom, *or* doctors' opinions. Yahweh {God} created our bodies to work perfectly, all of the time!

The extraordinary book quoted above, **HEAL YOUR BODY**, fills my new *"medicine cabinet!"* Any time I feel any *dis*-ease, any *dis*-comfort I open the book! It has helped me greatly, to live in ease and peace! Headache, pain in my shoulder, or pain in my neck, looking up the **WHY** in the book, deals with the emotion *BEHIND the pain*. In my mind, this book is a **definite MUST** in every household in the world! I believe medications could be thrown out, and instead heal our minds and bodies from the inside. Now, I did not learn this all overnight... it took me time to "un-program," as Bruce Lipton Ph.D. would say, the old beliefs I was raised with. (I do still keep a generic pain killer in my house, I embarrassingly admit. Once in a while I do not catch the feeling of stress and I will then take one, KNOWING I have work to do on my insides, my feelings and emotions, while this "band aide" is working for a few hours. I am still on my journey!)

Before, when I strictly believed ONLY in "The Medical Model" (meaning "doctors are GODS who know everything and everything they say is TRUTH") I used to think that people, like me now, were quacks! Complete lunatics who had totally lost their minds! Ha!!! **I guess I am now a quack!** And... happy to be one! *(I am actually laughing out loud as I write this!)*

Healed! Healthy! Living wholeheartedly in peace!

Having discovered what healed me, it then dawned on me that, tracing back to the moment the "jelly left my sacrum," I further discovered what had cursed me...

I recalled the day of the marriage, I was in a room with my best friend Tina, getting ready in my wedding dress, preparing myself for the *"I do."* When it came time to emerge from the room, both my feet felt like ten ton bricks. The same heaviness upon my feet that I had felt before, in the station wagon, I again felt loaded down, something preventing me from crossing the threshold and out of the room. Nothing in me wanted to go through with the wedding. I was scared. Sadly though, even with the strongest urge, I did not even reveal to Tina how I felt. I did not want to hurt or embarrass Red by leaving him at the altar. My mind, searching for anything good to sway my decision, thinking *"surely, Red is a 'good person,' right? I mean, he has never drank a drop of alcohol in his life, even when he often sings in bars. He refused to even touch the stuff. He is generally a kind and positive person. Why are my feet so determined NOT to go through with this?"* Looking back, I **now know**, even though I was not devoutly following Him at the time, it was Yahweh's {God's} spirit speaking to me **again**, weighing down my feet, attempting to guide me not to take this step. My warring mind, fighting against what I now know to be the truth, reasoning that it was normal to feel this, just the jitters, pushing me to ignore the true feeling in my feet, to walk out and do the, *"I do."*

> **"…if we are disbelieving, He is remaining faithful -- He cannot disown Himself."**
>
> *2 Timothy 2:13*

It was not long after this that I re-joined the same church (the "big box church" that I ended up leaving years later when Yahweh {God} said, "*Everyone here is dead*"), but Red did not join it right away. I was afraid, afraid of what would happen IF he did not give his life to Yahweh {God} too. I imagined the worst, confirmed yet further at the witnessing of some realities to those fears. I shared my deepest fears with no one, internalizing almost all of my feelings, burying my head in the sand deluding myself that "everything was great." I felt I was spiritually carrying Red. **I was now sinning**: believing I could bear the spiritual accountability for his actions (that which was to be between Red and Yahweh {God} alone).

I chose fear and worry, instead of trusting Yahweh {God}, an overbearing sin, the burden of which, unbeknownst to me then, led to manifesting in the physical as debilitating back pain… for *years.*

I have learned that any feeling of "dis-ease" in my body is a result of my own sin, missing the mark somewhere in my life. This is in alignment with what Louise Hay discovered and labeled as "probable causes," the fears and negative emotions that lead to physical symptoms. I now know that these "probable causes" are directly related to the sin itself.

Because of my choosing fear and worry, generating only my own negative emotions, I was bed-ridden for a month, suffered continuous excruciating back pain for more than eight years, with "*no hope of a cure.*" My literal change of mind, my repentance, the decision to cut the chains tying me to the spiritual weight of Red, severing light from darkness, was now generating the positive emotions that, overnight, had me rollerblading and joyously doing somersaults with my daughter, to my heart's delight!!! Wow! I am definitely *"happy to be called a quack,"* a quack who has abundant **freedom** and vibrant **health** to go with it!!

Now, just because I had *decided* to get a divorce, and *spoke* it to others (the power of which I had not totally understood at the time…) it was still a few WEEKS before I conjured up the courage to actually move out of the house… and about four MONTHS until I would finally legally file papers for a divorce.

I was still fiercely struggling within myself to take the step and now *walk out this decision.*

During the many arguments in the marriage for the many months previous to all this, the word "divorce" had been used as a threat to me. Now it was time to face "Goliath," to conquer the mountain and speak my truth, obey Yahweh {God} and follow Him alone, faithfully, wholeheartedly.

The time had come to *walk*... One night, while my daughter was upstairs in bed sleeping, I told Red that I wanted a divorce and I was moving out. He became very angry. Livid in fact. The most volatile I had ever seen him. I was petrified. He seemed to fill the entire room, his anger felt large as a mountain right inside the house, growing and filling the place, scarcely leaving me space to even stand. He was in a rage, yelling at me. I asked him to please lower his voice, my little angel's innocent ears my greatest concern. He refused. Beyond that, he threatened me further. My only defense a warning to call the police. After taunting my warning, a boldness came over me, and I did! I pressed the buttons and called the police. I feared for my life.

This was the first time an argument had gotten so out of hand. This was also the first time I had ever called the police, or even felt the *need* to.

(Looking back, I was not the "gentle and quiet" spirited person I am now, as I said before. It takes two to argue. So, I take the part of the responsibility that is mine to take, absolutely.)

I was done. I obeyed Yahweh {God}. I moved out.

> **"You are My friends, if you should be doing whatever I am directing you."**
>
> *John 15:14*

Miraculously, Red and I agreed that my daughter would live with me from Sunday evening until Friday evening, and with him on the weekends.

My sister, Christina, and her husband, graciously agreed to let my daughter and I live with them. I was so grateful for the room we moved into! Glad to be free! They did say, though, I must leave before their two new dogs arrived, in approximately five months. Their home was not big enough for the dogs *and* us.

Months later... in November of 2011, I finally found the courage to legally file papers for a divorce. Even locating the "correct courthouse" to file the paperwork was an entire palaver! Ugh. I went to the courthouse in the county I was currently living in, (while at my sister's house), and they said I had to file in the county that I had last lived together with Red. So, I went to that courthouse. THEY said I had to go to a different courthouse... (Each courthouse said a different thing regarding WHERE I was to file.) Again, Ugh.

Already emotionally exhausted, full of fear and dread, my mind a mess... I FINALLY found "the correct courthouse" and miraculously (Praise Yahweh {God}!) there was a KIND volunteer there who came up to me and asked if I needed help. I broke down and cried. Right there. I did not know what I was doing (my mind and spirit STILL warring, wondering IF I *was* doing what Yahweh {God} wanted me to do), and I was not 100% sure what legal paperwork I had to fill out. I gratefully accepted, "*Yes please, please help me.*" And the words, "*Thank you SO VERY MUCH! You are an angel,*" must have been proclaimed a thousand times that day. Having shared with me that they themselves had gone through the same struggle years prior, they were thus helping those in need, in need of a kind and loving "hand to hold" through this tumultuous and far from straight-forward process.

Since that day, that very day, I wanted to help others too… as I had been helped in so many areas of my life. (As Yeshua {Jesus} said, *"Freely you have received, freely give.")*

"Gratuitously you got; gratuitously be giving."

Matthew 10:8b

Blessed is the God and Father of our Lord Jesus Christ, the Father of pities and God of all consolation, Who is consoling us in our every affliction to enable us to be consoling those in every affliction, through the consolation with which we ourselves are being consoled by God…

2 Corinthians 1:3-4

Father,
I pray my experiences help the one reading this now. Even if it is for just you, dear reader, it will have been worth it. I pray you feel comforted that, whatever your struggle, "you are ***not the only one*** *going through it." I pray strength and peace over you, to continue walking... walking on this path, sometimes a lonely one to follow, but never alone! (As Yahweh {God} Himself is always with us... even if we do not feel Him near.) Blessings beyond to you, my fellow truth-seeker! In Yeshua's {Jesus'} Name,*
Amen.

I had researched on-line how to file for a divorce. Since I had a daughter with Red, there would be a statutory trial, no matter what else was agreed upon (or not) regarding worldly possessions, (for example: house, cars, clothes, kitchen items, furniture and so forth).

Before locating the correct courthouse, I had already written out a detailed list of all these worldly possessions, with a more-than-fair distribution of each. There were two used vehicles, I kept one; I kept my own clothes and personal paperwork, an air mattress, pillow and blanket and, additionally, some of my daughter's clothes and books; some of my daughter's toys, including her three-story doll-house, (leaving more than half of everything with Red). I did not ask for, nor want, anything else. Nothing. Over this, and many aspects of the divorce process, I would confide in my sister and her husband...

To my absolute horror, I soon discovered that they were regularly speaking with, as well as relaying to, Red everything I was doing!

WHAT?!? This was *not* ok with me ("tempering" my language as I write). Especially after the horrendous fight, Red's rage, the *threatening behavior,* and *the* fear for my life. My mind was reeling: "*Why would they choose to be friends with the man who threatened their own sister? What were they thinking? Did they not understand?* **Clearly not**. *After ALL that Christina had done for me... Why would she betray me now?*" It was beyond all comprehension.

As Deborah always says: "*Everyone is free to make their own choices, they are not free from the consequences of those choices.*"

My heart saddened. Some of those consequences were such that I had to stop being open with my own sister about my life. To my greater surprise, they could not fathom as to why. They could not see how breaching my confidence by sharing much of all I said and did, especially with the opposition... was in anyway a form of betrayal?!?

I had no option but to move out of their house. On my second trip to collect the remainder of our belongings, mine and my daughters... ***all*** the toys, her cherished doll-house, clothes, books, etc. were already outside on their front lawn. Door shut. Curtains closed.

I loaded up my truck, filled up with gas, literally kicked the dust off my feet, and drove out of town.

"Now, on entering into a house, salute it, and if, indeed, the house should be worthy, let your peace come on it. Yet if it should not be worthy, let your peace be turned back on you. And whosoever should not be receiving you, nor yet be hearing your words, coming outside of that house or city or village, shake off the dust from your feet."

Matthew 10:12-14

My mind, still reeling, I held onto the only constant in my life:

Yahweh {God}**!**

Now we are aware that God is working all together for the good of those who are loving God, who are called according to the purpose that, whom He foreknew, He designates beforehand, also, to be conformed to the image of His Son, for Him to be Firstborn among many brethren.

Romans 8:28-29

Jesus Christ, yesterday and today, is the Same One for the eons also.

Hebrews 13:8

My parents then made the exact same decision as Christina and her husband... they also continued to speak regularly to Red. I will admit, much as a result of my own inhibitions, believing I was to be quiet and only to speak of the good in people, over the ten years of the marriage

I did not tell the truth about his conduct with me to anyone. Not to family, not a single person, not even my best friend. Instead, I painted the "perfect picture" of him, having taken seriously what was taught me, often ringing in my ears, *"if you do not have anything nice to say, don't say anything at all."* I was protecting the man and the "colorful painting" I had conjured of his reputation as well. Much to my dismay, it came back to BITE ME… far beyond anything I could ever have imagined. Far, far beyond.

Again, as Deborah always says, *"We are free to make our own choices, we are not free from the consequences of those choices."*

To my recollection, there was only one instance I did say something and it seemed even that was "too little, too late," especially amidst all my "perfect picture painting." My daughter and I flew to Arizona for ten days to help take care of my dad after he had undergone back surgery. Nearing the end of the ten days, I was sitting on my parent's living room floor, and looking up at my dad, with tears in my eyes, I said, *"I do not want to go back, Dad. I do* ***not*** *want to go back."* He looked at me and said nothing.

I now see that it was the *worldly* life I had created that was falling apart. The family systems I was so deeply entrenched in. And this was just the beginning…

"If anyone is coming to Me and is not hating his father and mother and wife [and husband] and children and brothers and sisters, and still more his soul besides, he can not be My disciple. And anyone who is not bearing his cross and coming after Me, can not be My disciple."

Luke 14:26-27

Dr. Tom Taylor teaches on this Scripture above *(Luke 14),* on this exact phenomenon, in his **Light Up the Scriptures** study, he states:

How much indoctrination is there in our society, and even in Christianity, about the importance of family and family ties and all that family closeness? Along comes Yeshua, who says essentially that these relationships which we would think are sacred are the first ones that we are to detest if we are serious about following after Him.

Light Up the Scriptures study "*171 - Acting on Revelation or Emotion*"
by Dr. Tom Taylor. (Time 6:55 - 7:21)

Yahweh {God} was breaking down what I had built my way... and was even then, planning and building my life HIS way, for HIS glory. Little did I know it.

Praise Yahweh {God} for His patience.

I am SO grateful that He came to find His lost little sheep.

Now He told them this parable, saying, "What man of you, having a hundred sheep, and losing one of them, is not leaving the ninety-nine in the wilderness and is going after the lost one, till he may be finding it? And finding it, he is placing it on his shoulders, rejoicing. And, coming into the house, he is calling together the friends and the neighbors, saying to them, 'Rejoice together with me that I found my sheep that was lost!' I am saying to you that thus there will be joy in heaven over one sinner repenting, more than over the ninety-nine just persons who have no need of repentance."

Luke 15:3-7

And I am also grateful He continually sends "angels" (as I call them) to help me along my journey.

When I was a teenager I would PRAY continually and SING in church during worship and BEG YAHWEH {GOD} to *"use me for His will."*

Then I heard the voice of Yahweh saying: Whom shall I send? And who shall go to this nation? So I answered, Behold me! Send me!

Isaiah 6:8

My favorite scripture was (and still is):

As a deer is panting over the channels of water,
So is my soul panting for You, O Elohim!
My soul thirsts for Elohim, for the living El;
When shall I come and appear before Elohim?

Psalm 42:1-2

And it is one of my very favorite songs also, written by Martin Nystrom, *"As the deer."*

However, the older me admits that, while the younger me's spirit was willing to do His will, the flesh was still weak, yearning for the "American dream" life. As if to say, *"Oh Father, use me to do Thy will. I will serve You. I am all Yours, wherever, however… however, I have a few conditions. I would like a lovely home, stable income, responsible husband, obedient children, everything "working out just swimmingly."* Oh bless my younger me's definition of "my soul thirsts for Elohim…" I had much to learn of Yahweh's {God's} ways…

My life was NOTHING like what I was expecting when I was praying.

Nothing.

For My designs are not your designs,
And your ways are not My ways, averring is Yahweh.
For as the heavens are loftier than the earth,
So are My ways loftier than your ways,
And My designs than your designs.

Isaiah 55:8-9

As Dr. Tom Taylor always says (paraphrasing), *"If I had been the author and architect of my life, I would* ***NOT*** *have included 'that' experience!"*

Dr. Tom Taylor and Barbara Brown also include this helpful explanation in their book (emphasis mine):

> **Experiences that we wish had not happened** *(or were not happening)* **or wish had been different** *(or were different)*, **may test us**, like the sa-tan tested Job and Yeshua; they may threaten to distract, delay, disqualify and, if possible, destroy our resolve to trust the Father and participate in His purpose for our lives. Trials have boundaries and accomplish a purpose, both of which the Father determines. He plays no direct part in the trial itself, but sets its conditions and **provides "the sequel," or way of eventual escape.** [And then they quote James 1:13, 1 Corinthians 10:13 and Romans 5:3-5.]
>
> Rescuing God From the Rubble of Religion
> by Dr. Tom Taylor and Barbara Brown, MSE, page 148.

Neither would I have wished for what had happened in my life, nor what was about to happen in my life... but it did.

Here are some *other helpful* NON-RELIGIOUS tips, explanations and Bible studies regarding marriage and divorce they have published:

- ***GOD is* GOD *and* We Are Not** by Barbara Brown
  - ~ *Chapter 17 - Holiness Will Prevail*
  - ~ *Chapter 18 - Marriage… Battleground or Blessing?*

- **Light Up the Scriptures** studies by Dr. Tom Taylor
  - ~ *"49 - Neither Male nor Female"*
  - ~ *"50 - Christ Sets the Standard"*
  - ~ *"60 - Blood and flesh, Fight the Right Giants"*
  - ~ *"63 - Marriage and Divorce"*
  - ~ *"115 - What God Joins, We Must Protect"*

Yahweh is my Shepherd;
Nothing shall I lack.
In verdant oases, He is making me recline;
Beside restful waters, He is conducting me.
My soul He is restoring;
He is guiding me in the routes of righteousness,
on account of His Name.
Even though I should walk in the ravine of blackest shadow,
I shall not fear evil,
For You are with me;
Your club and Your staff, they are comforting me.
You are arranging a table before me in front of my foes;
You have sleeked my head with oil;
My cup is satiated (filled to overflowing).
Yea, goodness and benignity (mercifulness,
kindness and bountifulness ~ *CLKC*),
they shall pursue me all the days of my life,
And I will dwell in the house of Yahweh for the length of my days.

Psalm 23

Chapter 8

HIS WAYS ARE NOT OUR WAYS

If what Yahweh directs you to do is
"out of your box," you are in GOOD company!

For My designs are not your designs,
And your ways are not My ways, averring is Yahweh.
For as the heavens are loftier than the earth,
So are My ways loftier than your ways,
And My designs than your designs.

Isaiah 55:8-9

Since I began living *on my own* with my daughter, I searched for suitable nanny jobs who would accept the fact that my own young, 4-year-old daughter would be with me while working also. I found a LOVELY couple with a new-born baby seeking temporary help. Beyond accepting my situation, they were thrilled to have my daughter come with me! (What a blessing!) I always felt so guilty deep inside that my daughter would have to accompany me "to work." I made the best of it though! I would take their child and my daughter on walks, to play at parks, and to do art projects to get all creative. So, there was my daughter benefitting from this work arrangement, with all the freedom and creativity that I certainly would not have been able to provide her in any other occupation!

No trial has taken you except what is human. Now, faithful is God, Who will not be leaving you to be tried above what you are able, but, together with the trial, will be making the sequel (a way to escape, exit ~ *CLKC*) **also, to enable you to undergo it.**

1 Corinthians 10:13

Trust in Yahweh with all your heart,
And do not lean to your own understanding.

Proverbs 3:5

Then Yahweh {God} opened yet another door with my next and absolute *perfect* long term, live-in nanny and personal assistant job! Someone who was on the SAME spiritual (religion-free) path as I was... needed help and was more than willing for myself and my daughter to live with her and her daughter! Another angel, (I will call her Angelica). I believe that she was helping me as much if not more than I was helping her, bless her!!! Yahweh {God} does work in mysterious ways!

The job was located only forty-five minutes from my daughter's current Private Christian School, (which Christina had kindly paid up front for an entire year), and just two minutes across the state line in New Hampshire.

I set up a court date, legally requesting to move with my daughter for my new lovely job in a home on the lake in an upscale neighborhood. (Due to the timing of events, I actually moved a few days before the court date, as the job began immediately, and Yahweh {God} worked it out to be more convenient for myself and my new employer.) Knowing that I had already moved, Red informed the judge.

Red's living arrangement for my daughter, on the other hand (which the judge had been aware of for weeks), was that of a single room for the two of them to share in his sister's house, which was even more unacceptable in my view due to the fact that it was located on an unsafe street (to put it kindly) in a town with a widely known bad reputation... not to mention, the whole property had been infested with bedbugs as certified by a professional pest control company. Everything in the house had to be removed and washed/dried at high temperatures including linens and clothing; all furniture moved, and then everything in the property including carpets and floor boards chemically treated. Even after this, my daughter would repeatedly suffer from bites, the signature three-in-a-row bite patterns, on her arms and legs. As I said, I had previously shared my concerns for my daughter about all of this in court... however **no one besides me** seemed to care.

After a short recess and review of the case, the judge denied my request to move. That would be surprise enough if it stopped there. Not drawing the line at that judgment, the already agreed custody arrangement between Red and myself for my daughter was reversed, by order of the judge, such that I was allowed to care for my daughter now ONLY on the weekends, and she would live with Red throughout the entire week.

I was KNOCKED FOR A LOOP! *What? What just happened?* I sat in my car after court unable to drive, stunned. Angry. Lost. I pounded the steering wheel… crying. Asking Yahweh {God}, *"WHAT JUST HAPPENED?!?"*

My school house Scripture memorization (programming) kicked in on automatic:

For My designs are not your designs,
And your ways are not My ways, averring is Yahweh.
For as the heavens are loftier than the earth,
So are My ways loftier than your ways,
And My designs than your designs.

Isaiah 55:8-9

I am lifting my eyes to the mountains;
From where shall my help come?
My help is from Yahweh,
Maker of the heavens and earth.

Psalm 121:1-2

But, THIS was NOT SUPPOSED TO HAPPEN!

"Yet wait!" my mind warring, *"Maybe this was the way it was supposed to happen for reasons only Yahweh {God} knows."*

This is NOT how I would have written my life! No.

And, little did I know, that this was just the BEGINNING (in my opinion) of a long, drawn out, biased, grievous, untenable, and unjust court case and custody battle.

(I later came to believe, again my personal opinion, that the judge did not want me to switch counties nor states, and thus the possibility to also switch judges over this whole divorce and child custody court case. Unbeknownst to me at the time, courts in New England focus MOSTLY on the physical location [home] of the child, and thus IF my daughter would have lived in New Hampshire, I would have legally been able to change courts. Also, I most likely angered the judge by moving before I received official permission from the courts to move out of the state… even though it was literally only 2 miles across the state border, and not to mention a move for a job which not only supplied salary, but also room and board for both myself and my young daughter.)

The spirit of Yahweh {God} brought to my mind Abraham, when Yahweh {God} told him to sacrifice his son. Thus directing my mind BACK to YAHWEH {GOD}, the creator of the entire universe, Who knows ALL things, and has planned every day of mine before I was even born! And I was encouraged. I wanted to have faith as Abraham. Trust. Complete Trust. Obedience. Unquestioning obedience.

It came to pass after these things that the One, Elohim, He probed Abraham and said to him: Abraham!

And he answered: Here I am.

Then He said: Take now your son, your only one, whom you love,

Isaac, and go by yourself to the land of Moriah and offer him up there as an ascent offering on one of the mountains which I shall indicate to you.

So Abraham rose early in the morning, saddled his donkey and took his two lads and his son Isaac with him. When he had split the wood for the ascent offering, he set out and went to the place which the One, Elohim, had indicated to him. It was on the third day that Abraham lifted up his eyes and saw the place from afar.

Then Abraham said to his lads: You sit here with the donkey while I and the youth shall indeed go thus far; there we shall worship, and we shall indeed return to you.

Now Abraham took the wood for the ascent offering and placed it on his son Isaac while he took the fire and the knife in his hand; and the two of them went along together.

Then Isaac spoke up and said to his father Abraham: My father!

And he replied: Here I am, my son.

Now he said: Behold the fire and the wood; yet where is the flockling for the ascent offering?

Abraham answered: Elohim, He shall see for Himself as to the flockling for the ascent offering, my son.

And the two of them walked on together.

Genesis 22:1-8

Your eyes saw my embryo,
And my days, all of them were written upon Your scroll;
The days, they were formed when there was not one of them.

Psalm 139:16

And also, the spirit steered my mind to Joseph… none of his brothers liked him. In fact, they were planning to kill him, yet then sold him as a slave to the Ishmaelite's (the Ishmaelite's)! Joseph was unjustly placed in jail… yet one day, in accord with Yahweh's {God's} timing, he became second in command of all Egypt, and in that authority saved his brothers from the seven-year famine. Despite everything Joseph lived though, in the end he was *not angry* with his brothers. His attitude was of gratitude to Yahweh {God}. He knew that **Yahweh** {God} had a "bigger vision" for his life. He learned to give all glory to Yahweh {God}. He learned that "His ways are not our ways!"

Joseph replied to them: Do not fear! For am I in the place of Elohim? You devised evil against me, yet Elohim, He devised it for good in order to accomplish, as at this day, to preserve many people alive.

Genesis 50:19-20

So, after my tears had finally subsided, I looked up and said to Yahweh {God}, *"I trust You."* I did not completely feel it deep in my heart yet, however I **wanted** to trust Him… and I knew enough to speak it out loud, to continue saying it **until I *did* believe it.**

Deborah, knowing and practicing the power of the spoken word, had encouraged me to read a very helpful book called **The Tongue, A Creative Force** by Charles Capps. One of the most insightful books I have ever read, I would even say it literally changed my speech! It changed my life! The lesson I instantly saw and have since learned, kept close to my heart, fixed forefront in my mind, and *on the tip of my tongue…* was:

> Words are the most powerful thing in the universe… We must learn to use our words more effectively. The words you speak will either put you over or hold you in bondage.
>
> **The Tongue, A Creative Force** by Charles Capps, page 1.

Above, "put you over" means to "give you freedom." Also, Charles Capps shares a similar experience to mine. He writes:

> One morning as I was confessing the WORD, I stopped and said, "Lord, You know I don't believe all this I am saying is true in me." (It was that tradition coming through that made me feel like I was lying.) *I knew the Bible was true and it was in the Bible.*
>
> The Lord said, "That's all right, son. Just *keep saying what the WORD says until it becomes a part of you, then it will be true in you.*"
>
> So I kept confessing, "I have abundance and no lack; my God supplieth all my need," until it was formed in my spirit and became a part of me. *Then, I realized I had broken into a realm of faith that I never knew existed.*
>
> **The Tongue, A Creative Force** by Charles Capps, page 79.

Today, as I write this book years later, I can say I have progressed far on the path in trusting Yahweh {God}… finally!

Death and life lie in the grip of the tongue…

Proverbs 18:21a

The tongue of the wise uses knowledge well,
Yet the mouth of the stupid utters folly.
…
A healing tongue is a tree of life,
Yet words of subversion in it are a breaking of the spirit.

Proverbs 15:2 and 4

Yahweh is my Strength and my Shield;
In Him has my heart trusted,
And I have been helped
So that my heart is joyous,
And with my song am I acclaiming Him.

Psalm 28:7

Today, looking with 20/20 vision, when I said *"I trust you, Lord,"* after pounding the steering wheel… deep in my heart I believed that Yahweh {God} would do the SAME with me as He did with Abraham. I believed He would **immediately restore** my child as soon as I surrendered! Just as He did with Isaac. However, as I was climbing "OUT OF *my* box" it seems I was trying to place Yahweh {God} INTO one. Father, thank You for Your patience! I still had many lessons to learn about Yahweh {God}…

I want to highlight here what Charles Capps describes in his book:

> This is where the fight of faith is lost so many times, just one inch below the nose (the mouth).
>
> **The Tongue, A Creative Force** by Charles Capps, page 81.

I am (sometimes) grateful for my determination… in this case, it saved my LIFE, literally and spiritually, to KEEP WALKING, to KEEP GOING. No matter what was happening around me. No matter what I saw in the physical with my own, earthly eyes. I sought heaven's view, and kept speaking the word of Truth.

(for by faith are we walking, not by perception)

2 Corinthians 5:7

In the group of followers of Yahweh {God}, the "Sold-Out-Seekers," everyone would pray for me and my daughter. They were all SO kind and giving. They also did not extend me any worldly pity. Instead, they would encourage me to completely surrender my daughter, trusting Yahweh {God} to choose the best path, His best path, for both me and my daughter.

One day, my confidence was further cemented when a word from Yahweh {God} came through Deborah regarding the court case, *"This is an Iron-clad case."* I was so relieved! I was convinced it meant that the judge would grant that my daughter live with me… and soon!

Dr. Tom Taylor teaches in a **Light Up the Scriptures** study about something I had never before gleaned from the Scripture about Abraham and Isaac, how Abraham PROPHESIED (spoke) the outcome of his test INTO existence. In fact, Abraham did this TWICE within a brief period… once when speaking to his servants, and once when speaking to his son. Dr. Tom Taylor reads *Genesis 22:2-5* and then shares:

Genesis 22:2-5

Then He said: Take now your son, your only one, whom you love, Isaac, and go by yourself to the land of Moriah and offer

him up there as an ascent offering on one of the mountains which I shall indicate to you.

So Abraham rose early in the morning, saddled his donkey and took his two lads and his son Isaac with him. When he had split the wood for the ascent offering, he set out and went to the place which the One, Elohim, had indicated to him. It was on the third day that Abraham lifted up his eyes and saw the place from afar.

Then Abraham said to his lads: You sit here with the donkey while I and the youth shall indeed go thus far; there we shall worship, and we shall indeed return to you.

Now, you will notice something, and a friend of ours pointed this out, a dear brother in the Lord…: Abraham actually spoke, "and then we will come back to you." He does not say, "then I will come back to you," he said "then we will come back to you." I don't know if Abraham knew it or not, but he was speaking prophetically here, telling his servants, "you hang out here, we're going to go over there but we will be back, both of us."

Light Up the Scriptures study "65 - *Revelation-Obedience-Confirmation-Blessing*" by Dr. Tom Taylor. (Time 18:13 - 18:43)

Now… notice Abraham *(in Genesis 22)*, just a few verses later prophesy's the outcome again:

Now Abraham took the wood for the ascent offering and placed it on his son Isaac while he took the fire and the knife in his hand; and the two of them went along together.

Then Isaac spoke up and said to his father Abraham: My father!

And he replied: Here I am, my son.

Now he said: Behold the fire and the wood; yet where is the flockling for the ascent offering?

Abraham answered: Elohim, He shall see for Himself as to the flockling for the ascent offering, my son.

And the two of them walked on together.

Genesis 22:6-8

Notice also, "**Elohim, He shall see for Himself as to the flockling for the ascent offering, my son.**" Abraham PROPHESIED (spoke into existence) Yahweh {God} sending a flockling for the offering, instead of his son Isaac being the sacrifice. (And if you know the story, this is EXACTLY what happened, after the angel told Abraham to "stop," a ram appeared in the thicket in front of him!)

When we DIG into the Scriptures, and *pay attention to the* ***details…*** Yahweh {God} shows "**His ways**" and we would do WELL to follow in the footsteps of the "faithful of old." Wait, let me speak only to myself here… *I* would do well to follow in the footsteps of the "faithful of old," because my insides are AT PEACE when I *do* follow the examples of those of great faith in the **Bible**, as well as those with great faith alive today!

Yahweh {God} Himself CREATED light by SPEAKING it into existence. He spoke. And it was created! Done!

And Elohim said: Let light come to be! And light came to be.

Elohim saw the light that it was good. Then Elohim separated the light from the darkness. And Elohim called the light Day, and the darkness He called Night.

And evening came to be, and morning came to be: day one.

Genesis 1:3-5

And as the author of Hebrews writes, regarding the declarations of Yahweh {God}:

> **By faith we are apprehending the eons to adjust to a declaration of God, so that what is being observed has not come out of what is appearing.**
>
> *Hebrews 11:3*

This same principle applies with BOTH positive and negative words… and thus all CREATIONS in life. To me, it is a practical example of Yahweh's {God's} instruction "do not complain." HE created everything. HE knows (obviously) that words create.

> **All be doing without murmurings and reasonings…**
>
> *Philippians 2:14*

Again, as Charles Capps teaches in his book **The Tongue, A Creative Force** (emphasis mine):

> …I began to *dig* into the Word of God to see where I was missing it. I had never heard anyone preach on Mark 11:23-24, **"For verily I say unto you, That whosoever shall say unto this mountain, Be thou removed, and be thou cast into the sea; and shall not doubt in his heart, but shall believe that those things which he saith shall come to pass; he shall have whatsoever he saith. Therefore I say unto you, What things soever ye desire, when ye pray, believe that ye receive them, and ye shall have them."**

> *I am sure I had read it but it meant nothing to me. It was not in me.* I had no idea you could have what you say. But as I began to *prayerfully study* what Jesus said about WORDS, the mouth, and prayer, God began to reveal these things to me.
>
> I remember one morning I was praying and I said, "Father, I have prayed and *it is not working out*."
>
> He spoke inside my spirit just as plain, "What are you doing?"
>
> I said, *"I am praying."*
>
> He said, "No, you're not, you are complaining."…
>
> Now that shook me…
>
> Then He spoke into my spirit some things that totally transformed my life. He said,
>
> "…*You have bound Me by the words of your own mouth*. And it is not going to get any better until you change your confessions and begin to agree with My Word. *You are operating in fear and unbelief. You have established the words of the evil one in your behalf.* By your own mouth you have released the ability of the enemy; and if I did anything about it, I would have to violate My Word, and I can't do that."
>
> The Tongue, A Creative Force by Charles Capps, pages 73-75.

Not to beat a dead horse… but this is an IMPORTANT principle! When you speak you are **creating**… thus, if you complain, you are CREATING MORE THINGS *to complain about!* When you speak about what you DESIRE in life, positively… you are CREATING *more positivity into your life (and the negativity OUT of it)!* Simple. Yet, now take it deeper, to the level *before* your speech, that of **your thoughts**… and apply the SAME principle! Changing your thoughts *will* change your speech. That means you can train your mind which, ultimately, will change your life.

As I was learning to WATCH what I speak, and how my words create… I remembered Barbara Brown's description on how Yahweh {God} helped her to use her words effectively. She writes in her book ***GOD is* GOD *and* We Are Not**:

> Years ago, God was trying to help me to be quiet, stay out of everyone else's business, and not always insert my opinions. I just couldn't get this, "shut up" thing. I really thought everyone needed to know what I thought and, of course, do what I told them. Help me, Jesus! I knew I was wearing out God's patience and that I was close to failing my test. I cried out to God, "Please put a watch on my mouth, so I'll quit sinning against You with it."
>
> God said, "It's your mouth; you put a watch on it!"
>
> I begged God to help me pass this class. One day, He said, "OK, Barbara, I'm going to help you. Go out to the garage and get a roll of duct tape." I did. Then He said, "Write 'Ecclesiastes 5:1-7' on it." I did. "Now, put the tape on your mouth."
>
> "Oh, God, MY mouth?" I was horrified…
>
> As I went through the day, people who saw me ran to find a Bible, dust if off, and look for Ecclesiastes 5:1-7. I learned to be quiet when the Spirit convicts me; that my words and opinions are of little value compared to the wisdom of God. If I continue talking when He has drawn the line, I see Him with a roll of duct tape in His hand, and I know that if I don't shut up NOW, I could be wearing it on my mouth again.
>
> [She quotes Ecclesiastes 5:1-7 in her book.]

> If you've never heard God tell you to be quiet, I question whether you've heard Him say anything. We have to close our mouths and open our ears to hear what He has to say!
>
> *GOD is* GOD *and* We Are Not
> by Barbara Brown, MSE, pages 137-139.

She goes on to say (emphasis mine):

> Have you ever tape-recorded your conversations? You could have your own personal dress rehearsal to see whether you're speaking life or death over your circumstances. <u>Listen to your words</u>, <u>for God surely is</u>.
>
> Silence can't be misquoted.
>
> *GOD is* GOD *and* We Are Not
> by Barbara Brown, MSE, page 139.

Bless Yahweh {God}, He sent me across the path of Barbara Brown, such an angel: the bold, strong, faith-filled, "*afraid of NOTHIN' and NO ONE*" guide, who will follow Yeshua {Jesus} through anything and everything. She shared that her boldness was once likened to: "**Benaiah… from Kabzeel was a man of many valiant deeds... Once, on a snowy day, he went down and smote a lion inside a cistern.**" *(Read 2 Samuel 23:20 where Benaiah jumped down into a pit where a lion was stuck, and killed it.)* She has personally spoken the words of Yahweh {God} to even U.S. presidents and kings. She has **complete, unmovable trust** in Yahweh {God}! Her prayers to Yahweh {God} stop earthquakes, (yes earthquakes… and much more)! Just like Yeshua {Jesus} said:

> **"Greater than these will you be doing."**
>
> *John 14:12*

I wanted to learn to control my tongue, so I took a piece of tape and placed it over my mouth. (However, I did not have the guts to go out in public with it on my mouth… I hoped I would LEARN the lesson if I just taped my mouth at home.)

> **… <u>be ambitious to be quiet</u>, and to be engaged in your own affairs** (business)…
>
> *1 Thessalonians 4:11a*

> **"He [Jesus] must be growing, yet <u>mine it is to be inferior</u>."**
>
> *John 3:30*

Through all this, indeed throughout my life, I was learning about **who Yahweh** {God} **REALLY was**, not the "formerly amazing but now dead 'god'" that I had been taught about in religion. I will admit in some areas I was ***far*** from a *"quick learner."*

One Biblical principle that I had rarely seen lived out in "big box churches" or religion (or anywhere frankly), was shunning. I venture to guess, dear reader, that this very act being carried out may be a new experience to you also? So, I thought it would be helpful to share in detail on this word (precept) of Yahweh {God}. As I have already mentioned, I had read all the Scriptures for over thirty years... however, I had not personally paid much (if any) attention to this, to shunning. Which, in fact, whether I knew about it or not does not matter at all, as it is in the Word of Yahweh {God}, and thus to be heeded.

Shunning is a principle that Yahweh {God} teaches throughout the Bible, incorporating it with guarding what is inside us, guarding the spirit inside us so it may grow and flourish... as opposed to wither and perish.

> **The ideal thing committed to you, guard through the holy spirit which is making its home in us.**
>
> *2 Timothy 1:14*

We are in charge of what goes into our ears, our eyes, our minds... everything. And thus Yahweh {God}, through Paul, David, Job, Amos, Yeshua {Jesus} amongst others, teaches us the following about protecting ourselves from evil:

> **Now this know, that in the last days perilous periods will be present, for men will be selfish, fond of money, ostentatious, proud, calumniators, stubborn to parents, ungrateful, malign, without natural affection, implacable, adversaries, uncontrollable, fierce, averse to the good, traitors, rash, conceited, fond of their own gratification rather than fond of God; having a form of devoutness, yet denying its power. These, also, shun.**
>
> *2 Timothy 3:1-6a*

Yahweh {God} is serious. He does not joke. He knows what He is talking about. He knows what people are like... and He also knows that a little leaven is leavening the whole batch, *(read Matthew 16:1-12)*. So, He knows what will happen when we are around others who are: selfish, fond of money, ostentatious, proud... ungrateful... implacable, adversaries... having a form of devoutness, yet denying its power.

Additional Scripture teaching on shunning includes:

> **Yet be testing all, retaining the ideal. From everything wicked to the perception, abstain.**
>
> *1 Thessalonians 5:21-22*

Above, *"abstain"* is the same as shun... stay away!

> **Now I am entreating you, brethren, to be noting those who are making dissensions and snares beside the teaching which you learned, and avoid them, for such for our Lord Christ are not slaving, but for their own bowels, and through compliments and adulation are deluding the hearts of the innocent. For your obedience reached out to all. Over you, then, am I rejoicing. Now I am wanting you to be wise, indeed, for good, yet artless for evil.**
>
> *Romans 16:17-19*

Above, *"avoid"* them is the same as shun... stay away from them!

Now if anyone is not obeying our word through this epistle, let it be a sign to you as to this man [woman], not to commingle with him [her], that he may be abashed…

2 Thessalonians 3:14

Above, *"not to commingle"* is the same as shun… stay away from!

This same principle is in the Old Testament also:

A wise man is fearing and withdrawing from evil,
Yet the stupid one is congenial and trusting to it.

Proverbs 14:16

Seek after good, and evil not at all, that you may live,
And so Yahweh Elohim of hosts shall come to be with you, just as you say.
Hate evil and love good,
And put right judgment in the gateway…

Amos 5:14-15a

There was a man in the land of Uz. Job was his name. This man was flawless and upright, fearing Elohim and keeping away from evil.

Job 1:1

There are countless other Scriptures, speaking of avoiding evil, running from evil, standing aloof, a season to fling away... etc. *(Read also 1 Timothy 4:7-8, 2 John 1:9-11, Matthew 18:15-18, 1 Corinthians 5:11-13, 2 Timothy 2:16-18, Ecclesiastes 3:1-8, Proverbs 4:14, 1 Corinthians 10:14, 1 Peter 3:11, Proverbs 3:7, 1 Timothy 6:9-11, Proverbs 4:27, Titus 3:9-11.)*

Dr. Tom Taylor teaches on shunning, and directly after reading *2 Timothy 3:1-6*, (quoted just a few pages earlier in the book), Tom explains shunning as follows:

> *Get away from these people. Shun them! This is like when a Jew would marry a gentile, if ever that would happen, that they would be cut off from their own families. They would be dead to them. That's what is in here.*
>
> **Light Up the Scriptures** study "*91 - Only by the Spirit of God will you know what you are dealing with*" by Dr. Tom Taylor. (Time 21:06 - 21:24)

I encourage you to listen to this entire **Light Up the Scriptures** study, as it is overflowing with wisdom on Paul's teachings, from Yahweh {God} Himself, on protecting ourselves and our spirits from others... with the act of *shunning*.

Shunning, to me, could be described as the adult version of disciplining a child by placing them on a *time-out*... if your child runs out into the street, or touches fire, you will most likely NOT kindly and gently tell them not to do that. Well, that is not how I taught my daughter. No. I was firm, strong and disciplining. I was serious. I meant business. I wanted to instil the seriousness of the action of, for example, running out into a street alone. While she, I am sure, did not ENJOY the experience of being disciplined, she DID learn not to run out into the street. (Well, it took a few times of these strong, serious-toned chats for her to learn, "*STOP. LOOK. And LISTEN. Then, only walk into the street holding Mama's hand, or another adult's hand.*")

As all humans on this earth that I know… we are all a "work in progress." Thus, to my knowledge, regarding the people I personally knew in the radical followers of the **Bible**, the "Sold-Out-Seekers" group, every single person was shunned… and more than once. Including myself. Life sure is a journey…

Now, while being shunned is NOT fun at all, excruciating is a more accurate descriptive word, it taught me to seek Yahweh {God} and HIM ALONE. (And, I will mention, the ONLY reason that it was excruciating to me… was because I was relying on people on earth, more than in Yahweh {God} Himself. Ohhh, forgive me Father.)

Deborah and Daniel taught me that what you learn and live through, YOU can then teach others. Meaning, when someone is strong enough to stand up to you and call you out on your own sin, THEN, later in life, you will ALSO have that same strength to stand up to others' sins, others whom Yahweh {God} will place in your life. (This pertains to being only positive, not gossiping, shunning… and any other sin.)

Now, the *importance* of shunning is like the *importance* of disciplining a child also, that being the greater good to the individual through firm but fair and necessary teaching:

He who keeps back his club hates his son,
Yet he who loves him is early to discipline him.

Proverbs 13:24

Train up a youth in accordance with his proper way;
Even when he is old he shall not withdraw from it.

Proverbs 22:6

Shunning by a leader, just like discipline by a parent can be heart-breaking to the one delivering it, yet essential to the recipient's spiritual growth, to learn and live by the seriousness of Yahweh's {God's} word, precepts and instructions. To not shun when required by Yahweh {God} is to thus be in sin yourself, tolerating what Yahweh {God} Himself will not tolerate; not to mention the danger you are placing others in, especially if you are a leader, and allowing harmful leaven to stay in the group Yahweh {God} has given you to shepherd, instead of guarding and protecting the flocks' precious spirits. *(Again read Matthew 16:1-12)* There are many accounts of this also throughout the **Bible**, for example in the Old Testament, Eli the priest did not discipline his sons according to the Word of Yahweh {God}, and thus Samuel became the next priest, instead of Eli's sons. *(Read 1 Samuel chapters 2-4)*

We must put on the panoply as equipment of defence and attack with which to quench the leaven of evil, the evil spirit that can and will try to bring you or others down! Leaders must use wisdom and have on their own panoply to be able to even spot when a member of the body of Christ needs to be disciplined and shunned. *(Read Ephesians 6:11-17)*

That all said, because of my own missing the mark (or sinning)... I myself was shunned one day by the "Sold-Out-Seekers."

Now this know, that in the last days perilous periods will be present, for men will be selfish, fond of money, ostentatious, proud, calumniators, stubborn to parents, ungrateful, malign, without natural affection, implacable, adversaries, uncontrollable, fierce, averse to the good, traitors, rash, conceited, fond of their own gratification rather than fond of God; having a form of devoutness, yet denying its power. These, also, shun.

2 Timothy 3:1-6a

I was far from perfect... One day, after my employer, Angelica, had moved to a new home, I took a big part of the day to unpack all of *my* belongings and organize *my* allotted part of the house (for myself and my daughter). So self-focused, I spent most of the day making a "calm and comfortable" environment for my daughter (when she came for the weekends), instead of WORKING that day. Not to mention I did not tell (nor ask) my employer if I could take a few hours off. No. I JUST DID IT. It was a deliberate act of selfishness, not communicating at all. (Now, I do believe IF I had told her my thoughts, she would have been FINE with it... probably even agreed with me.)

Another one of the reasons that I was shunned... was that my former religious beliefs, so engrained in me, were "**having a form of devoutness, yet denying its power,**" and I had chosen to continue living with this programming of lies as an adult for most of my life. I was steeped in religion, instead of believing and following only the truth. In order to protect the rest of the group of "Sold-Out-Seekers" from my own leaven of selfishness and denying of Yahweh's {God's} power, the leaders thus obeyed the Scriptures, and shunned me. *(Read 2 Timothy 3:1-6a)*

Let me explain, for example: for YEARS and YEARS when I would receive bio-energetic treatments and while the simple "muscle test" was performed on me, being asked to think *"God is good,"* my arm would **go weak**. (This meant, that while in my head I was thinking, *"God is good... God is good... God is good...,"* my body TRULY did NOT BELIEVE it. And our bodies **cannot** and **do not lie**, including during bio-energetics and energy treatments.)

Dr. Tom Taylor explains (emphasis mine):

In 1990, my earliest mentor in this field showed me how my physical body was directly connected to – and would make instantaneous changes according to – my thoughts, feelings, and beliefs. The simple "muscle test" he performed was so astonishing that I made him repeat it several times. Suddenly, a new awareness dawned and it has never left: **My physical, mental, emotional, and spiritual well-being affects every area of my life and is entirely up to me.** I also realized that if this was true for me, then it was true for everyone around me.

Your Personal Roadmap to Whole Body Cleansing
by Barbara Brown, MSE and Dr. Tom Taylor, page 106.

Because I was working for and living with a follower of Yeshua {Jesus}... being shunned meant I was also let go from my job, as well as instructed to leave the home I was living in, kicked out on a snowy night...

So, on that cold night in the middle of winter, I packed up everything into (and strapped on top of) my truck. I drove off the property without a CLUE what to do. In less than one day I suddenly had no job. No home. Bills to pay. And to top it all off, my young daughter was coming to stay with me for the weekend (as she did every weekend), which was literally in just a few days.

I drove to Walmart, the only place open and with lights on at 8 pm. I was so scared. Too scared to even cry. I walked into Walmart and just stood there, about twenty feet inside the doors. I looked around, still not having one CLUE what to do. A complete stranger walked up to me and asked if I was ok. They said, *"You look lost. Here is $60. This is all the cash I have on me. There is a hotel down the road. Go there and spend the night."* I was in a daze, the kind gesture not registering completely. I quietly uttered, *"Ok"* and *"Thank you."* **Yahweh** {God} **had sent me an angel!** In Walmart! Let me just put this another way. An angel, whose heart He had moved to help me, with no way of knowing that I was jobless and homeless, came up to me out of the blue in a store and gave me $60 and advice on what to do with it.

Thank You Father for always guiding me, for always taking care of me! Thank You for sending angels to help me... **EVERYWHERE I go.**

This humble one called, and Yahweh heard,
And from all his distresses, He saved him.
Encamping is the messenger of Yahweh around those fearing Him,
And He shall liberate them.
Taste and see that Yahweh is good;
Happy is the master who takes refuge in Him.
…
The righteous cry out, and Yahweh hears,
And from all their distresses He rescues them.
Near is Yahweh to the broken of heart,
And those crushed of spirit He shall save.

Psalm 34:6-8 and 17-18

Behold, I shall be sending a messenger before you to keep you in the way and to bring you to the place which I have prepared.

Exodus 23:20

I checked-in to a room at the hotel, and sat on the chair still feeling completely lost. Lost and scared… in a panic. I needed a job. I needed a home. In just a few days my daughter would be coming to stay with me for the weekend! AHHHHHH!

For My designs are not your designs,
And your ways are not My ways, averring is Yahweh.
For as the heavens are loftier than the earth,
So are My ways loftier than your ways,
And My designs than your designs.

Isaiah 55:8-9

Trust in Yahweh with all your heart,
And do not lean to your own understanding.
In all your ways acknowledge Him,
And He Himself shall straighten your paths.

Proverbs 3:5-6

O, the depth of the riches and the wisdom and the knowledge of God! How inscrutable are His judgments, and untraceable His ways! For, who knew the mind of the Lord? or, who became His adviser? or, who gives to Him first, and it will be repaid him? seeing that out of Him and through Him and for Him is all: to Him be the glory for the eons! Amen!

Romans 11:33-36

So, panic stricken and short of answers, I decided to ask a couple who lived in the neighboring state, and with whom I had worked for years previously, if my daughter and I could stay with them for a few months.

After staying there a few months, I found a small apartment in New Hampshire, and moved in.

This was the **first time in my life that I had lived alone**. **EVER**. It was terrifying. I was such a "people person," and had yet to learn to **enjoy** being alone with Yahweh {God}.

The day I moved, dusk creeping into the day and remnants of snow still on the ground, my truck broke down just short of the state line. What more could happen? How much more could I take? I arrived outside my new "questionable" apartment block, shrouded in the darkness of night, by tow truck! All I owned was with me, all in and strapped on top of my truck… which was strapped on top of a tow truck. An air mattress, a blanket and pillows, clothes (both mine and my daughters), some toys for my daughter, her doll-house and, of course, my **Bible**.

Not wanting to hang around outside in the dark too long in this particular area, I clambered with my belongings up to a dark, cold and completely empty apartment for which I had no furniture. None.

I had no one to call. No one to talk to. No one to help me. No one to comfort me. Not a soul.

I believe this was Yahweh's {God's} plan…
to get me to turn to Him FIRST,
and Him ALONE.

There shall not come to be other elohim for you in preference to Me.

… for I, Yahweh your Elohim, am a jealous El…

Exodus 20:3 and 5

> **Yahweh is my Shepherd;**
> **Nothing shall I lack.**
> **In verdant oases, He is making me recline;**
> **Beside restful waters, He is conducting me.**
> **My soul He is restoring;**
> **He is guiding me in the routes of righteousness,**
> **on account of His Name.**
> **Even though I should walk in the ravine of blackest shadow,**
> **I shall not fear evil,**
> **For You are with me;**
> **Your club and Your staff, they are comforting me.**
> **You are arranging a table before me in front of my foes;**
> **You have sleeked my head with oil;**
> **My cup is satiated** (filled to overflowing).
> **Yea, goodness and benignity** (mercifulness,
> kindness and bountifulness ~ *CLKC*),
> **they shall pursue me all the days of my life,**
> **And I will dwell in the house of Yahweh for the length of my days.**
>
> *Psalm 23*

As Brother Lawrence wisely states (emphasis mine):

> That in his trouble of mind, he had consulted nobody, **but knowing only by the light of faith that GOD was present**, he contented himself with directing all his actions to Him, *i.e.,* doing them with a desire to please Him, let what would come of it.

And again he shares:

> Take courage! God often allows us to go through difficulties to purify our souls **and to teach us to rely on Him more** (1 Peter 1:6-7).
>
> The Brother Lawrence Collection – An Christian Classic – Practice and Presence of God, Spiritual Maxims, The Life of Brother Lawrence by Brother Lawrence, Kindle page 15 and 103 of 139.

I just looked up *1 Peter 1:6-7* from Brother Lawrence's book quote above, and must share it with you here (just in case you had not already run to look it up yourself):

> **...in which you are exulting; briefly at present, if it must be, being sorrowed by various trials, that the testing of your faith, much more precious than gold which is perishing, yet, being tested by fire, may be found for applause and glory and honor at the unveiling of Jesus Christ...**
>
> *1 Peter 1:6-7*

Deborah often says ... *"God just wants YOU!"* Meaning He wants you ALL to Himself, no one and nothing in-between. Nothing. No one.

Dr. Tom Taylor also shares this precise lesson in his **Light Up the Scriptures** study where he says (emphasis mine):

> *They (the Israelites) were entirely lost without Him and dependent upon on Him. Which is... if I could say it, I believe **exactly** where the Father wants us, because THAT is the truth of things.*
>
> **Light Up the Scriptures** study *"180 - Pause for further instructions"* by Dr. Tom Taylor. (Time: 13:42 - 13:58)

I praise the Lord for His patience with me! And I thank Him for sending his spirit, the consoler, and for The Word, for the **Bible**... and ALL the faithful followers "of old" and their examples you and I have to follow:

"And I shall be asking the Father, and He will be giving you another consoler, that it, indeed, may be with you for the eon -- the spirit of truth, which the world can not get, for it is not beholding it, neither is knowing it. Yet you know it, for it is remaining with you and will be in you."

John 14:16

At my first defense no one came along with me, but all forsook me. May it not be reckoned against them! Yet the Lord stood beside me, and He invigorates me, that through me the heralding may be fully discharged, and all the nations should hear; and I am rescued out of the mouth of the lion. The Lord will be rescuing me from every wicked work and will be saving me for His celestial kingdom: to Whom be glory for the eons of the eons. Amen!

2 Timothy 4:16-18

Yet David encouraged himself in Yahweh his Elohim.

1 Samuel 30:6

One of my FAVORITE, most inspiring chapters in the ENTIRE **Bible**, and indeed throughout my entire life too, is *Hebrews 11*. I needed some encouragement in this trying time... So I read this over and over. Again and again. I have always loved to soak up every word of this chapter of inspiring faith... thinking about each devout follower... imagining myself in their shoes and being GRATEFUL for my own, having suffered so much less than they, some having been physically beaten, some tortured, some executed, some even sawn in two! It is so inspiring for me... hearing how OTHERS have lived their lives for and to Yahweh {God}! In faith... not seeking an earthly reward, their faith not shaken whatever their persecution! (I had to include these verses below!) I pray you are as encouraged as I am, and more so!

Now faith is an assumption of what is being expected, a conviction concerning matters which are not being observed; for in this the elders were testified to. By faith we are apprehending the eons to adjust to a declaration of God, so that what is being observed has not come out of what is appearing.

Hebrews 11:1-3

From *Hebrews 11:1-3* (above), oh that my conviction concerning matters not being seen be steadfast as a rock. Knowing, being certain of, in complete faith, speaking "declarations of Yahweh {God}" into my life!

By faith Enoch was transferred, so as not to be acquainted with death, and was not found, because God transfers him. For before his transference he is attested to have pleased God well.

Hebrews 11:5

From verse 5 (above), oh that I be as Enoch... attesting to please Yahweh {God} well!

By faith Abraham, being called, obeys, coming out into the place which he was about to obtain to enjoy as an allotment, and came out, not versed in where he is coming. By faith he sojourns in the land of promise… For he waited for the city having foundations, whose Artificer and Architect is God.

Hebrews 11:8-10

From verses 8-10 (above), oh that I continue to live as faithful as Abraham… following Yahweh {God}, step by step, LOOKING ONLY for heaven, "whose Artificer and Architect is God {Yahweh}." Focusing not on what I see, or anything on THIS earth, but focusing on Yahweh {God}, walking with Him where His glory surrounds us! Amen and Amen!

In faith died all these, not being requited with the promises, but perceiving them ahead and saluting them, and avowing that they are strangers and expatriates on the earth.

Hebrews 11:13

From verse 13 (above), oh that I be devout until my last breath. I pray this often… *"Father, keep me faithful until my last breath or until Yeshua {Jesus} descends, as I am ascending, and meet Him in the clouds!" (Read 1 Thessalonians 4:16-17)*

Yet now they are craving a better, that is, a celestial; wherefore God is not ashamed of them, to be invoked as their God, for He makes ready for them a city.

Hebrews 11:16

From verse 16 (above), oh I DO crave a better... I crave life in the celestial, with my Father in Heaven! Amen!

By faith Abraham, when undergoing trial, has offered Isaac, and he who receives the promises offered the only-begotten, he to whom it was spoken that "In Isaac shall your seed be called," reckoning that God is able to be rousing him from among the dead also; whence he recovers him in a parable also.

Hebrews 11:17-19

From verses 17-19 (above), oh that I continue to trust Yahweh {God} all the days of my life, KNOWING He raises people from the dead, He parts seas, He does ANYTHING HE DESIRES! (Yet in my life also, just as Shadrach, Meshach and Abed-nego, I choose to BE FAITHFUL even if Yahweh {God} does NOT do miracles! **His will be done,** as Yeshua {Jesus} Himself prayed. Amen.)

By faith Moses, becoming great, disowns the term "son of Pharaoh's daughter," preferring rather to be maltreated with the people of God than to have a temporary enjoyment of sin, deeming the reproach of Christ greater riches than the treasures of Egypt, for he looked away to the reward.

Hebrews 11:24-26

From verses 24-26 (above), oh that I too disown being called a "family member" on this earth (of blood relatives). I only look forward to my reward with the One True, Living Yahweh {God}! As Yeshua {Jesus} Himself said to His followers, "**Who is My mother, and who are My brothers?... anyone whoever should be doing the will of My Father Who is in the heavens...**" *(Matthew 12:48 and 50)*

By faith they crossed the Red Sea as through dry land, attempting which, the Egyptians were swallowed up.

Hebrews 11:29

From verse 29 (above), oh to know, in every cell of my being, every passing moment, that He alone is Yahweh {God}, Who decides who shall pass and who shall be swallowed up. Thank You Father for straightening my paths... for walking with me... guiding me. Thank You that I am faithful, my name **written in the Lambkin's scroll of life!** *(Revelations - The Unveiling of Jesus Christ 21:27b)*

By faith the walls of Jericho fall, being surrounded on seven days.

Hebrews 11:30

From verse 30 (above), oh that any "walls" in my path on this journey crumble and fall... in a moment, from a word spoken of the Father, and obedience walked out on my part. Amen! (Can you just IMAGINE all the dust and rubble in the air, when the walls of Jericho fell! What an awe-inspiring and miraculous sight!)

And what still may I be saying? For the time will be lacking for me to relate concerning Gideon, Barak, Samson, Jephthah, David, besides Samuel also, and the prophets, who, through faith, subdue kingdoms, work righteousness, happened on promises, bar the mouths of lions, quench the power of fire, fled from the edge of the sword, were invigorated from infirmity (weakness ~ *CLKC*), became strong in battle, rout the camps of aliens, women obtained their dead by resurrection.

Now others are flogged, not anticipating deliverance, that they may be happening upon a better resurrection. Yet others got a trial of scoffings and scourgings, yet still more of bonds and jail. They are stoned, they are sawn, they are tried, they died, murdered by the sword; they wandered about in sheepskins, in goatskins, in want, afflicted, maltreated (of whom the world was not worthy), straying in wildernesses and mountains and caves and the holes of the earth.

And these all, being testified to through faith, are not requited with the promise of God concerning us (the looking forward is to something better), that, apart from us, they may not be perfected.

Hebrews 11:32-40

From verses 32-40 (above), oh that the faith of each of these named above be etched in my memory… each miracle listed… unleashing my energy and spirit to embody THESE! Forget anything on this earth, Tamra, live HERE, IN HEAVEN'S VIEW! Join the masters of valor of old! You are not being flogged, nor scourged, nor hurt at all! You are BLESSED! Stoned, sawn in two… ugh, beyond imagining.

Oh Father, if ever I think I have it tougher than I can handle, I am reminded that my life is easy compared to these… **and** all that Yeshua {Jesus} lived through! Bless You Yeshua {Jesus}! My body flinches when I picture the abuse, beatings and scourgings Yeshua {Jesus} suffered and bore alone… continuous beatings with chipped bone pieces on the end of whips, ripping flesh from flesh. And that being only the beginning, leading to an even weightier ordeal. Not to mention those "**of whom the world was not worthy**," who stood strong, steadfast, devout, unmovable and unshakeable for Yahweh {God}! Thank You Father for all who have gone before me… so I may be inspired and encouraged by them to walk the walk of faith that leads to freedom.

I love that entire chapter... *Hebrews 11*, how I am strengthened spiritually directing my focus back on Yahweh {God}, Who is always with me... no less so alone in my apartment, with a broken-down truck.

I found a local car mechanic, the owner was a **kind and honest** old man. (Miraculous... a kind and honest mechanic!) Another angel Yahweh {God} sent me! He admitted that the cost of repairs were greater than the value of the truck itself. Bless him, Father. So, I went to a used car lot, and having been told, *"You have perfect credit! You can have any car on the lot,"* I purchased a comfortable, reliable used car. And now a car-loan to pay also. The "honest mechanic" helped me MUCH over the next few years... He always went the extra mile for me, and charged MUCH LESS than his regular prices when helping me.

Yahweh {God} is faithful. He continued to take care of me. Looking back now, today, yes, I admit that during and after the move I did not FEEL Yahweh {God} was taking care of me. I felt lost, abandoned and scared. BUT, I KNEW I could not go back... I was not sure which way was forward, which was the right step, but I just took one small step at a time. And I kept walking.

Change is so difficult to see when you are amidst its fog. Again, precisely what Bruce Lipton, Ph.D. states in an interview, which now, today, makes complete sense to me... (emphasis mine):

> *...the only way you really see the change is to look back.* ***In the process of change, you don't see it*** *<u>because it's live action</u>. It's only when you look back, and go, "Well, how were those actions?" Now you have review, you can see;* ***in the midst... it's process. You do NOT see the changes happening now... until you look back.***
>
> Quotes from a podcast with Bruce Lipton Ph.D. at:
> BruceLipton.com/the-frontier-sciences-evidence-based-practises-principles-guiding-you-to-transform

The famous *"Footprints in the Sand"* poem comes to mind also.

Thank You Father in Heaven,
Thank You for always being WITH me and never giving me more than I can handle. (Though often what I thought was the extent to which I could bear happened FAR BEFORE Your thoughts and Your ways both led and pushed me to go…)
Thank You for Your path… Your wisdom… Your strength!
Amen.

No trial has taken you except what is human. Now, faithful is God, Who will not be leaving you to be tried above what you are able, but, together with the trial, will be making the sequel (a way to escape, exit ~ *CLKC*) **also, to enable you to undergo it.**

1 Corinthians 10:13

**Fling your granted burden on Yahweh,
And He Himself shall sustain you;
He shall not allow the righteous to slip for the eon.**

Psalm 55:22

Be steadfast, and be resolute! Do not fear... for Yahweh your Elohim, He is the One going with you; He shall neither neglect you nor forsake you.

Deuteronomy 31:6

I kept thinking my life would get better. I kept thinking... *"Surely it CANNOT get any worse. I am at my wit's end, Lord!"*

Chapter 9

YAHWEH GIVETH AND YAHWEH TAKETH AWAY...

BLESSED be the Name of Yahweh!

Yahweh, He gives,

and Yahweh, He takes away.

Blessed be the Name of Yahweh.

Job 1:21

And he said... Yahweh, He gives, and Yahweh, He takes away. Blessed be the Name of Yahweh.

Job 1:21

Oh, my life was *far* from getting better...

One weekend when my daughter was staying with me, she woke up at 11 pm SCREAMING. She screamed uncontrollably for an HOUR STRAIGHT. Nothing I did would console her. In my desperation, not knowing what else I could possibly do, my daughter's screams still filling the air, I called Barbara Brown on the phone.

The odd sign here and there, with symptoms surfacing, were leading my suspicions into disarray. Her mannerisms as well as both her visible and emotional state of mind suggested many other **strange** things had been happening to my daughter. TOO MANY "little things" were apparent to doubt them any longer. I took my daughter to the doctor, and my worst fear was confirmed.

My daughter was showing signs of abuse, (alleged, I must state for legal reasons).

I received court approval (from the local courthouse where my daughter physically lived during the week) to bring my daughter for a week of "new-science" holistic treatment (including bio-energetics), out of state. (And, for my daughter's protection, a restraining order was placed on Red preventing any and all contact with her.)

My daughter had been raised natural and holistic from my womb onwards, and this alternative, new-age, bio-energetic treatment was the ideal solution. I had high expectations of these treatments for my daughter from the top bio-energetic specialists in the nation... their program and expertise was impeccable, and most importantly their faith and gifts of healing and miracles were directly from Yahweh {God} above! Again, it is said of Dr. Tom Taylor:

> Other doctors called him, came to him for help, or sent him their "hopeless cases."
>
> **Rescuing God From the Rubble of Religion**
> by Dr. Tom Taylor and Barbara Brown, MSE, page 1.

As I shared in the first chapter, Barbara Brown has performed many miracles through the power of Yeshua {Jesus} throughout her lifetime. You can read all about them in her book ***GOD is* GOD *and* We Are Not**. (A few include giving sight to a blind boy, healing cripples in her athletic store, along with many more.) When you are at **The Ministry Center** for treatment with Barbara Brown and Dr. Tom Taylor, you can feel ***the presence of Yahweh*** *{God}*… it is strong, pure in spirit, and holy.

So, my daughter and I embarked on an airplane to Texas, for what **The Ministry Center** terms a "fly-in program" of treatment from **Whole Life Whole Health**. During the program they *turned* the *"8 Master Keys to Unlock Your Total Health,"* with daily bio-energetics treatments, health and wellness classes, non-evasive help and healing, and care from **The Ministry Center** including powerful, miraculous prayer.

> **You will serve Yahweh your Elohim, and He will bless your bread and your water. And I will take away illness from among you.**
>
> *Exodus 23:25*

Better a ration of greens when love is there
Than a fattened ox when hatred is with it.

Proverbs 15:17

The operative petition of the just is availing (is able, is of strength ~ *CLKC*) **much.**

James 5:16b

My daughter was visibly and audibly suffering. She had a HUGE GASH on her leg, complained of terrible stomach pains and cramping, as well as having a rampant yeast infection. The life in her spirit (the twinkle in her eyes, the spark previously brightening up in her soul like fireworks) was now completely snuffed out. Her middle-of-the-night-wakings in utter terror were regular.

My emotions still a wreck when we first arrived, my heart constantly breaking at the mere sight of my daughters beyond miserable countenance. Two or three times per day we both received bio-energetics treatments, and both Barbara Brown and Dr. Tom Taylor prayed for us constantly. Out loud, in their minds, and in the spirit. Bless them Father in Heaven! We were fed healthy meals, including specially formulated *"Barbara's Ultimate Power Breakfast"* shakes *(amongst many organic ingredients, this included blended chard, spinach, kale, beet, radish, frozen berries, spirulina, and fresh home-made almond milk)!* We drank only the best filtered, alkaline water. We even enjoyed swimming in a salt-water pool a few times!

This all-encompassing treatment, even before the end of that week, **healed my daughter** of all the physical aspects listed above. Further still, she began sleeping soundly again throughout the *entire* night! Praise the Living Yahweh {God}!!!

The relief to my heart… inexpressible.

Most importantly, the JOY (the twinkle, the sparkle) in her EYES and LIFE in her **SPIRIT reignited** as well! Praise Yahweh {God}! *(I am almost in tears now, remembering the visible, energy rich JOY twinkling in her eyes. The miraculous return of LIFE in her SPIRIT that week was exhilarating! Praise His Holy Name!)*

He [Yahweh] said to me: Son of humanity, shall these bones live? And I answered, My Lord Yahweh, You know.
…
When I prophesied as He had instructed me, the spirit came into them, and they lived…

Ezekiel 37:3 and 10a

(Read the entire life-giving, inspiring account of Ezekiel 37:1-14.)

Behold, I shall bring up wholeness and health for it, and I will heal them and reveal to them the sweet-smell of peace and truth.

Jeremiah 33:6

… the throng marvels, observing the mute speaking, the maimed sound, the lame walking and the blind observing. And they glorify the God of Israel.

Matthew 15:31

Only the best was good enough for my daughter, especially in her then horrific predicament, a treatment center where "worst case patients" were sent to the internationally known wellness expert, Dr. Tom Taylor. So, to Texas we went, being the ONLY place I was confident of finding this level of expert, specialist treatment.

Bio-energetics has since grown more widespread in "popularity" since 2012, though it is STILL not being broadcasted on the news, nor taught in medical universities, to my knowledge!

As I quoted in a previous chapter… Bruce Lipton Ph.D., world renowned scientist, speaker, epigenetics specialist and author of his best-selling book, **The Biology of Belief**, stated in an interview (emphasis mine):

> *So, the medical industry is led by this pharmaceutical industry, which has got its hands in the FDA, (which is the Federal Drug Administration in the United States). It is still run by these pharmaceuticals.* ***The medical schools teach by funding, and funding comes from big organizations like the pharmaceutical industry, so you teach what is in their interest.*** *So, medical schools do not fully go into this new area of healing and* ***all*** *that is fundamentally the direction we need. Why? Corporate interest.*

He went on to say:

> *And we have to wake up now. And the wake up is this:* ***"I want to be healthy!" Yeah but that hasn't been a mission.*** *When you go to the doctor, he doesn't say, "Listen, before I give you the pill, I want you to do all these exercise things and eat this way and I want you to stay healthy and THEN I'll give you the pill." No, no, no…* ***We have to take care of ourselves: eat healthy, eat organic, do exercises, move… you gotta use this machine, use it or lose it! It applies to EVERY part***

of our human body, from mind to toes, use it or lose it. And we're not being encouraged with the idea of this. We're not in harmony. We're not in health.

Quotes from a podcast with Bruce Lipton Ph.D. at:
BruceLipton.com/the-frontier-sciences-evidence-based-practises-principles-guiding-you-to-transform

I believe, (or should I say, my personal deduction today leads me to believe), that Red thought I was not going to return to New England with my daughter, as if my intent was some elaborate kidnapping excursion. So, would you believe it, my blood relative Christina obtained legal custody of my daughter from the New England judicial system! Having then flown down to Texas, she went to a courthouse to present the custody papers, and two hours, **yes only two hours, before my daughter and I were returning ourselves on our own flight to New England**, (as I had planned, purchased and promised to the court in New England the week prior), my blood relative Christina *tore my daughter out of my hands.*

A police officer came to present the official documents that Christina had obtained pertaining to legal guardianship of my daughter. There was nothing I could legally do. *What could I possibly do? Go against the police? Go against the court system?* No, never. So… while my mind escalated to HURRICANE proportions, LITERALLY… I calmly (as calm as a storm could muster) performed a "joyful" explanation to my own daughter that she would, instead, be going with her auntie on an airplane! Having accomplished her healing and overcome her own inner turbulence *(by the grace of Yahweh {God})* I made it sound FUN to her, turning it into a grand adventure. I did NOT want her to be upset nor stressed… not again… not to feel unprotected and vulnerable. (I have still wondered to this day if that was the best and wisest decision… to lie to her and protect her emotions… at that moment, instead of telling her the scary truth. She was 5-years-old... I only wanted her to continue living in the peace and the JOYFUL SPIRIT she had won back! Yahweh {God} alone knows...)

I hugged her, holding her close, kissed her, and walked her out to the police car. As we were approaching the car, Tom ran out to her, his last step falling to his knees, placed his hand on her head and blessed her. He prayed a father's blessing over her and angels to guard and protect her.

Back in the house I was baffled. Speechless. Frankly, we *all* were! My mind was REELING! *WHAT JUST HAPPENED?*

It is definitely a skill to learn, specifically in times of trial, to not try to "figure out" what is happening nor why, that which is beyond human understanding... and to always **remember Who is Yahweh** {God}, and who is *not* (me)! I know I personally had "room to grow" in this area...

Who gauges the spirit of Yahweh
And is informing Him as a man of His counsel?
With whom does He take counsel?
And who is giving Him understanding,
Is teaching Him in judgment's path,
Is teaching Him knowledge
And is informing Him the way of understanding?
Or who has given to Him first,
And it shall be repaid to him?

Isaiah 40:13-14

Behold, El is my Salvation;
I shall trust in Him and not be afraid,
For my Strength and my Melody is Yah, Yahweh,
And He became mine for salvation.

Isaiah 12:2

I flew back to New England two hours later, just as had always been planned. Christina had legal custody of my daughter for a few weeks. I spoke to my daughter on the phone when permitted, calls predominantly nursing her tears, as she begged to see me... *(What do you say to a 5-year-old who has been ripped from your arms? How do you hold back that you want to be together more than she does?)*

MUCH to my surprise... even BEYOND my surprise... at the court hearing, to my horror Red subsequently received full custody of my daughter, both legal and physical. And I was granted merely visiting rights, and ordered to only see my daughter **with professional, paid supervision**! *Me!?!*

Yahweh {God} alone knows what lies my daughter has been told over the years...

However:

I DO KNOW MY YAHWEH {GOD},
and HE IS A YAHWEH {GOD} OF MIRACLES!!!

I have sometimes thought of Isaac, and the years after his being tied to an altar to be sacrificed. What went through his mind? Did he focus on the continual FAITH of his father Abraham? Or did he wallow in self-pity? Yahweh {God} alone knows. Can you imagine growing up with Abraham as a parent though? "**A man of great faith**" according to Yahweh {God}! Wow! What incredible faith-obedience Isaac surely must have learned…

Now, clearly, I did not agree with the judge's decision. So, I went to the appeals court. I saw it as the only just and right action. Years later, having heard this whole horror story, a lawyer in New England said to me, *"YOU went to the appeals court? You represented yourself? You? MOST LAWYERS do not even do that! They just do not have the guts to appeal a judge's decision!"* (Just like doctors are NOT gods… neither are judges.)

My case was heard at the appeals court. However, (looking back), because I presented my appeal on the basis of *why* I believed I should have custody of my daughter rather than Red, INSTEAD of WHY the previous custody judgement was in error, (slight difference it would seem, but all the difference in a courtroom), my appeal was denied.

I was in utter lostness, my world was turned upside-down! Again!

Crying out to Yahweh {God}, asking Him, *"WHAT IN THE WORLD WAS HAPPENING?!?"* I still made a point of declaring, *"Your will be done."* I encouraged myself by recalling Abraham's obedience to sacrifice Isaac, and the pure excellence and trust of Job. Even after all his children were killed and all his earthly possessions stolen. Even after his body was in unbearable pain… what endurance, what FAITH he kept! What TRUST in Yahweh {God}! Job STILL said:

> **…Yahweh, He gives, and Yahweh, He takes away. Blessed be the Name of Yahweh.**
>
> *Job 1:21*

The words of the prophet Habakkuk came to mind:

> **Though the fig tree is not budding,**
> **And there is no crop on the vines,**
> **Though the yield of the olive is emaciated,**
> **And the plantations yield not food,**
> **Though the flock is severed from the fold,**
> **And there is no herd in the paddocks,**
> **Yet I shall be joyous in Yahweh;**
> **I shall exult in the Elohim of my salvation.**
>
> *Habakkuk 3:17-18*

I held onto the words of the Psalms and Isaiah:

> **He who is dwelling in the concealment of the Supreme**
> **Shall lodge in the shadow of Him Who-Suffices.**
> **I shall say of Yahweh: My Refuge and my Fastness,**
> **My Elohim, in Whom I trust.**
> **For He Himself shall rescue you from the snare of the trapper,**
> **From the plague of woes.**
> **With His pinions shall He overshadow you,**
> **And under His wings shall you take refuge;**
> **A large shield and encircling-guard is His faithfulness.**
>
> *Psalm 91:1-4*

> **Bless Yahweh, my soul,**
> **And all within me, bless His holy Name!**
> **Bless Yahweh, my soul,**
> **And do not forget any of His well-dealings,**

Who is pardoning all your depravity,
Who is healing all your ailments,
Who is redeeming your life from ruin,
Who is crowning you with benignity (mercifulness, kindness and bountifulness ~ *CLKC*) and compassion,
Who is satisfying your future with good,
So your youth is renewed like the vulture's.
Yahweh is the One executing acts of righteousness
And right judgments for all those being exploited.

Psalm 103:1-6

Youths may faint and be wearied,
And choice young men may stumble, yea stumble,
Yet those who are expectant in Yahweh,
they shall rejuvenate with vigor;
They shall ascend on pinions like vultures;
They shall run and not be wearied;
They shall walk and not faint.

Isaiah 40:30-31

Indeed You Yourself shall light up my lamp, O Yahweh;
My Elohim, He shall brighten my darkness,
So that by You I may run over a stone dike,
And by my Elohim I may leap a barricade.
The One, El, His way is flawless;
The word of Yahweh is refined;
He is a Shield to all who are taking refuge in Him.

Psalm 18:28-30

Every week, and limited to only *once* per week, I was allowed to see my daughter. And only under professional supervision. Supervision I then, for the most part, had to pay for myself. I made the MOST of it, as BEST I COULD! I was upbeat and energized, effervescent at the joy of just *being* with my lovely little daughter! I brought art projects, cooking recipes, toys and games to play with her! We (with paid supervision, of course) would go to parks, to indoor trampoline places... we had the MOST FUN that could be compressed into an hour, two at most! Though she would be sad, and most often tearful when we were required to separate.

My heart broke, in silence, in steadfastness. *(Tears are trickling down my face as I write this.)*

One day, weakness getting the better of me, I tripped again, missed the mark. Sinned.

I loved my daughter... absolutely adored her! And so, one day after spending my allotted time with her, and having said good-bye in the parking lot... she ran back to me and, arms outstretched, asked if I would eat lunch with her and Red at a local restaurant. My heart tugged at me, knowing this was the last scenario in which I would ever want to be with her. However, I wanted to spend AS MUCH time with her as I could, and I would do ANYTHING to put that endearing smile back on her face. So, I said, "*Yes.*" (Ugh. Oh Tamra, when would you learn?!?) It was the most miserable meal... an air of much tension and anger, as well as blatant arrogance on the part of Red, only punctuated with downright condescension. (Sadly, I bore his contempt, just to spend those few more precious moments with my daughter.) Later, when I shared with my true family of Yahweh {God}, the "Sold-Out-Seekers," what I had done, they were all aghast at my decision. (It took me a while to understand why.) They shared the following Scripture with me (as well as others):

> **With such a one you are not even to be eating.**
>
> *1 Corinthians 5:11b*

I realized that my daughter had become an idol to me... I had placed her above Yahweh {God}. Father forgive me. I felt so ashamed... so embarrassed that I had completely missed how walking into the shroud of wickedness that day was a sin, in complete disobedience to my Father in Heaven. He had been waving a red flag in my spirit but my heart was so focused on my daughter, I was blind to the signs. (I realized that day, that Red had used my daughter as a pawn, a bait to me... and I bit straight through to the hook.)

I fell to my knees, heavy of spirit. Lost. Saddened by my previous choices, seeking the Father's forgiveness.

I learned from this experience though. Praise Yahweh {God}. I repented. It *never* happened again.

I slowly continued on the long and arduous path to "let go" of my precious daughter... and give her into the hands of Yahweh {God}, where in truth, she *already* was. I was simply learning His ways.

I kept crying out to my Father in Heaven... NOT understanding His ways, pleading redemption. In the midst of innumerable tears, I spoke Yeshua's {Jesus'} own immortal words, *"**Your will** be done, Father."* Still, I just could not completely wrap my head around my having no part in my daughter's upbringing!?! It made no sense to me whatsoever. Bringing my attention back to Yahweh {God}, I played and replayed the life of Joseph in my mind... whose life He had planned also! (Every detail.) And this same Yahweh {God} planned my life and that of my daughter, in ways I could not yet comprehend for the good of us who love Him...

For My designs are not your designs,
And your ways are not My ways, averring is Yahweh.
For as the heavens are loftier than the earth,
So are My ways loftier than your ways,
And My designs than your designs.

Isaiah 55:8-9

O, the depth of the riches and the wisdom and the knowledge of God! How inscrutable are His judgments, and untraceable His ways! For, who knew the mind of the Lord? or, who became His adviser? or, who gives to Him first, and it will be repaid him? seeing that out of Him and through Him and for Him is all: to Him be the glory for the eons! Amen!

Romans 11:33-36

In one of my troubled moments, Deborah reminded me of the Scripture:

I will repay to you for the years which the locust devoured…
Then you will eat, yea eat and be satisfied,
And you will praise the Name of Yahweh your Elohim,
Who deals with you marvelously;

Joel 2:25-26

I held on to this Scripture, repeating it often in prayer: *"Thank You Father for repaying the years which the locust devoured!"*

My own interpretation of the previous word I had received from Yahweh {God}, *"This case is Ironclad,"* to me had meant Yahweh {God} would open the eyes of the judge to "see the light of truth" and give *me* full custody of my daughter. Well… Yahweh {God} had intended it differently… He alone knew the true, full meaning and the **precise timing** of His word to come to pass (as His Words always do). *"Remember Hebrews 11, Tamra,"* I told myself.

I would wonder: *"How could this POSSIBLY be right, just and, in all wisdom, the best and healthiest outcome for my daughter? This was madness surely, worldly madness."* Maybe that was it. As I was learning, when occurrences just do not seem to go how you would have thought, how you would expect, and seem as worldly madness… **remember** and **KNOW** that Yahweh {God}, being in a Higher Plain, is always directing everything for our good, for those loving Him.

Now we are aware that God is working all together for the good of those who are loving God, who are called according to the purpose…

Romans 8:28

A prayer for my daughter today, and for ALL Yahweh's {God's} children out there:

Father,
I pray for my little girl,
I pray angels guard and protect her.
I pray Your will be done, in each of our lives.
I know Your ways are higher than ours…
I do not understand all that
has happened in my life…
Though I trust You, Father in Heaven.
Your will be done!
Yours alone.
Thank You for all I have learned…
Thank You for all I am learning…
I pray my daughter knows You
as I know You,
I pray she sees You as I see You.
Truth. Love. Grace. Strength. Power.
Everything IS possible!
I believe.
Wrap Your arms around my daughter,
guard and protect her,
In Yeshua's {Jesus'} Holy Name I pray,
Amen. Amen and Amen.

Because you are precious in My eyes,
You are glorified, and I Myself love you…

Isaiah 43:4a

May Yahweh bless you and keep you;
May Yahweh light up His face toward you and be gracious to you;
May Yahweh lift His face to you and appoint peace for you.

Numbers 6:24-26

Alas, my Lord Yahweh! Behold, You Yourself made the heavens and the earth by Your great vigor and by Your outstretched arm;
Nothing at all is too marvelous for You…

Jeremiah 32:17

Chapter 10

FORGIVENESS

Forgiving the unforgivable…
from deep in the heart.

"Father, forgive them, for they are not aware what they are doing."
Luke 23:34

My life's afflictions PALE in comparison to what Yeshua {Jesus} lived through… *being falsely accused and arrested, tortured, flogged on several occasions multiple times with chords intertwined with sharp bone fragments, bleeding and wounded, a crown of thorns impaled into His head, stakes pounded into his wrists and ankles, and finally lifted up to hang on the cross until death…* all for me.

Even when I was raped at knife-point… and even through those years of a horrific, unimaginable, biased custody battle and divorce trial (completely devoid of justice, I add), along with my precious daughter being torn from my arms when I was protecting her, my life does **not even come CLOSE** to what Yeshua {Jesus} suffered, for me. *To give me the gift of grace!*

However, I learned a **valuable lesson from Yeshua** {Jesus} and the grace He gave us all EVEN WHILE HANGING ON A CROSS. It did not take Yeshua {Jesus} years of therapy, nor bio-energetics treatments to forgive. No. He did it IN THE MOMENT! Even when Yeshua {Jesus} felt as though His Father abandoned Him in His final hours (*read Matthew 27:46*). What a kind and gracious example to give us… to give me. THANK YOU Brother Yeshua {Jesus}! Thank You for ALL You suffered through, to give me life and grace today.

Dr. Tom Taylor wrote about a personal vision he had with Yeshua {Jesus}, helping express the depth and personal nature of the love Yeshua {Jesus} gives each of us. His incredibly moving book, **You Think YOU Have It Tough?**, helps me to always remember that whatever I go through bears little weight in comparison to Yeshua's {Jesus'} life and walk. Dr. Tom Taylor writes:

Yeshua held out His hands, resting them on the table, palms up. I saw the scars where the nails had been driven into His flesh.

"Has anyone done this to you yet?" He asked, pointing to His wrists. There was, of course, no answer needed to His question…

There, kneeling in the garden, Yeshua became to me fully identified with all mortal humanity. He was only a few hours away from suffering one of the most brutal, painful, and publicly humiliating deaths imaginable. Crucifixion caused death by the slow suffering of dehydration, or asphyxiation from the weight of a man's body restricting his lungs. Victims were left hanging for as long as it took them to die… This was what Yeshua faced, and He wanted out if at all possible! Who could blame Him?...

[It was ordered for] Yeshua to be flogged. They stripped His back, tied Him to a stake, and brought out a short whip with several leather chords coming out of a thick handle. Metal discs with sharp edges were knotted into the cords, together with bone fragments. I was horrified when I saw the whip, which was designed to tear flesh off a man's body down to the bone. The pain that this punishment inflicted, together with the loss of tissue and the bleeding it produced often killed its victim.

Once on the hill of Golgotha… Though He never resisted throughout the ordeal, the soldiers held Him down, pressings His arms flat on the crossbar. One of them took a huge mallet and holding a long thin spike over Yeshua's wrist just above the end of His palm, pounded it directly through the flesh. The sound of steel tearing through skin, muscle, and vessels, was sickening. The process was repeated with Yeshua's other wrist; then His feet…

Yeshua was pinned, literally, and He was in tremendous pain of a kind that I cannot fathom. When the soldiers set the pole upright,

> Yeshua's weight shifted downward, stretching the fresh wounds in His hands and feet. All I could do was watch and weep…
>
> **You Think YOU Have It Tough?** by Dr. Tom Taylor, pages 14, 35, 48-49 and 56-57.

I humbly encourage you to read the whole book for yourself. You will never be the same again. This book is truly anointed, the words come alive, the vision Tom had with Yeshua {Jesus} and the Father… every time I read it, *I am RIGHT THERE WITH them.*

I will say it again, I cannot stress enough… that my life PALES in comparison to all Yeshua {Jesus} lived through on this earth and then forgave others for…

PALES.

As I shared in the first chapter, I had a much harder time finding something to be GRATEFUL for regarding the horrific, life-threatening rape at knife-point experience at age 17, than I did in *forgiving* Blake.

Everyone in my life made SUCH A BIG DEAL about what had happened to me, that I quickly learned I could get attention and "love" (what I *thought* was love at the time) from it.

However, in the beginning I refused to go to therapy. Though I did wonder WHY it had happened. I wondered *WHY* Blake did what he did to me. I went to the library one day, months later, and searched for books to explain to me WHY people hurt others.

I found a book, (I do not recall the title), explaining that people who hurt others have THEMSELVES BEEN HURT (often as young children). I felt bad for Blake. I imagined the HORRENDOUS childhood (and life) he must have had, to be able to do such an unspeakable act to me. I did not excuse his actions. (I had taken him to court and he went to jail for four years.) Unthinkable as it might seem, having read that book, my heart did go out to him though. For, in my understanding, he must have had a BEYOND INDESCRIBABLE life to be able to do such a thing.

I forgave him.

I did not ever want to see him nor talk to him again, but I did forgive him. (I did tell my Father in Heaven, IF He, Yahweh {God}, wanted me to speak to Blake... I would. I did not want to... but I would, *"Your will be done, Father,"* I told Him in my heart of hearts.)

However severe the life experiences and pain I had lived through were, remembering Yeshua's {Jesus'} forgiveness of those who conducted unspeakable acts against Him brought this Scripture to my mind:

> **"For if you should be forgiving men their offenses, your heavenly Father also will be forgiving you. Yet if you should not be forgiving men their offenses, neither will your Father be forgiving your offenses."**
>
> *Matthew 6:14-15*

Yeshua's {Jesus'} words, *on the cross*, have also helped me **immensely** in my life.

> **"Father, forgive them, for they are not aware what they are doing."**
>
> *Luke 23:34*

My Father in Heaven taught me to speak it (to be encouraged by it) AS I WALKED THROUGH the horrific, long, drawn-out trial and divorce, during which *almost all* of my family, (whom I subsequently call blood relatives), completely turned against me. Countless times throughout my life the spirit of Yahweh {God} reminded me that Yeshua {Jesus} said:

Now it was reported to Him, saying that "Thy mother and Thy brothers stand outside wanting to see Thee." Now He, answering, said to them, "My mother and My brethren are these who are hearing the word of God and doing it."

Luke 8:20-21

"You should not be inferring that I came to be casting peace on the earth. I did not come to be casting peace, but a sword. For I came to pit a man against his father, and a daughter against her mother, and a daughter-in-law against her mother-in-law. And the enemies of a man are those of his household.

"He who is fond of father or mother above Me is not worthy of Me. And he who is fond of son or daughter above Me is not worthy of Me.

"And he who is not taking his cross and following after Me is not worthy of Me.

Matthew 10:34-38

My biological parents, (I will refer to them as Caren and Roger), flew out to New England for the divorce trial, unbeknownst to me that they were even attending, until they called and asked if I would like to meet them at a restaurant. They had flown out to support Red. *WHAT?!?*

I agreed to meet them. They did not recognize me upon their arrival. I actually held the door open for them, and they walked right past me, not noticing me at all. I took a breath, prayed, entered the restaurant, and sat down across the table from them.

That day, I ***felt*** Yahweh {God} near me and with me. (Bless You Father in Heaven. Thank You!)

The energy around Caren and Roger was devoid of the spirit of Yahweh {God}. It was serious, tense, stubborn and religious. It was palpable. I said to them, *"I want to tell you both the whole truth."* I literally saw in the spirit, a line in the sand being drawn down the middle of the table. A line between myself, and Caren and Roger. Just like when Joshua "drew a line" and said, "Choose this day whom you will serve."

> **Yet if it is displeasing in your eyes to serve Yahweh, choose for yourselves today whom you shall serve, whether those elohim that your fathers had served when they dwelt across the Stream, or whether the elohim of the Amorite in whose land you are dwelling; yet I and my house, we shall serve Yahweh.**
>
> *Joshua 24: 15*

They looked at me questioningly. Untrusting. And Roger slowly, cautiously said, *"Ok…"*

I told them everything: Yahweh {God} speaking to me saying, *"Light cannot live with darkness;"* my back being COMPLETELY HEALED from the day I said, *"I am getting a divorce;"* everything about my daughter waking up and screaming uncontrollably for an hour at 11 pm months prior; about the doctor visit; about how my daughter was miraculously healed and healthy again in Texas with bio-energetics treatments, prayer and nutritious foods; about my daughter continually asking to come live with me when I was allowed to see her. I told them much much more. I told them everything.

Caren and Roger are Lutherans, devout, strict Lutherans. They also believed completely, hook-line-and-sinker, in "the medical model." Looking back, writing this today, I am not surprised at the choice they made that day. It took me years to leave "the medical model" belief system that had been engrained in me... But, Yahweh {God} was giving them one last chance that day. One last chance to "pick a side" before court in mere days. Caren was being the devout wife, not saying a word. Not one. She would shake her head sometimes in disgust and disbelief that I would even say such things. *"Such nonsense,"* I could almost hear her thinking. And Roger, he asked me a few questions, but then shut down. I felt his energy. He did not want to hear the truth, the whole truth, either... in the end.

I prayed for them, as Yeshua {Jesus} set the example:

"Father, forgive them, for they are not aware what they are doing."

Luke 23:34

Yet where sin increases, grace superexceeds...

Romans 5:20b

Bless those who are persecuting you: bless, and do not curse...

Romans 12:14

I had done my part, as Barbara Brown and Dr. Tom Taylor teach:

1. Show up.
2. Pay attention.
3. Share your truth.
4. Let go of the outcome.

Your Personal Roadmap to Whole Body Cleansing
by Barbara Brown, MSE and Dr. Tom Taylor, page 95.

I had shown up, remaining spiritually strong. I paid attention to my spirit throughout and to the energy around me, to the words used. I spoke only the truth. I let go, knowing that they were free to make their choice, and face its consequences.

I drove home. Amazed at what I had just seen in the spirit, the line being drawn in the sand, that Yahweh {God} trusted me enough to show me His view, *Heavens View*. Just as Yahweh {God} would show His prophets visions, so He opened my eyes again, to see in the spirit also. Bless His Holy Name!

And I was also saddened at the decision Caren and Roger had made. My heart went out to them. They were doing "the best they could" and "the best they knew." I understood the religious spirit that was deeply rooted in them. I had been trapped there myself. I also understood the medical model and family belief systems that were engrained in them, boxing them in. I had been trapped there too. That said, I also understood that the truth was making me free:

"… and the truth will be making you free."

John 8:32b

I also understand Yahweh's {God's} ways, and how He treats His kids (His chosen ones). He says:

"If the world is hating you, know that it has hated Me first before you. If you were of the world, the world would be fond of its own. Now, seeing that you are not of the world, but I choose you out of the world, therefore the world is hating you.

"Remember the word which I said to you, 'A slave is not greater than his lord.' If Me they persecute, you they will be persecuting also. If My word they keep, yours also will they be keeping. But all these things will they be doing to you because of My name, seeing that they are not acquainted with Him Who sends Me.

John 15:18-21

I shall indeed bless those blessing you,
And I shall curse the one maledicting you.

Genesis 12:3

However, I know I had climbed (or was still climbing) **out** of those "boxes," those systems. So, I know it IS POSSIBLE! *Easy? No.* **Possible.** Yes. But not alone.

"With men this is impossible, yet <u>with God</u> <u>all is possible</u>."

Matthew 19:26

> **Now Jesus said to him, "Why the if? You are able to believe. All is possible to him who is believing."**
>
> *Mark 9:23*

I prayed again, knowing that if Yeshua {Jesus} could, so could I:

> **"Father, forgive them, for they are not aware what they are doing."**
>
> *Luke 23:34*

Hence, as a result of the choice of their decision, to support, believe, and befriend Red, I then stopped speaking to them. I kept away from them, (thus shunning them).

The morning of court, I walked in alone, carrying all of my evidence for trial, folders and binders of notes, and of course, my **Bible**. Not one person sat with me nor behind me, supporting me. (Though I *now know* Yahweh {God} and a host of angels were there that day, standing with me!) Caren and Roger sat in the exact middle of the court room. After a few hours, they both moved to sit completely on the other side, the side of the defendant, Red. Months prior, Roger had agreed to testify against me in court. However, he had changed his mind weeks after his initial decision… and I believe Yahweh {God} gave him (or will give him) grace for that. Caren was also asked to testify against me. She said no immediately. Bless her.

Christina and her husband did both testify against me.

When I realized they were testifying against me, I asked the judge to have them leave the courtroom until the time of their testimony. (I did not want them to have any understanding of what was said in court, prior to giving their own testimonies.) The judge approved my request.

The trial ended up lasting more than one day. It was scheduled to reconvene a few weeks later.

Upon completion of that first day, I was relieved that part was over. (Yet dreading the upcoming final day of trial.)

Sadly, I had not yet learned to BE STILL, ("**Relax and know that I am Elohim.**" *Psalm 46:10*). I felt so much fear, that peace, His true peace, could not reach me. Father, forgive me.

Be steadfast, and be resolute! Do not fear... and do not be terrified because of their presence, for Yahweh your Elohim, He is the One going with you; He shall neither neglect you nor forsake you.

Deuteronomy 31:6

Do not worry about anything, but in everything, by prayer and petition, with thanksgiving, let your requests be made known to God, and the peace of God, that is superior to every frame of mind, shall be garrisoning (protect with a military force ~ *CLKC*) **your hearts and your apprehensions in Christ Jesus.**

Philippians 4:6-7

...the weakness of God is stronger than men.

1 Corinthians 1:25b

I read these stories and Scriptures repeatedly over the next few weeks:

Elisha replied, Do not fear, for those with us are more than those with them.

Now Elisha prayed and said, O Yahweh, unclose, I pray, his eyes so that he may see. Yahweh unclosed the eyes of the lad, and he saw, behold, the hill was full of horses and chariots of fire round about Elisha.

2 Kings 6:16-17

(Read the whole story, 2 Kings 6:8-23!)

Yet, answering Him, Peter said, "Lord, if it is Thou, order me to come to Thee on the waters." Now He said, "Come!" And, descending from the ship, Peter walks on the waters, to come to Jesus.

Matthew 14:28-29

(Read the whole story, Matthew 14:22-33!)

Do not be mindful of the former things,
And do not consider those preceding.
Behold, I am doing a new thing; Now it is sprouting;
Do you not know it?
Indeed, I am placing a way in the wilderness,
Tracks in the desolation.
The animals of the field shall glorify Me,
Wild jackals and ostriches;

For I provide water in the wilderness,
Streams in the desolation;
To give drink to My people, My chosen.
This people I have formed for Myself,
And they shall recount My praise.

Isaiah 43:18-21

Yet I was saying to you: You should not be terrified, and you should not fear them. Yahweh your Elohim Who is going before you, He Himself shall fight for you according to all that He did for you in Egypt before your eyes, and in the wilderness where you saw how Yahweh your Elohim carried you, just as a man carries his son, in all the way you went until you came to this place. Even in this matter you were not believing in Yahweh your Elohim, Who was going before you in the way to explore for you a place for you to encamp, in fire by night, to show you the way by which you should go, and in a cloud by day.

Deuteronomy 1:29-33

And answering, Jesus is saying to them, "If you have faith of God, verily, I am saying to you that whosoever may be saying to this mountain, 'Be picked up and cast into the sea,' and may not be doubting in his heart, but should be believing that what he is speaking is occurring, it shall be his, whatsoever he may be saying.

Therefore I am saying to you, All, whatever you are praying and requesting, be believing that you obtained, and it will be yours."

Mark 11:22-24

Do you not know? Or do you not hear?
The Elohim eonian is Yahweh,
Creator of the ends of the earth;
He does not faint Nor is He wearied;
There is no fathoming of His understanding.
He is giving vigor to the faint,
And to one who is without virility He is increasing staunchness.
Youths may faint and be wearied,
And choice young men may stumble, yea stumble,
Yet those who are expectant in Yahweh
shall rejuvenate with vigor;
They shall ascend on pinions like vultures;
They shall run and not be wearied;
They shall walk and not faint.

Isaiah 40:28-31

Elohim is our Refuge and Strength,
A very providing Help in distresses.
Therefore, we shall not fear when the earth is made to change,
Or when the mountains slide into the heart of the seas.
Its waters clamor; they foam;
The mountains quake at its swelling.
...
Yahweh of hosts is with us;
Our Impregnable Retreat is the Elohim of Jacob.

Psalm 46:1-3 and 11

Be steadfast and be resolute; do not fear and do not be dismayed because of the king of Assyria and because of the presence of all the throng that is with him, for with us is more than with him. With him is an arm of flesh, but with us is Yahweh our Elohim to help us and to fight our battles. And the people were supported by the words of Hezekiah king of Judah.

2 Chronicles 32:7-8

(Read the whole story where Yahweh {God} kills 185,000 men in the enemy camp, 2 Chronicles 32:1-23!)

Unfortunately, my faith was still weak. And I would feel fear again. I was growing though, My Father in Heaven was strengthening my faith and my spirit muscle! HE STOOD BY ME at every moment, even though I did not always feel His presence there. Looking back, I KNOW He was there with me!

A few weeks later, I was back in court for the final day of trial.

Over the whole trial, testimonies were heard from a doctor, the court appointed representative of my daughter, and others. Christina and her husband both testified against me. I then cross-examined them both, as with everyone who was called for the defence to the witness stand. Christina cried on the witness stand, looking straight at me with tears rolling down her face, she saying, *"I want my sister back, the old Tamra!"* I thought: *"Really? The one who was overweight, on anxiety and depression medications, the one who HAD a depleted disk in her sacrum 'for life' according to doctors? Miserable and stressed… You want THAT PERSON BACK?!? What!?! Why?"* (The Scripture study of Dr. Tom Taylor came to mind, which I shared about previously, when he said, "*We ought **never** to change who we are to suit **anyone**, other than the Father Himself…*")

I cross-examined Red on the witness stand also. He denied almost every question I asked. I was at a loss. I wanted to shout, *"YES YOU DID!"* Though I knew it would not do any good at all. Yahweh {God} knew the truth, so I held onto that.

"For nothing is hidden which shall not become apparent, neither concealed which should not by all means be known and come to be apparent."

Luke 8:17

"Now nothing is covered up which shall not be revealed, and hidden which shall not be known…"

Luke 12:2

I was examined by Red's lawyer. I was on the witness stand for hours…

As I was representing myself and, clearly, not a "professional lawyer," the judge did give me "grace," stepping in a few times when, I believe, Red's lawyer was over-questioning me, or overstepping the mark by attempting somewhat questionable court conduct.

When the trial was finally over, the judge went into deliberation.

I was in shock at how Christina and her husband testified lies against me. They seemed completely blinded to the truth, or not prepared to face the consequences of it, aligned as they were with Red. Now, I do not know why I was so shocked… Yeshua {Jesus} Himself said that, **"he who is receiving you is receiving Me…"** a Scripture I knew all too well that applied here:

"He who is receiving you is receiving Me, and he who is receiving Me is receiving Him Who commissions Me."

Matthew 10:40

"If the world is hating you, know that it has hated Me first before you. If you were of the world, the world would be fond of its own. Now, seeing that you are not of the world, but I choose you out of the world, therefore the world is hating you."

John 15:18-19

"Happy are you whenever they should be reproaching and persecuting you and, falsifying, saying every wicked thing against you, on my account. Rejoice and exult, for your wages are vast in the heavens. For thus they persecute the prophets before you."

Matthew 5:11-12

The judge's decision took what felt like FOREVER... over two months. On the exact same day of the year that I had gotten married, the judge signed the divorce decree, twelve years later. (That is how Yahweh {God} works! He is into the details!)

I was finally FREE!!!

Free of the persecution and the lies, and free of that which had manacled me to them, my name. Actually, I had a new name! I refused to return to my maiden name, refused to be connected to "dead" people, people who chose to not believe me, to not believe the truth and pursue it, those who chose the side of the enemy.

The details of the divorce judgement were unconscionable... I was even ordered to pay off all credit cards, (all the debt of which had been incurred by both parties throughout the term of the marriage).

And worst of all… my daughter was ordered, by the judge, to be raised solely at the hand of Red. Even after ALL my *expositions* regarding his manipulation of my young daughter, his lack of nutrition given to her, and his actions toward her (to say the least).

What is happening in the world?!?

I did some research, and to my *absolute SHOCK and HORROR*, this actually happens to many, many mothers. Children are being given to biological dads, EVEN when it was clear that that decision was not the most healthy outcome for the child. (Including when the biological dad was abusive!) WHAT, how can that even be legal, never mind ethical?!?

Additional research today, in 2021, includes the following findings. An article titled *"Family court crisis: courts placing children with abusive parents with tragic results,"* in the **Child Welfare Monitor**, states the following shocking information (emphasis mine):

> A four-month investigation by Gillian Friedman in the *Deseret News* found that **in many cases family courts are failing to protect children**, allowing unsupervised visits or even custody to abusive parents. **These decisions are resulting in physical and sexual child abuse** and sometimes homicide.
>
> Why would family courts put a child in danger by allowing unsupervised contact with a dangerous parent? One reason, experts told Friedman, is that judges and custody evaluators hired by

> courts often do not believe the claims of danger from the other parent who is trying to protect the child. As the director of CJE told Friedman, "**In custody proceedings, family courts often see a parent's allegation of child abuse as no more than a tactic to undermine the other parent's custodial rights to the child — and therefore not a credible accusation." Several of the mothers interviewed by Friedman reported that their attorneys told them not to allege abuse for fear that these allegations would lead to an adverse custody ruling.**
>
> **Child Welfare Monitor** article *"Family court crisis: courts placing children with abusive parents with tragic results"* (gathered on July 14, 2021) at: ChildWelfareMonitor.org/2019/10/15/family-court-crisis-courts-placing-children-with-abusive-parents-with-tragic-results

In 2019, **George Washington (GW) Law Faculty Publications & Other Works** presented the following final report to the funder, (the National Institute of Justice), titled, *"Child Custody Outcomes in Cases Involving Parental Alienation and Abuse Allegations"* by Joan S. Meier (George Washington University Law School, jmeier@law.gwu.edu), Sean Dickson, Chris O'Sullivan, Leora Rosen, and Jeffrey Hayes. I will share only the opening paragraph here (underlining emphasis mine):

> Arguably the most troubling aspect of justice system response to intimate partner violence is custody courts' failure to protect children when mothers allege the father is abusive. Family courts' errors in assessing adult and child abuse, and punitive responses to abuse allegations, have been widely documented.

> The report later adds the following proven facts:

> These data powerfully affirm the reports from the field, that women who allege abuse - particularly child abuse - by a father are at

> significant risk (over 1 in 4) of losing custody to the alleged abuser. (Importantly, this rate applies even in cases where the fathers appear not to have claimed alienation to defeat the abuse claim.) Even when courts find that fathers **have** abused the children or the mother, they award them custody 14% of the time. **In cases with credited child physical abuse claims, fathers win custody 19% of the time.**
>
> **GW Law Faculty Publications & Other Works** report *"Child Custody Outcomes in Cases Involving Parental Alienation and Abuse Allegations"* by Joan S. Meier, Sean Dickson, Chris O'Sullivan, Leora Rosen, and Jeffrey Hayes (gathered on July 14, 2021) at: Scholarship.Law.GWU.edu/cgi/viewcontent.cgi?article=2712&context=faculty_publications

An updated version of the above report was also published in the **Journal of Social Welfare and Family Law** in 2020, slightly more academic and peer-reviewed, the report now titled, *"U.S. child custody outcomes in cases involving parental alienation and abuse allegations: what do the data show?,"* written by Joan S. Meier at George Washington University Law School, Washington D.C., discloses the same unimaginable and horrific proven statistics as well. The paper's abstract includes the following (emphasis mine):

> Family court and abuse professionals have long been polarized over the use of parental alienation claims to discredit a mother alleging that the father has been abusive or is unsafe for the children. **This paper reports the findings from an empirical study of ten years of U.S. cases involving abuse and alienation claims.** The findings confirm that mothers' claims of abuse, especially child physical or sexual abuse, increase their risk of losing custody, and that fathers' cross-claims of alienation virtually double that risk. Alienation's impact is gender-specific; fathers alleging mothers are abusive are not similarly undermined when mothers cross-claim alienation.

The journal goes on to say (emphasis mine):

> …the data tells us nothing about why the courts deemed the mothers to be worse parents than the fathers accused of abuse, nor how severe any credited abuse was. However, **the experiences of myriad lawyers, advocates and litigants in custody/abuse cases is that courts and ancillary professionals frequently react to mothers' claims of paternal abuse – particularly child abuse – with hostility and criticism** (Meier 2003, Meier and Dickson 2017). It is likely, therefore, that many of these mothers were penalized with loss of custody at least in part because they reported the father to have abused themselves or their children, and the court did not believe them.
>
> **The Journal of Social Welfare and Family Law** report *"U.S. child custody outcomes in cases involving parental alienation and abuse allegations: what do the data show?"* by Joan S. Meier (gathered on September 17, 2021) at: https://doi.org/10.1080/09649069.2020.1701941

I feel sick to my stomach, my own court case and life having added to these beyond disturbing statistics. I was afraid to continue with the research… afraid of the results I would continue to find.

As I have personally found:

Healing is not found in the courtroom,
nay not anywhere in the world,
only in YAHWEH {GOD}!

Father,
Bless the children,
All the children of the world!
Father, I know that You can heal, in an INSTANT, every person, every child.
Father, use me, use my story of complete healing, complete surrender, complete forgiveness and gratitude to give hope and healing to a lost and dying world.
And let us all remember Yeshua {Jesus} and ALL that He lived through to give us GRACE, HOPE, PEACE and LOVE!
I choose to Praise You Father!
I choose to keep my eyes focused on YOU alone!
Give mountains of strength to all who read this, to all on this earth!
In Yeshua's {Jesus'} name I pray,
Amen.

The Scripture comes to my mind:

No trial has taken you except what is human. Now, faithful is God, Who will not be leaving you to be tried above what you are able, but, together with the trial, will be making the sequel (a way to escape, exit ~ *CLKC*) **also, to enable you to undergo it.**

1 Corinthians 10:13

As I write this, I battle with feeling pity, worldly sorrow and emotional overwhelm. I encourage myself, as I do you too, dear reader, with the following words from chapter one... *"Find one thing you are grateful for."* Even if it feels like a huge leap to take, a ravine too far to cross, I encourage you to leap with me:

> **And let the peace of Christ be arbitrating in your hearts, for which you were called also in one body; and become thankful.**
>
> *Colossians 3:15*

What if Yahweh {God} allowed me to go through this... knowing I would come out *"on the other side"* living free and living the victory one day, so that I, with all humility, strength and faith, may help you...

> **Blessed is the God and Father of our Lord Jesus Christ, the Father of pities and God of all consolation, Who is consoling us in our every affliction to enable us to be consoling those in every affliction, through the consolation with which we ourselves are being consoled by God...**
>
> *2 Corinthians 1:3-4*

Barbara Brown prays for everyone who has been hurt by a "father" or "dad" on this earth, to heal any hurts sinned against us, gently pointing us to look toward the Father of us all, Our Father in Heaven, and not focusing on what is happening on this earth, in this present wicked eon *(read Galatians 1:4)*. I encourage you, as I myself have been encouraged, to include anyone, not just a "father" or "dad," who may have hurt you or, indeed, someone you know. She writes in her book, **Rescuing God From the Rubble of Religion:**

"...I pray that as He [Yahweh] puts His big arms around His children and brings them into His heart, they know that they are loved and safe.

And my days, all of them were written on Your scroll; The days, they were formed when there was not one of them. (Psalm 139:16)

"Father, You knew what each of us would need to go through, to be all You've called us to be. I'm not second-guessing Your plan, or the path on which You have taken each of us; but, Father, I am crying out for Your mercy and grace. Manifest Your presence in each of our lives and heal the memories of the past.

"Forgive us for any judgements we have had against our biological fathers. We don't know what makes people do what they do, but You said, whose sins we forgive, You forgive; so, we proclaim all pardon for anyone's sins, because if we don't forgive, we can't be forgiven *(See Matthew 6:14-15).*

"Father, let Your glory fall and bring all Your children to Yourself. Thank You for Your strategy for the victory in everyone's life. I pray we get beyond anything that has happened in this earthly, fleshly realm, and come into Your presence, where You make all things new.

> **'So that, if anyone is in Christ, there is a new creation: the primitive passed by. Lo! There has some new!'**
>
> (2 Corinthians 5:17)

Rescuing God From the Rubble of Religion
by Dr. Tom Taylor and Barbara Brown, MSE, page 37-38.

Dr. Tom Taylor and Barbara Brown also dedicate an entire chapter titled *"Who's In Charge Here?"* in this same book, **Rescuing God From**

the Rubble of Religion, answering head-on the age-old question *of "How can Yahweh {God} be **in charge** if there is so much evil in the world?"* I encourage you to read this chapter. Frankly and in all sincerity, read the entire book!

I continued to pay money to be supervised during the precious few hours I was allowed to spend time with my young daughter, only 6-years-old at the time.

I became the "black sheep" at my daughter's school. Red became quite popular among all the mothers, and to anyone who would listen, he would tell *his story…* All of the parents heard "through the grapevine" of this small Private Christian School, and rapidly my reputation was dragged through the mud (to say the least). No one spoke to me any more… I was considered with distain, as if I was leprous.

I am insignificant and despised,
Yet I do not forget Your precepts.

Psalm 119:141

"Happy are you whenever they should be reproaching and persecuting you and, falsifying, saying every wicked thing against you, on my account. Rejoice and exult, for your wages are vast in the heavens. For thus they persecute the prophets before you."

Matthew 5:11-12

I learned to rise above it. Such cruelty would not deter me from seeing my daughter. I learned to not look at their faces, to keep my gaze straight along the path of truth, literally, the truth only Yahweh {God} knew. That is all that matters. I taught myself to not remember the past, what my relationships with others *used to be like…* but instead to enjoy what little time I had with my precious child.

Do not be mindful of the former things,
And do not consider those preceding.
Behold, I am doing a new thing; Now it is sprouting;
Do you not know it?
Indeed, I am placing a way in the wilderness,
Tracks in the desolation.

Isaiah 43:18-19

I repeated this Scripture many, many times… per day! I did not know what the "new thing" Yahweh {God} was doing was, but I did know HE was doing it. I *knew* to speak His Word into my life. I continued to see my daughter (when I was legally allowed) for the school's public celebrations at Christmas, on Mother's Day, and on a few other rare but cherished occasions. My daughter would RUN UP to me excitedly shouting *"MAMA!"* and throw her arms around me and hug me. She would beg me to let her come home with me. *(What do you say to that? You can't say what you want to say, nor do what you know to be best. I broke down inside… again and again.) "Soon…"* I said to her, *"soon you will. I am doing all I can."*

I would pray over and bless my daughter every time I said good-bye, *"Big angels guard and protect you."*

However, as time passed and lies seeped below the surface, the hurt and sadness she was feeling soon *turned* to blaming me, and her words of *"this is all your fault,"* shattered my heart when I would see her at supervised visitations for one or two hours on the weekends. Of course, what would you expect from a 6-year-old missing her mother, while not understanding what the courts can sometimes do, nor the real evil that often occurs in the world? Yahweh {God} alone knows what she would hear and absorb throughout the week.

Again, the Scriptures came to my mind:

"Father, forgive them, for they are not aware what they are doing."

Luke 23:34

It is intelligence for a man when he postpones his anger,
And it is his beauty to pass over a transgression.

Proverbs 19:11

"Now brother shall be giving up brother to death, and father, child, and children shall be rising up against parents... And you shall be hated by all because of My name. Yet he who endures to the consummation, he shall be saved."

Matthew 10:21-22

"Are you supposing that I came along to give peace to the earth? No, I am saying to you, but rather division. For from now on there will be five in one home divided, three against two, and two against three will be divided, father against son and son against father, and mother against daughter and daughter against mother…"

Luke 12:51-53a

Here are some additional Scriptures that I have found helpful to me now, even today. I pray they help YOU also, if you need them:

Thus says Yahweh your Redeemer, the Holy One of Israel: I am Yahweh your Elohim, Who is teaching you to benefit, Positioning you in the way you shall go.

Isaiah 48:17

…And I shall direct you in the way that you should go;
I shall indeed give counsel with My eye upon you.

Psalm 32:8

Now may the God of peace, Who is leading up our Lord Jesus, the great Shepherd of the sheep… be adapting you to every good work to do His will, doing in us what is well pleasing in His sight, through Jesus Christ, to Whom be glory for the eons of the eons. Amen!

Hebrews 13:20-21

Yahweh is my Shepherd;
Nothing shall I lack.
In verdant oases, He is making me recline;
Beside restful waters, He is conducting me.
My soul He is restoring;
He is guiding me in the routes of righteousness,
on account of His Name.
Even though I should walk in the ravine of blackest shadow,
I shall not fear evil,
For You are with me;
Your club and Your staff, they are comforting me.
You are arranging a table before me in front of my foes;
You have sleeked my head with oil;
My cup is satiated (filled to overflowing).
Yea, goodness and benignity (mercifulness,
kindness and bountifulness ~ *CLKC*),
they shall pursue me all the days of my life,
And I will dwell in the house of Yahweh for the length of my days.

Psalm 23

A master's steps are directed by Yahweh;
How then can a man understand his way?

Proverbs 20:24

Throughout my life, there have been other events in which I have followed Yeshua's {Jesus'} example in forgiving others… some of them include:

- While going through all the changes in my life, learning to hear and heed the spirit, leaving behind my "old boxes" (boxes of "the medical model," of "family systems," of "big box religion") and of ALL the lies the world and religion teach… I would sometimes go for a drive, on short "get-a-ways" to hiking parks out in nature.

  One day, I drove up north to a small town with a lovely nature park. I went for a peaceful walk, through forests, by bubbling brooks, the smell of pine wafting all around me, caught in the beautiful bliss of walking with my Father, Yahweh {God}! Upon returning to the parking lot, still at a distance, I saw someone with their head IN my car! They had forced the back door, and were rummaging through my belongings! I yelled: *"HEY!!!"* And the man quickly stood up, shut the door, and ran to his own truck.

  I ran toward him and boldly asked, *"WHAT are you doing?"* The man responded that he was hungry and wanted some food. While not entirely believing him, I was reminded of the Scripture, "If your enemy should be hungering, give him the morsel" *(read Romans 12:20),* so I took some crackers from my car and boldly walked over to his truck and asked if he would like some? He was shocked, and timidly asked why I was being so nice to him after what he had done? I stated that the Scripture says "give a hungry person food" *(read also Isaiah 58:7)* and walked away, a little scared and mistrusting of him.

  I forgave him immediately and Praised Yahweh {God} for an opportunity to live out His Scriptures! (Despite being a little shaken, I was grateful for the strength Yahweh {God} had given me. In times past I would have kept my mouth shut and simply driven away scared, instead of being Yeshua {Jesus} to someone.

- When I was young, around 10-years-old, all my siblings were going to the mall together, my two oldest sisters and my two brothers. I asked if I could accompany them, and they agreed. However, vacuuming my bedroom on that Saturday afternoon, I finished to find that they had all left for the mall, *without me.* I felt completely abandoned. Unloved. Unwanted. I was crushed. For years and years I was hurt and angry about this seemingly small but significant event (in *my* heart). I eventually gave it to Yahweh {God} and forgave them. (I admit, I was, no doubt, a pain in the neck to the oldest three siblings, "the baby brat sister," when I was young. I wanted to do *everything* they did… and they did not want a "tag-a-long" baby sister to look after!) I now know that, quite often, while we might know what we are doing we are short-sighted as to the consequences of our actions. Forgiveness is the only route, and the only one Yeshua {Jesus} takes.

- Finally, Red, (and many others mentioned in this book). I forgive him, for all he has done. (Again, I myself am not perfect… far far from it. I know I need forgiveness also. And, I forgive myself too.) For, just as Deborah says, *"There is nothing you have done that I could not do, and nothing I have done that you could not do. All ground is level at the cross."* Red is a child of Yahweh {God} also. The Scripture comes to mind, "**Let the sinless one of you first cast a stone…**" *(Read John 8:7)* I thought I had forgiven him, forgiven everyone, completely.

  However, writing this book brings up memories… memories that I had buried deep. Also, I noticed that I got emotional when editing these chapters with a dear friend. I can almost hear in my mind Daniel saying, *"this means you are not completely 'over' these events, not 100% surrendered."* Father forgive me. As I have learned from Dr. Tom Taylor and Barbara Brown, and thus included with all other accounts in life, when forgiving, I place ALL in front of the cross, forgive all, forgive myself, thank Yahweh {God} for all that I learned, and place everything and everyone in Yahweh's {God's} hands.

Stand up, and walk away. Praising Yahweh {God}, looking forward, and focusing on Him alone.

Let us keep our eyes firmly on Yeshua {Jesus}... remembering that we are only sojourners in this world, and looking to the day we are in heaven with Him and our Father, Yahweh {God}! Come Yeshua the Messiah {Jesus Christ}, come!!!

Not that I already obtained, or am already perfected. Yet I am pursuing, if I may be grasping also that for which I was grasped also by Christ Jesus. Brethren, not as yet am I reckoning myself to have grasped, yet one thing -- forgetting, indeed, those things which are behind, yet stretching out to those in front -- toward the goal am I pursuing for the prize of God's calling above in Christ Jesus.

Philippians 3:12-14

Imagine what this would look like, if EVERYONE forgave, if EVERYONE had a true heart to hear and heed Yahweh {God}! One day... every knee will bow... oh what a GLORIOUS DAY that will be! As Corrie Ten Boom said:

And for all these people alike, the key to healing turned out to be the same. Each had a hurt he had to forgive.

Corrie Ten Boom quote (gathered on June 7, 2021) at:
EverydayPower.com/corrie-ten-boom-quotes

While I have forgiven many people for many things, I am still maturing in the Lord... though not perfect (not on this earth). In one area of life I am in process of forgiving someone close to me, (every day closer to the finish and thus to Yahweh's {God's} complete peace)! And it would do me well to forgive *myself* much more in every-day life also. (This would mean releasing the chains of guilt, cutting the cord of condemnation, and freeing the way to ultimate peace, His peace. Amen!)

"Father, forgive them, for they are not aware what they are doing."

Luke 23:34

"But to you, who are hearing, am I saying: Love your enemies. Be doing ideally to those who are hating you. Bless those who are cursing you. Pray concerning those who are traducing you."

Luke 6:27-28

"Therefore I am saying to you, All, whatever you are praying and requesting, be believing that you obtained, and it will be yours. And whenever you may be standing praying, be forgiving, if you have anything against anyone, that your Father also, Who is in the heavens, may be forgiving you your offenses. Now if you are not forgiving, neither will your Father Who is in the heavens be forgiving your offenses."

Mark 11:24-26

As Barbara Brown writes in her book, ***GOD is* GOD *and* We Are Not**:

> When we really understand that God is sovereign, we learn how to walk the "slave and his master" story in *Luke 17:7-10*, knowing we're just supposed to be God's kids and serve Him. Then, even through our tests, we can love everyone God has brought into our lives, knowing they can't do anything He doesn't allow, and they're helping to produce His best in us.
>
> ***GOD is* GOD *and* We Are Not**
> by Barbara Brown, MSE, page 120.

And, as both Dr. Tom Taylor and Barbara Brown write in their book, **Rescuing God From the Rubble of Religion**:

> ***Give thanks for everyone and everything in your life.*** Love it, change it, or leave it and start over. Whichever option you choose, learn from every experience; repent where you fall short of the ideal; forgive, bless, and walk on in love, peace and joy!
>
> **Rescuing God From the Rubble of Religion**
> by Dr. Tom Taylor and Barbara Brown, MSE, page 155.

Father in Heaven,
Thank You for each and every day of my life.
Thank You for every person whom
You have placed in my path, know today,
and will yet meet...

Thank You for ALL I have learned in the past, for all I am learning today, and for all I will learn in the future.
YOU ALONE are YAHWEH {GOD},
and there is NO OTHER.
I would not choose to re-live many days of the past, however I thank you for each of the days that led me closer to You.
I would not have "signed myself up" for
half of what I have lived through…
However, that is why
YOU ARE YAHWEH {GOD}, and I am not.
YOU know ALL things.
YOU created ALL things.
I surrender all.
As I used to sing in church as a teen…
"I surrender all."
I sing today… "I surrender all."

Father, I ask that you bless every person
I have ever met, friend or foe.
Yeshua {Jesus} said, "Bless those who curse you, bless and do not curse."
So, Father, I bless everyone in my life:
past, present, and future.
There is nothing someone else has done,
that I could not have done myself,
And there is nothing I have done,
that someone else could not
have done themselves.
All ground is level at the cross.
Thank You for Your gift of GRACE…
May it flow to each and every person in my life: past, present, and future,
As well as to your child, reading this…

Grant forgiveness, grace, life, peace and love
to each and every child of Yours, Father.
Open their eyes to see YOU and YOU alone,
Not who "religion" portrays You to be,
but the TRUE, LOVING Father
Who You really are and always have been!
Show everyone that THEY are
precious to YOU,
That You would leave the ninety-nine
and seek to find THEM, the one,
(just as You did with me)!
I only pray You are smiling down
on me, Father.
I only ask that I be found faithful until my last breath or until I am ascending as Yeshua {Jesus} is descending!
Bless everyone…
In Yeshua's {Jesus'} Holy Name,
Amen. Amen. And Amen.

Show us, O Yahweh, Your benignity (mercifulness,
kindness and bountifulness ~ *CLKC*),
And grant us Your salvation.
Do let me hear what the One, El, shall speak;
Yahweh indeed, He shall pronounce well-being to His people,
To His benign ones,
To those who turn back their heart to Him.
Yea, His salvation is near to those fearing Him,
That glory may tabernacle in our land.

Psalm 85:7-9

Chapter 11

CALLED TO FOLLOW YAHWEH (AGAIN)...

Greater than these things and more will you do!

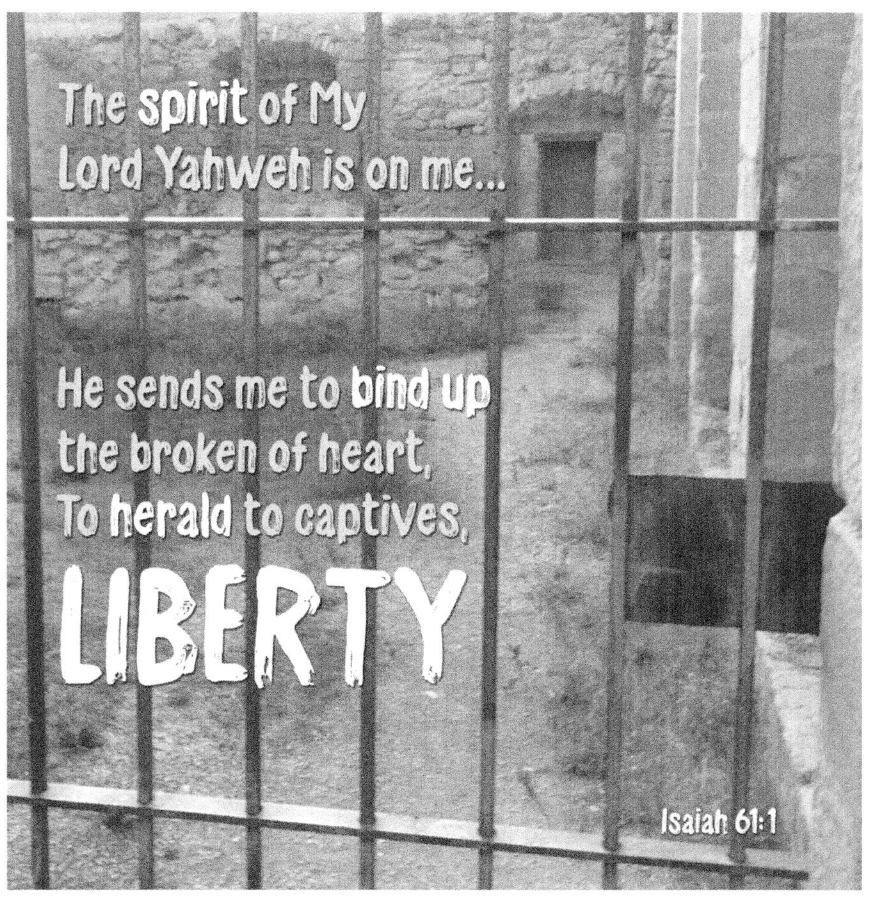

> The spirit of My Lord Yahweh is on Me
> Because Yahweh anoints Me to bear tidings to the humbled;
> He sends Me to bind up the broken of heart,
> To herald to captives, liberty,
> And to the sightless, unclosed eyes,
> And to the bound, emancipation,
> To herald an acceptable year for Yahweh,
> And a day of vengeance for our Elohim;
> To comfort all mourners,
> To establish rejoicing for Zion's mourners,
> To give them beauty instead of ashes,
> …
> Yet you shall be called priests of Yahweh;
> Ministers of our Elohim, it will be said of you;
> The estate of nations you shall eat,
> And in their glory you shall vaunt.
> Instead of your shame, a double portion,
> And for mortification, they shall be jubilant in their portion;
> Therefore they shall tenant a double portion in their land,
> And rejoicing eonian shall become theirs.
>
> *Isaiah 61:1-3a and 6-7*

I heard *the call* of Yahweh {God}!

Well, a quick side-note here: My Father in Heaven kindly reminded me that this was NOT the first "calling" I had heard. Actually, (embarrassingly) I had received the call a couple of years earlier...

My whole life I had heard accounts of others "hearing the call" and did not completely understand what it meant, nor what it sounded like, nor even what it felt like.

I had heard that first call not long after leaving the "big box church," while still living with (and married to) Red who had chosen to stay in religion where "*everyone is dead.*" One day, while I was spending time in the presence of Yahweh {God} and reading the Scriptures, my heart was suddenly and completely LIT ON FIRE! My entire body was consumed with the spirit, with Yahweh {God}. I desired to give my entire life, my every breath to HIM, to do HIS will, HIS work *alone.* **NOTHING else in the world mattered**. Nothing. Only HIS will, HIS purpose, HIS delight.

Light on my feet, floating almost, I set off to the house of fellow followers, Elena and her husband (I will call him Henry), for one of the weekly meetings of "Sold-Out-Seekers" and servants of Yahweh {God}, to also share with them what I was going to do... how I was going to follow my new life path. My plan was to pack up my clothes and drive to the "Sold-Out-Seekers" Organization, to serve Deborah and Daniel, in Virginia, about 800 miles away. (This was before they moved their organization to Texas.) I would just show up on their doorstep, and give my life, my every breath to Yahweh {God}! I was excited at the prospect yet afraid at the same time, with doubt and fear already edging their way in, "*What would they say? How would they react? Would they be happy or angry? Would they accept my heart to serve... or close the door in my face as some freaked out, overzealous but misguided child of Yahweh {God}?*"

While faith fought with fear, I had no answers... but I simply could not care. I was overwhelmed with the ONLY thing in life that mattered, Yahweh {God} and HIS will on earth! While all these thoughts were running through my mind, on the drive to Elena and Henry's house in New England... I saw a big dumpster and immediately felt led to throw away anything of my old life that didn't belong in my newly called life. I drove right up next to it and threw in cd's and a crate full of items, *and*, with a deep pain and sorrow tugging at my heart, I discarded my daughter's car-seat, that signified so much more… yet I was determined to obey Yahweh {God} no matter the cost of His calling.

Now, walking beside the sea of Galilee, He perceived two brothers, Simon, termed Peter, and Andrew, his brother, casting a purse net into the sea, for they were fishers. And He is saying to them, "Hither! After Me, and I will be making you fishers of men!" Now immediately leaving the nets, they follow Him.

And, advancing thence, He perceived two others, brothers, James of Zebedee and John, his brother, in the ship with Zebedee, their father, adjusting their nets. And He calls them. Now, immediately leaving the ship and their father, they follow Him.

Matthew 4:18-22

"If anyone is coming to Me and is not hating his father and mother and wife [and husband] and children and brothers and sisters, and still more his soul besides, he can not be My disciple. And anyone who is not bearing his cross and coming after Me, can not be My disciple."

Luke 14:26-27

As I drove closer and closer to Elena and Henry's house, doubt was now flooding my mind, crashing in like tidal waves against my decision. By the time I arrived, I had already convinced myself that I was crazy, and, sadly, had changed my mind to continue the "rat-race" of life as usual. I told my spiritual family at the meeting what I **had thought** to do… and laughed it off.

On my drive home that night, I returned to the big dumpster and parked right next to it again. I climbed in to retrieve my daughter's car-seat, (one of the pivotal items along with my daughter herself, that I had been previously prepared to leave behind for the call on my life). Now, mere hours later, I was taking her back from the safe arms of Yahweh {God}, thinking I knew a better way. I had placed my daughter above Yahweh {God}, letting fear overcome faith, a decision that would cost a hefty price. I went home, sad in heart, deflated in spirit, yet comforting myself with my *"comfort zone box"* lie that, *"this was a much more practical and reasonable path to follow."*

> **<u>All be doing without</u> murmurings and <u>reasonings</u>...**
>
> *Philippians 2:14*

"Oh Tamra!" scolding myself... **Yahweh** {God} **ALONE knows** if I had gone through with the leading of HIS SPIRIT that day, would I have saved myself YEARS of hell in court battles yet to come and so much wasted time and emotions? The whole transition to my new life in ministry, serving Yahweh {God}, could possibly have been so much easier! Oh man!

I am so thoroughly embarrassed to share this above... However, I am convinced (and convicted) to share the truth, the whole truth. I pray you can *learn* from my mistakes, and have the courage to "Go" **when** the spirit tells you to *"Go!"* It reminds me of the Israelites in the desert, and that their journey could have taken a mere eleven days. Yes, eleven days.

(It is eleven days' journey from Horeb by the Mount Seir road unto Kadesh-barnea.)

Deuteronomy 1:2

However, because of their unbelief and disobedience, it took them forty years of roaming the wilderness! Through my own lack of faith at times, my "walk" was to take a good number of loops around the wilderness too, as I discovered...

I felt worse than Peter when he was distracted by the waves while walking on the water toward Yeshua {Jesus}! Most likely, at some point in my life I judged him for this and thought... *"Well, I would never do that."* Ugh.

Yet, answering Him, Peter said, "Lord, if it is Thou, order me to come to Thee on the waters." Now He said, "Come!" And, descending from the ship, Peter walks on the waters, to come to Jesus.

Yet, observing the strong wind, he was afraid. And, beginning to sink, he cries, saying, "Lord, save me!" Now immediately Jesus, stretching out His hand, got hold of him and is saying to him, "Scant of faith, why do you hesitate?"

Matthew 14:28-31

Not only did I look at the wind and waves... I sank, Yeshua {Jesus} standing right there with His hand held out to me, unnoticed by me as my eyes were NOT on Him.

Looking back, I turned from "my breaking" here. I did not believe that Yahweh {God} could be asking something so "abnormal" or "*out of Tamra's box*" in my life. I had a lot to learn!

Dr. Tom Taylor discusses when "the breaking" is necessary in one of his **Bible** studies titled "*114 – Keep Coming and Never Stop Short*":

> *It seems to me that the phenomenon we call "breaking" is only necessary when we have become stiff and rigid by our own devices, (it's a natural process of growing up in this eon), and by our own opinions, decisions that have* **excluded** *God, His will and His purpose for us. Now we become pots that are unusable and must be broken – sometimes shattered to bits – until we can be remade into vessels of honor, usable by the potter for His will and purpose rather than ours.*
>
> Light Up the Scriptures study "*114 - Keep Coming and Never Stop Short*"
> by Dr. Tom Taylor. (Time: 21:16 - 21:56)

Oh man…! Well, as Dr. Tom Taylor sees it: "*Yahweh {God} is* ***NOT*** *up in heaven wringing his hands, wondering WHAT just happened? He knows!* ***He knows ALL things!*** *Praise His Holy Name!*"

> **O Yahweh, You have investigated me and are knowing me;**
> **You Yourself know my sitting down and my rising up;**
> **You understand my thought from afar;**
> **My path and my pallet You have measured off,**
> **And for all my ways You have made provision.**
> **For though there be no declaration on my tongue,**
> **Behold, O Yahweh, You know it all.**
> …

For You Yourself achieved the making of
my innermost being;
You overshadowed me in my mother's belly.
…
Your eyes saw my embryo,
And my days, all of them were written upon Your scroll;
The days, they were formed when there was not
one of them.

Psalm 139:1-4, 13 and 16

Did I not **know** the testaments to faith, having read them over and over? The story of Abraham's test with his son Isaac? The abhorrent account of Yeshua's {Jesus'} arrest, crucifixion and death? Paul's life of hardships and persecutions? David's life of oppression before becoming king? Gideon's battles even when he felt unworthy? I believe I thought that Yahweh {God} would not require such an "unnatural" test in MY own life… Others in the **Bible**? Yes. Me? Surely not. "*It could not be possible*!" I thought. Yes… lots to learn…

Dr. Tom Taylor and Barbara Brown include a perfect explanation of "His ways" in their book **Rescuing God From the Rubble of Religion**:

> We must maintain a teachable spirit, remembering that God thinks differently from human beings. Believing the best about Him first, rather than considering Him negligent or malicious, will lead to better answers.
>
> **For my designs are not your designs,**
> **And your ways are not My ways, averring is Yahweh.**
> **For as the heavens are loftier than the earth,**

So are My ways loftier than your ways,
And My designs than your designs.

(Isaiah 55:8-9)

Rescuing God From the Rubble of Religion
by Dr. Tom Taylor and Barbara Brown, MSE pages 137-138.

So, like I said... I then heard ***the call*** of Yahweh {God}! Again! (After the above calling, over one year previous.) Praise Yah {God} for HIS grace, mercy and patience.

It is by Yahweh's benignities that we have not come to end,
that His compassions are not finished;
They are new every morning;
great is Your faithfulness...

Lamentations 3:22-23

One relaxing weekend afternoon, I was in a small meeting in New England with the "Sold-Out-Seekers," the true followers of Yeshua {Jesus}. No religious teachings nor doctrines! Only true seekers of Yahweh {God}, seeking His will in our lives! (There were just three of us together that day.)

We were encouraged by Deborah to read Isaiah chapters 40 through to 66, the end of the book of Isaiah.

As I listened to the words of Isaiah… **I heard the call of Yahweh** {God}**!** My whole body came alive! Once again it lit my spirit on fire. I wanted to get up THAT SECOND and GO! GO AND DO! (I could barely contain myself to finish listening to the entire Scripture reading…)

I felt most on FIRE during two particular sections of the reading, at first in Chapter 42:

I, Yahweh, I call You in righteousness,
And I shall hold fast to Your hand;
I shall preserve You
And give You for a covenant of the people,
For a light of the nations,
To unclose the eyes that are blind,
To bring forth the prisoner from the enclosure,
And those dwelling in darkness from the house of detention.
I am Yahweh; that is My Name,
And My glory I shall not give to another,
Or My praise to carvings.
The former things, behold, they came;
Now I will tell the new;
Ere they are sprouting I shall announce them to you.
Sing to Yahweh a new song,
His praise from the end of the earth…

Isaiah 42:6-10a

And again in Chapter 61:

The spirit of My Lord Yahweh is on Me
Because Yahweh anoints Me to bear tidings to the humbled;
He sends Me to bind up the broken of heart,

To herald to captives, liberty,
And to the sightless, unclosed eyes,
And to the bound, emancipation,
To herald an acceptable year for Yahweh,
And a day of vengeance for our Elohim;
To comfort all mourners,
To establish rejoicing for Zion's mourners,
To give them beauty instead of ashes,
...
Yet you shall be called priests of Yahweh;
Ministers of our Elohim, it will be said of you...

Isaiah 61:1-3a and 6a

I SHOUTED IN MY MIND, as willing as Isaiah was to his own calling:

So I answered, Behold me! Send me!

Isaiah 6:8b

...with everyone whose spirit the One, Elohim, had roused to go up to rebuild the House of Yahweh Who is in Jerusalem.

Ezra 1:5b

I looked around expecting to see the same excitement and fire in the others... but saw nothing close to the feeling inside of me. I was confused... I did not understand why the others did not feel the same as I did. The message ignited my spirit. I was ON FIRE to GO! To FOLLOW YAHWEH {GOD} with my whole heart, with my entire strength, with my every breath. Nothing else mattered. Nothing. And I knew that what anyone else did or said was of no consequence, just as when Yeshua {Jesus} said to Peter:

Now Peter, being turned about, is observing the disciple whom Jesus loved… Peter, then, perceiving this one, is saying to Jesus, "Lord, yet what of this man?" Jesus is saying to him, "If I should be wanting him to be remaining till I am coming, what is it to you? You be following Me!"

John 21:20-22

Today, I understand that every person, every child of Yahweh {God} has a DIFFERENT calling, (which is why the others did not hear as I did in that moment, nor have the same feeling that I had to "GO").

Now all these one and the same spirit is operating, apportioning to each his own, according as He is intending.

For even as the body is one and has many members, yet all the members of the one body, being many, are one body, thus also is the Christ.

…

Now you are the body of Christ, and members of a part, whom also God, indeed, placed in the ecclesia, first, apostles, second, prophets, third, teachers, thereupon powers, thereupon graces of healing, supports, pilotage, species of languages. Not all are apostles. Not all are prophets. Not all are teachers. Not all have powers. Not all have the graces of healing. Not all are speaking languages. Not all are interpreting. Yet be zealous for the greater graces…

1 Corinthians 12:11-12 and 27-31a

Again, the most faithful followers I knew, true followers of Yahweh {God}, were Deborah and Daniel. Since I was (or felt) "new" at this, the best way I could think of to obey the call on my life this time was to go learn from others who were further on the path than I was... I wanted to do ANYTHING I COULD to help... to help them in serving Yahweh {God} and helping others at their organization, "Sold-Out-Seekers." I would do ANYTHING! I did not care. WhatEVER Yahweh {God} wanted, *"Here am I, send me!"* my mind was SHOUTING.

Jesus... is rising from dinner and is laying down His garments, and, getting a cloth, He girds Himself.

Thereafter He is draining water into the basin, and begins washing the feet of the disciples and wiping them off with the cloth with which He was girded.

...

"If, then, I, the Lord and the Teacher, wash your feet, you also ought to be washing one another's feet. For an example have I given you, that, according as I do to you, you also may be doing."

John 13:3-5 and 14-15

Blessed is the God and Father of our Lord Jesus Christ, the Father of pities and God of all consolation, Who is consoling us in our every affliction to enable us to be consoling those in every affliction, through the consolation with which we ourselves are being consoled by God...

2 Corinthians 1:3-4

> **For <u>better is a day in Your courts</u> than a thousand elsewhere;**
> **<u>I would choose to sweep in the house of my Elohim</u>,**
> **Rather than abide in the tents of wickedness.**
>
> *Psalm 84:10*

I called Deborah and told her about the effect the reading had on me. (I was like an EXCITED LITTLE KID!) She was glad… though not as giddy and excited as I was. I was ready to pack up all my belongings in that hour, walk out the door and drive to Texas at THAT very MOMENT. (And this time, go through with it.) As wiser followers of the way, while both Deborah and Daniel were happy for me, first they tested me… to make sure this spirit, my spirit, was truly from Yahweh {God}:

> **Beloved, do not believe every spirit, but <u>test the spirits</u> to see if they are of God…**
>
> *1 John 4:1a*

> **And you will remember all the way which Yahweh your Elohim caused you to go these forty years in the wilderness, that He might make you humble, <u>to probe you so as to know what is in your heart</u>, whether or not you shall observe His instructions.**
>
> *Deuteronomy 8:2*

Deborah warned me (at least twelve times, literally, over the next few weeks) that I would be *"working my tail off,"* **on purpose** for Yahweh {God} at "Sold-Out-Seekers." (Before she was saved, she was a hard working business woman, with many many earthly riches. And she was raised by two strict, hard-core parents!) She was contagiously energetic, positive, and **on a mission** to DO YAHWEH's {GOD's} WILL, whatever the cost. Every day. All day. From early morning till late at night.

Daniel was "God's workhorse" (as he called himself). Yahweh {God} would often wake him up around 4 am, and he would simply follow the leading of the spirit... read and study the Word; heal, help and advise others on their path; write books; edit devotionals; as well as create and design everything from videos to brochures to websites until 11 pm... almost every day, 365 days of the year! And I was told, if I was truly called to **this** ministry, I was expected to *"hit the ground running"* the moment I arrived.

I was not deterred. I knew I was called there... I sang out, *"Yes! Here am I! Send ME!"*

Deborah also said, that this would be the MOST FULFILLING "work" I had ever done, living for ***Yahweh's*** *{God's}* ***purpose!***

...that the God of our Lord Jesus Christ, the Father of glory, may be giving you a spirit of wisdom and revelation in the realization of Him, the eyes of your heart having been enlightened, for you to perceive what is the expectation of His calling, and what the riches of the glory of the enjoyment of His allotment among the saints, and what the transcendent greatness of His power for us who are believing, in accord with the operation of the might of His strength...

...

...and subjects all under His (the Messiah's) feet, and gives Him, as Head over all, to the ecclesia which is His body, the complement of the One completing the all in all.

Ephesians 1:17-19 and 22

"The spirit of the Lord is on Me,
On account of which He anoints Me to bring
the evangel to the poor.
He has commissioned Me to heal the crushed heart,
To herald to captives a pardon,
And to the blind the receiving of sight;
To dispatch the oppressed with a pardon.
To herald an acceptable year of the Lord..."

Luke 4:18-19

"The infirm (weak ~ *CLKC*) be curing, the dead be rousing, lepers be cleansing, demons be casting out. Gratuitously you got; gratuitously be giving."

Matthew 10:8

I recalled, on a previous trip to Texas, saying to Deborah: *"Do you remember a few months ago you said to me, 'You are the only person I could live with, Tamra.'?"* She looked at me and said, *"That is very interesting you would say that."* That is all she said. A big smile grew on my face. I was learning "the power of words," prophecy and speaking things into existence... I had learned not to speak of anything negative NOR to complain. And I knew, as soon as I had said those words, that SOMETHING then happened. I did not know exactly what it was... I just knew something had happened as I spoke those words... Today, I now know I was creating with the power of the spoken word, *speaking things into existence!*

And Elohim said: Let light come to be! And light came to be. Elohim saw the light that it was good.

Genesis 1:3-4a

By the word of Yahweh, the heavens were made,
And by the spirit of His mouth, all their host.
...
For He spoke, and it came to be;
He enjoined, and it stood firm.

Psalm 33:6 and 9

As Charles Capps states in his book, **The Tongue, A Creative Force**:

> *Words are the most powerful thing in the universe...* We must learn to use our words more effectively. *The words you speak will either put you over or hold you in bondage.*
>
> **The Tongue, A Creative Force** by Charles Capps, page 1.

Above, "put you over" means to "give you freedom."

Since I was a little girl, I *loved*, and I mean LOVED, listening to the story of Samuel, how he had the privilege of growing up *living* **in the temple** with **the Ark of the Covenant**. With Yahweh {God}! IN HIS PRESENCE! I felt as if I was about to be living a similar life... serving Yahweh {God}. A dream come true, a prayer answered, from a young, young age. From drawing pointless circles with my feet in the desert, to now following a clear, CALLED path.

2:21 …the lad Samuel grew up in the presence of Yahweh.

…

3:1 The lad Samuel was in the ministry before Yahweh under Eli the priest. In those days the word of Yahweh had become rare; there was no vision being unfolded.

…

3:3 The lamp of Elohim was not yet quenched, while Samuel was lying down in the temple of Yahweh where the coffer of Elohim was.

1 Samuel 2:21b and 3:1 and 3

(Read the whole account, 1 Samuel chapters 1-3.)

The day finally came when "the door was opened" and I was invited to move to "Sold-Out-Seekers" in Texas! My entire body was ALIVE and SINGING!!!

My heart bubbles over…!

Psalm 45:1a

…yet God, being rich in mercy, because of His vast love with which He loves us…

Ephesians 2:4

Bless Yahweh, my soul,
And all within me, bless His holy Name!
Bless Yahweh, my soul,
And do not forget any of His well-dealings,
Who is pardoning all your depravity,
Who is healing all your ailments,
Who is redeeming your life from ruin,
Who is crowning you with benignity (mercifulness, kindness and bountifulness ~ *CLKC*) and compassion,
Who is satisfying your future with good,
So your youth is renewed like the vulture's.
…
Yahweh has established His throne in the heavens,
And His kingdom rules among all.
Bless Yahweh, all His messengers,
Masters of valor, doing His word,
So as to hearken to the voice of His word!
Bless Yahweh, all His hosts,
Who are ministering to Him,
Doing what is acceptable to Him!
Bless Yahweh, all His works,
In all places of His rule!
Bless Yahweh, my soul!

Psalm 103:1-5 and 19-22

I informed the courts that I was beginning a new life serving in ministry and was moving to Texas. Multiple times I requested and proved that my daughter would have an *excellent life* with me in my new life in ministry, living in a home within a closed community, safe for children (a stark comparison to where she lived at the time). She would have her very own bedroom (instead of sharing a bedroom with Red), attend an excellent

Public Christian School, while enjoying wholesome, healthy food and a happy home-life!

The court was dead-set against it all, and refused to let my daughter move out of state with me.

I told my young daughter I was moving to Texas. She clung to my neck, tears streaming down her cheeks. (As heart wrenching as it was to tell my daughter this… **the call** was strong enough in me that "I left everything to follow Him!" And, I KNEW that YAHWEH {GOD} could restore her to me the very next day… if He wanted to!) I told my daughter that *"I would prepare a room for her in my new home."*

I packed up my car, the spirit in me joyous and flowing as I walked out my "Yes" to Yahweh's {God's} leading, and drove to my new beginning…

As I drove through and out of New England, (less than a mile from where my daughter lived), I cried. "**Lowing as they went**" came to mind from the Biblical account where the Philistines, wanting to rid themselves of the plagues Yahweh {God} had sent upon them, returned the Ark of the Covenant, transported on a cart by two young cows, each leaving behind them their own young calves born only hours earlier:

> **…They took two young cows, recently freshened firstlings, and hitched them to the cart; yet their young they detained at home.**
> **…**
> **The young cows went straight ahead on their way in the direction of Beth-shemesh. They went along a single highway, lowing as they went; and they did not withdraw to the right or left…**
>
> *1 Samuel 6: 10 and 12*

"<u>And everyone who leaves</u> houses, or brothers, or sisters, or father, or mother, or wife [or husband], **or <u>children</u>, or fields, <u>on account of My name</u>…"**

Matthew 19:29a

Another "child of Yahweh {God}" (a teenager, I will call her Violet) was moving to "Sold-Out-Seekers" also, for her new beginning!... and I joyously brought her on the 1800 mile drive. We made a "little adventure" of it! We visited Niagara Falls… we blasted and sang along to WORSHIP MUSIC as we passed beautiful fields in the lovely countryside and many, many hay bales! (I love road trips! Always have…always will!) We listened to the **Bible** on audio recording, as well as devotions, and more worship music for the whole five-day journey!

We arrived at "Sold-Out-Seekers" in Texas. I was completely energized! I unpacked and "got to work." I LOVED IT! I LOVED EVERYTHING ABOUT IT! A new life… for Yahweh {God}!

…I shall sing of Your strength
And be jubilant each morning over Your benignity (mercifulness, kindness and bountifulness ~ *CLKC*)…

Psalm 59:16a

Chapter 12

HOLY SPIRIT UNIVERSITY

Unique classes and path for each chosen vessel!

Therefore we also, from the day on which we hear, do not cease praying for you and requesting that you may be filled full with the realization of His will, in all wisdom and spiritual understanding, you to walk worthily of the Lord for all pleasing, bearing fruit in every good work, and growing in the realization of God; being endued with all power, in accord with the might of His glory, for all endurance and patience with joy...

Colossians 1:9-11

My life changed overnight, wonderfully, from "swimming in a sea of sharks" in the ocean to diving into the deep end of "Holy Spirit University" as Deborah calls it, *"A specific, special path of classes just for you, chosen and set in motion by Yahweh {God} Himself, before you were even born!"*

Here in Texas, *no one knew me!* No ruined reputation nor unjust defamation of character, no one even knew I had a child... unless I told them. I had learned quickly months prior, that **many would judge me**: *a mother of a young child who was not raising her own daughter?* I also learned that I had only One Judge, and to **hear and heed** His word alone:

...and that you be ambitious to be quiet, and to be engaged in your own affairs, and to be working with your hands, according as we charge you...

1 Thessalonians 4:11

Soon after I arrived in Texas, my other brother (I shall call him Dan), upon hearing from other blood relatives that I had moved to Texas to follow my *call of Yahweh {God}*, sent me a supportive text message saying, *"Congratulations. Good for you!"* Bless him Father!

At "Sold-Out-Seekers" first thing in the morning they held **Bible** meetings. Deborah read **Bible Gateway's** Scripture verse of the day, followed by the whole chapter from which that particular verse was drawn. They would then read **My Utmost for His Highest**, a daily devotional by Oswald Chambers. Deborah and Daniel's discussions flowed wherever the spirit led them, relating the Scriptures and learnings with present day life. Sometimes these morning meetings would last twenty minutes... and other times two to three hours! They would completely flow with the spirit, no limits at all placed on their *precious time in Yahweh's {God's} presence!*

A piece of my serving and training as an assistant minister was to help guide Violet there at "Sold-Out-Seekers." I knew that she did not love being in Texas, to say the least. She dearly missed her friends in New England; she looked back often, messaged old friends, and did not seem to rejoice in "her new life." She would murmur and complain when performing little tasks, like mopping the floors. (I was not personally aware of all of her training there, nor of all the details in her life. I was simply an assistant at the organization, and would see her for a few hours here and there throughout the day. So, there were many other things going on with her, conversations had that I was not privy to...) One day she was told to leave, (shunned, you could say). Days later she returned to live in New England.

<u>All</u> be doing <u>without murmurings</u> and reasonings...

Philippians 2:14

<u>Nor yet be murmuring</u> even as some of them murmur, and perished by the exterminator.

1 Corinthians 10:10

Be rejoicing in the Lord always! Again, I will declare, be rejoicing!

Philippians 4:4

Deborah and Daniel lived by and spoke the utmost importance of positivity at "Sold-Out-Seekers." Daniel said, *"You CAN do anything! STOP saying you cannot. I do not want to hear it."* And Deborah shared her learnings on the journey... *"IF you have to complain about something, you have TWO minutes. Then stop. Never speak of it again. SPEAK ONLY POSITIVE from then on!"* Also, saying often, *"Thoughts are things."* And Daniel would share that everything, **everything** is about energy.

How compelling, to fully understand the importance of guarding your own spirit from the attitudes, opinions and negativity of others, precisely as the Scriptures say…

Then the superintendents will continue to speak to the people and say: Whoever the man be who is fearful and timid of heart may go and return to his house so that the heart of his brothers may not be melted as his own heart is.

Deuteronomy 20:8

Everything done at "Sold-Out-Seekers" was with complete excellence. Everything. Thus, it was expected of me also. (From crafting correspondence to careful stewardship with money, including every dime spent; from picking up others' trash at public parks to mopping floors at the organization; from quality, nutritious food selection to its preparation; and everything in-between!)

All, whatsoever you may be doing, work from the soul, as to the Lord and not to men...

Colossians 3:23

Therefore we also, from the day on which we hear, do not cease praying for you and requesting that you may be filled full with the realization of His will, in all wisdom and spiritual understanding, you to walk worthily of the Lord for all pleasing, bearing fruit in every good work, and growing in the realization of God; being endued with all power, in accord with the might of His glory, for all endurance and patience with joy...

Colossians 1:9-11

Bless them Father, for all they do, grant them a double-blessing and beyond. Before I arrived, their home was peaceful, tranquil and free from "young spiritual children." I know they gave this up in order to train up a new minister in the ways of Yahweh {God}...

Now we are asking you, brethren, to perceive those who are toiling among you and presiding over you in the Lord and admonishing you, and to deem them exceedingly distinguished in love, because of their work. Be at peace among yourselves.

1 Thessalonians 5:12-13

Let elders who have presided ideally be counted worthy of double honor, especially those who are toiling in word and teaching…

1 Timothy 5:17

Be persuaded by your leaders, and be deferring to them, for they are vigilant for the sake of your souls, as having to render an account, that they may be doing this with joy, and not with groaning, for this is disadvantageous for you.

Hebrews 13:17

Daniel and Deborah were well educated in caring for the only body Yahweh {God} gave them, and they included many greens on their plates. They had learned in their journeys much about the mind and how it works, as well as energetic treatments for the body (also called bio-energetics). They graciously gave me energetic treatments to remove "blockages" when I felt stuck. Stuck in past beliefs, stuck in fear, stuck in overwhelm or plain stuck. This was an unspeakable help, and such a blessing! I must add here, I *loved* when Deborah would pray over me before a treatment. She would place her hand on my forehead, bring the power of Yahweh {God} down by speaking healing *into* my body, and I would sometimes be healed from the prayer alone! Nothing would show up, no energetic *"blocks"* that would need to be treated with bio-energetics! The power of prayer is miraculous! Thank You Father!

And with His welts comes healing for us.

Isaiah 53:5b

"Verily, verily, I am saying to you, he who is believing in Me, the works which I am doing he also will be doing, and greater than these will he be doing, for I am going to the Father. And whatever you should be requesting in My name, this I will be doing, that the Father should be glorified in the Son. If you should ever be requesting anything of Me in My name, this I will be doing."

John 14:12-14

There were also fun times at "Sold-Out-Seekers..." a few months after arriving I celebrated my birthday, and Deborah so kindly surprised me with a present EVERY MORNING for a week straight before my birthday!!! Each morning she gave me a piece of luggage... by the time my birthday came, I had an entire matching set! It was LOVELY! What a surprise!!!

We would go on some fun outings also... Deborah and I went horse-back-riding one day! I loved it! (It was hot though... summer in Texas! That was the first and last time we did that. LOL.)

I shall acclaim You, O Yahweh, with all my heart;
I shall indeed recount all Your marvelous works.
I shall greatly rejoice and be glad in You;
I shall surely make melody to Your Name, O Supreme.

Psalm 9:1-2

Praise Yah.
Indeed it is good to make melody to our Elohim;

Psalm 147:1

Traveling with Deborah was exciting! Regardless of being out "in the world" or at the "Sold-Out-Seekers" organization, Deborah had her eyes and ears fixed on Yahweh {God}, to speak all He wanted her to minister to others as the spirit led her. She was a straight talker, never "beating around the bush," certainly no sugar-coating, and instead speaking only what **Yahweh** {God} wanted others to hear including encouragement, piercing questions, blunt answers, rebukes and everything in-between. Yahweh {God} would reveal much about them to her, including their thoughts, their past, their current needs and more! On her journey, she had learned to be obedient to His leading and His voice when ministering to others. She would not try to figure out Yahweh {God}… but simply SPEAK when and ALL HE directed her to speak!

I witnessed Daniel ministering to others as well, during phone and video calls or when others came to "Sold-Out-Seekers." He truly is the wisest and most humble man of Yahweh {God} that I have ever met. He is the epitome of the Scripture: "**…be ambitious to be quiet, and to be engaged in your own affairs, and to be working with your hands…**" *(1 Thessalonians 4:11)* He LIVED his words of wisdom to *"not give advice unless asked. People who do not ask for your wisdom do not want it, are not ready to hear it and thus will not heed it anyway. It will simply be a waste of your time and words."* What an impartation I received! What a blessing to witness Yahweh's {God's} servants, speaking His word with His heart to His children. Thank You Father!

Just as Yeshua {Jesus} spoke only what His Father directed:

> **"…seeing that I speak not from Myself, but the Father Who sends Me, He has given Me the precept, <u>what I may be saying and what I should be speaking</u>."**
>
> *John 12:49*

I learned to simply keep my mouth shut and watch. Watch and learn. Taking NO ATTENTION for myself. NONE. I was still learning to hear the spirit, and "making it my AMBITION to lead a quiet life" was the best way to learn. I **know** it took me longer to learn than they wanted... Bless them Father.

> **...and that you <u>be ambitious to be quiet</u>, and to <u>be engaged in your own affairs</u>, and to be working with your hands, according as we charge you...**
>
> *1 Thessalonians 4:11*

Thus I was trained as a holy woman of Yahweh {God} on how to speak and minister to men and women. No flirting with men, none. (Same goes for men: no flirting with women.)

> **A decadent human, a lawless man**
> **Is one who goes about with a perverse mouth,**
> **Who winks with his eyes, who declares with his feet,**
> **Who signals with his fingers...**
>
> *Proverbs 6:12-13*

No attention seeking, no spirit of neediness, only to "live above and beyond reproach" (in all integrity, blameless) as a holy woman (or man) of Yahweh {God}.

(Well, obviously exceptions to this are married couples, yes, they should flirt with and *encourage only each other*, and often! Also, when Yahweh {God} leads two single people to date, as He knows the hearts of all, after prayer and testing of the spirits, then some flirting or encouragement is ok. *This is my own opinion.)*

Barbara Brown teaches in her book about living in purity and holiness. If and when possible, men deal with men and women deal with women.

> Let's jump right into the holiness issue. This is not about legalism, but purity before God and one another. Never let the grace of our Lord be an excuse for fleshly indulgences. There is a reason for the fence that separates the men from the women at the Wailing Wall in Jerusalem, even today.
>
> > ***As obedient children, do not be conformed to the former lusts which were yours in your ignorance, but like the Holy One Who called you, be holy yourselves also in all your behavior; because it is written, "You shall be holy, for I am holy."***
> >
> > (1 Peter 1:14-16 NASB)
>
> When guys deal with guys and girls deal with girls, a standard of holiness is established to keep out "flesh treats" and spiritual adultery. After all, it was God Who said, "Be holy for I am holy."…
>
> > ***Be of sober spirit, be on the alert. Your adversary, the devil, prowls around like a roaring lion, seeking someone to devour.***
> >
> > (1 Peter 5:8 NASB)
>
> *GOD is* GOD *and* We Are Not
> by Barbara Brown, MSE, page 177.

Deborah has such a selfless and giving spirit when speaking with anyone. She is fulfilled by Yahweh {God} in every area of life, she needs NOTHING nor wants anything from anyone. She has become "safe" around both men and women. People are drawn to her… drawn to the spirit of Yahweh {God} in her.

Faithful is the saying: "If anyone is craving the supervision, he is desiring an ideal work." The supervisor, then, <u>must be irreprehensible</u> (blameless, unrebukable ~ *CLKC*)...

1 Timothy 3:1-2a

Additional valuable lessons I learned along the same lines as no flirting... were no flattery and no familiarity.

For <u>neither did we at any time become flattering in expression</u>, according as you are aware; neither with a pretense for greed, God is witness; neither seeking glory from men, neither from you, nor from others, when we could be a burden as Christ's apostles.

1 Thessalonians 2:5-6

He who reproves a man shall find more grace afterward <u>Than he who is slick of tongue</u> (flattering).

Proverbs 28:23

So that we, from now on, are <u>acquainted with no one according to flesh</u>.

2 Corinthians 5:16a

(Read more Scriptures on flattery including: Psalm 12:2-3, Proverbs 26:28, Job 32:21-22, Luke 20:21, and many more...)

I was utterly shocked the day Deborah told me she did NOT want flattery. I was sitting in her office, when she shared that she did not want me to flatter her, nor praise her practically **at all**. I wanted to encourage her all the time, telling her how wise she was. She, on the other hand, thought these words were a waste of time and was wisely guarding her own heart, keeping her eyes focused on Yahweh {God} from Whom the wisdom came. (Another characteristic for me to learn!)

The first evening I had ever spent time with her was in a small gathering of followers of Yeshua {Jesus}, ("Sold-Out-Seekers"), everyone seated in chairs around the living room in a circle. I sat at her feet, with my hand on her knee. I wanted to be as CLOSE to her (to her SPIRIT actually, to the spirit of Yahweh {God} IN her) as possible. I was glued to her. I was literally drinking from her spirit... filling up my own spirit from Yahweh {God} above.

I believe this was fine... for a time. And later, while I did not realize it, nor want to, frankly, the time came to grow up and out of this, into maturity. I adored her, yes! There was such LIFE in her! The spirit of Yahweh {God} was so strong in her.

As Barbara Brown herself explains in her book:

> I was drawn to those who were filled with the Holy Spirit and I wanted what they had, because they were so vibrant with life.
>
> *GOD is* GOD *and* We Are Not
> by Barbara Brown, MSE, pages 217-218.

There is a fine line between flattery and encouragement. *"Pray for a spirit of discernment,"* I was advised... repeatedly and for many different reasons.

Both Deborah and Daniel, (any and EVERY single time someone praises them), respond adamantly, "***Praise Yahweh** {God}**!***" They take NO praise for themselves. None. They give ALL glory to Yahweh {God}! This was completely NEW *and refreshing* to me... to see it lived out in every-day life! They are serious about giving ALL the glory to Yahweh {God} alone, to Whom all the glory belongs!

Not to us, O Yahweh, not to us,
But to Your Name give glory,
On account of Your benignity (mercifulness, kindness and bountifulness ~ *CLKC*)**, on Your faithfulness.**

Psalm 115:1

...you may be learning not to be disposed above what is written, that you may not be puffed up, one over the one, against the other. For who is making you to discriminate? Now what have you which you did not obtain? Now if you obtained it also, why are you boasting as though not obtaining?

1 Corinthians 4:6b-7

"Worthy art Thou, O Lord, our Lord and God,
To get glory and honor and power;
For Thou dost create all,
And because of Thy will they were, and are created."

Revelations - The Unveiling of Jesus Christ 4:11

All this came upon king Nebuchadnezzar when at the end of twelve months he was walking about on the housetop of the royal palace of Babylon. The king was responding to all this by saying, Is not this Babylon the Great that I myself have built for the royal house with the might of my safeguarding walls and for the esteem of my honor!

While the declaration was still in the mouth of the king, there was a voice that fell from the heavens: This has been decreed for you, king Nebuchadnezzar, that the kingdom has passed away from you. From mortals are they shoving you away, and with the animals of the field is your abode. They shall feed herbage to you, like oxen. Thus seven seasons shall pass on over you until you know that the Supreme is in authority in the kingdom of mortals, and He gives it to whomsoever He will.

In the same hour the declaration gathered on Nebuchadnezzar...

At the end of the days, I, Nebuchadnezzar, lifted up my eyes to the heavens, and my knowledge was returning onto me. Then I blessed the Supreme, and I lauded and honored Him Who is living for the eon, since His jurisdiction is an eonian jurisdiction, and His kingdom is with generation after generation.

Daniel 4:28-34

(Read the whole account in Daniel 4.)

So that, let no one be boasting in men…

1 Corinthians 3:21

On to the next: Familiarity.

As Dr. Tom Taylor states: *"familiarity will kill you."* He shares in a **Light Up the Scriptures** study:

> *I tell ya, just from personal experience only, it is a fearful thing to set aside what you know to be true, who you know you are in Christ, and what you know the call of God is on your own life in a spirit of familiarity, with the world and with people. It is perilous, it is dangerous and it'll kill'ya. It'll take you right out from underneath the operation of God... of your gift, soul and call. And it is not necessary.*

He goes on to say:

> *In the midst of our most joyful, affirming and even playful experiences, are we in the greatest danger of ignoring our spiritual alertness and astuteness, and even setting aside our panoply, our armor, our weapons of both offence and defense, leaving ourselves wide open to massive attack with the singular goal of destroying our calling and our walk with God in this eon? That is openly the goal of such attacks.*
>
> **Light Up the Scriptures** study *"119 - Have we died with Him"*
> by Dr. Tom Taylor. (Time: 13:13 - 13:52 and 17:45 - 18:24)

In his **Light Up the Scriptures** study, *"154 - Least of all,"* he describes what happened when even Yeshua's {Jesus'} own disciples became *familiar* with Yeshua {Jesus} Himself:

> *The Messiah gave Paul a new paradigm, a complete revelation, because He chose to; but also because the familiarity with Yeshua in*

*the flesh blinded the eyes of the other apostles. They had become Yeshua's '**own country**,' and His home, in which He had no honor. Barbara read that scripture before in Matthew 13:57:*

> ***A prophet is not dishonored except in his own country...***

And it said right before that, it says in the first part of verse 57 there in Matthew 13:

> ***And they were snared in Him.***

They could not get past the fact, "Hey this is Joseph the carpenter's son, we know this guy."

*The Messiah found His twelfth apostle while the others were "drawing straws!" It is Paul's revelation alone, delivered directly by the risen Lord, which describes YaHoVeH's **purpose of the eons** (Ephesians 3:11), which includes all mankind in a previously unheard of, grand celestial destiny.*

Light Up the Scriptures study "*154 - Least of all*"
by Dr. Tom Taylor. (Time: 1:03:51 - 1:04:58)

And again in his study "*89 – God Cuts Deep to get the Cancers Out*" both Dr. Tom Taylor and Barbara Brown speak of the utter dangers of familiarity (emphasis mine):

*Tom said: ...**we would do well to be on our guard for familiarity**, or the temptation to be casual in our relationships, our speech, all of our actions... because as the Apostle Paul wrote "Our lives are not our own, we died with Christ, so that He may live in us and we in Him." Therefore, you and I are His ambassadors to everyone we meet, and God is watching. I pray He is smiling!*

... our focus has to be certain and narrow. Our commitment must be unwavering and steadfast. And our awareness must be alert and ready for anything and everything God may be speaking, showing or doing in our lives, and in the lives of those around us.

And Barbara shared: ...I would encourage each of you to break the powers of a familiar spirit, and deal boldly with whatever God has before you...

... and what God is doing is inviting all of us to get our pots clean, so He can flow His presence through us. And so, in my life, I have wound up in many situations that had I ***not had a familiar spirit*** *involved, had I not gotten into worldly sorrow, had I not wanted more for people than they wanted for themselves... if there is no investment, if there is no exchange, then you are caring more for their lives than they do.*

... but we have a tendency, because we want the best for everybody, we want them to make it! And if there is ANY... ***ANY familiarity****, any wrong spirit,* ***the enemy can use that relationship to take you down.***

Light Up the Scriptures study "*89 - God Cuts Deep to get the Cancers Out*" by Dr. Tom Taylor. (Time: 5:16 - 6:14 and 22:11 - 23:45 and 26:08 - 26:27)

I must say, it is quite easy to fall into this... into familiarity. Just as Deborah and Daniel would teach, it takes SERIOUS WORK to put on (and keep on) your armor of Yahweh {God}, the panoply *(read Ephesians 6:10-17)* and to GUARD the ideal thing committed to us.

It IS possible though!

Today in life, it has ***finally*** become almost second nature to me... to WATCH and GUARD in the spirit. Things once acceptable to do at the beginning of "the walk," are no longer acceptable to Yahweh {God} and His spirit as I matured… no longer helpful nor serving in my walk with Him. Just as Paul himself said:

> **When I was a minor, I spoke as a minor, I was disposed as a minor, I took account of things as a minor. Yet when I have become a man, I have discarded that which is a minor's.**
>
> *1 Corinthians 13:11*

> **The ideal thing committed to you, guard through the holy spirit which is making its home in us.**
>
> *2 Timothy 1:14*

My walk with Yahweh {God} is the only thing that matters. Doing His will, His way.

> **From the rising of the sun unto its setting,**
> **Let the Name of Yahweh be praised.**
>
> *Psalm 113:3*

Yahweh {God} gave me many words through both Deborah and Daniel over the years. I share with you a written word, below... Ohhh that I had listened to and obeyed *this* word, I would have saved myself many months (years, actually) of walking around in the wilderness. Ugh. (Well, that is all for another book.)

It is a NEW day! So, gently bringing my mind back to the present, Praise Yahweh {God} for ALL I have learned, as I now put the very word I heard into practice in my life today… and may I encourage you as I share this word with you, dear reader, to place YOUR name where mine is… and receive this word for yourself also… (emphasis mine):

> *Tamra:*
>
> *Do not struggle or strive to excel, or even to please; rather, "**Relax, and know that I am God.**" Your intelligence and your capacity is as sure and unquestionable as your worth. You need to speak the truth about yourself <u>that agrees with My word about you</u>. When you diminish yourself, you diminish Me, both within yourself and before others. You need not be timid any longer, but assertive - not aggressive, but righteously assertive. This is a skill I am teaching you.*
>
> *Do not fear, but trust Me. Receive the comfort of knowing that you are where I have placed you at this time. Much of your preparation has already been completed, but I am repairing your damage, and replacing the old with the new, like you replaced your damaged wheel and the worn out parts on your car today. Notice that someone else inflicted the damage to your wheel, <u>but I made it new</u>. You have sustained damage to yourself that you need never experience again **<u>if</u> you will care for the one I created as much as I do.***

Praise Yah {God} for His love and kindness, *to each and every one of us…* His perfect creations!

And He is saying to them, "Hither! You yourselves come privately into a place in the wilderness and rest briefly."

Mark 6:31a

Because you are precious in My eyes,
You are glorified, and I Myself love you…

Isaiah 43:4a

Yahweh, your Elohim, is in your midst;
The Masterful One, He shall save.
He shall be elated over you with rejoicing;
He shall renew you in His love;
He shall exult over you with jubilant song.

Zephaniah 3:17

Chapter 13

HE ENCOURAGED HIMSELF IN THE LORD

Turn to Yahweh alone!

It was very distressing to David, for the soldiers spoke of stoning him because all the soldiers were bitter in soul, each man for his sons and for his daughters.

Yet David encouraged himself in Yahweh his Elohim.

1 Samuel 30:6

Mere months after moving to Texas… saying "*YES*" to my calling… living my new life for Yahweh {God}… another UNTHINKABLE happened.

I admit (I confess), since I began writing this book, I had worried (albeit in the back of my mind) how I was going to write this chapter… about these next events. Last night, I put down the notepad, closed my eyes, and the Scriptures I know by heart came to mind:

"Now, whenever they may be giving you up, you should not be worrying about how or what you should be speaking, for it shall be given you in that hour what you should be speaking, for not you are speaking, but the spirit of your Father is speaking in you."

Matthew 10:19-20

The spirit of My Lord Yahweh is on Me
Because Yahweh anoints Me to bear tidings to the humbled;
He sends Me to bind up the broken of heart,
To herald to captives, liberty,
And to the sightless, unclosed eyes,

And to the bound, emancipation,
To herald an acceptable year for Yahweh…

Isaiah 61:1-2a

(This Yeshua {Jesus} Himself read in the synagogue, see Luke 4:17-20.)

The hand of Yahweh came on me. He brought me forth by the spirit of Yahweh and stopped me in the midst of a valley. It was full of bones… and behold, there were exceedingly many on the surface of the valley, and behold, they were very dry.

He said to me: Son of humanity, shall these bones live?

And I answered, My Lord Yahweh, You know.

Ezekiel 37:1-3

(Read the whole account in Ezekiel 37:1-14.)

While the Scriptures do not pertain exactly to my situation… the lessons from Yahweh {God} are the same… This morning, a few hours after waking, Yahweh {God} flowed into my mind, He downloaded to me what to write! BLESS HIM! I felt guilty… guilty of the sin of worrying, dreading this moment. Sad for not trusting in HIM. I am still learning!

As Brother Lawrence lives and breathes Yahweh's {God's} grace in his own life, he gently encourages himself after his mind strays. He shares (emphasis mine):

…we must serve GOD in a holy freedom; we must do our business faithfully; without trouble or disquiet, recalling our mind to GOD

> **mildly, and with tranquility, as often as we find it wandering from Him.**
>
> The Brother Lawrence Collection - An Christian Classic - Practice and Presence of God, Spiritual Maxims, The Life of Brother Lawrence by Brother Lawrence, Kindle page 45-46 of 139.

So... after gently bringing myself back to the NOW, with no condemnation *(read Romans 8:1),* I shall tell you about the next UNTHINKABLE:

Ready?

Not long after arriving in Texas with the "Sold-Out-Seekers," I mailed a letter to Red. While I was still afraid of him, I cared more for the well-being of my daughter. Since he was now raising my daughter, I reminded him that Yahweh {God} was watching all that he was doing. I wrote of my calling from Yahweh {God}; as well as stating how he had ill-treated me and blocked any real relationship between myself and my daughter. I then included the following Scripture and wording:

> "There is nothing covered up that will not be uncovered, or hidden that will not become known. What you have spoken in the dark will be heard in the light, and what you have whispered behind closed doors will be proclaimed on the housetops." *(Luke 12:2-3)*
>
> Angels of the LIVING GOD will guard and protect my little girl's body, mind, and spirit, until she comes home with me, her loving mother, to Texas.
>
> Tamra Jean
> Daughter of God
> Mother of my precious daughter

Less than a month later, I received a phone call from a child services department in New England saying that charges of sexual abuse to my daughter had been filed … against me. ***Against ME! What?!?*** It did not take long to surmise who had done the filing. The charge was simply preposterous.

I was actually under investigation for charges of sexual abuse of my own daughter?!?

Deborah and Daniel kindly and selflessly put almost everything in their lives on hold to help me in every way they could. Bless them Father! Advised to do so as quickly as humanly possible, I faxed in a letter of appeal to this trumped up, ludicrous, slanderous lie, and absurdly false charge!

More ludicrous still… after an incredibly short investigation, *myself personally only having been spoken to once for a mere twenty minutes in what was unmistakably a rushed and disorganized conversation,* I was found guilty. *GUILTY! WHAT?!?*

This wrong judgment could not stand uncontended. Determined, I set out to **clear my name** of this horrendous, unthinkable and unfounded LIE. The "Sold-Out-Seekers" *GRACIOUSLY* paid for a lawyer to appeal the court judgement and clear my name. So, with the greatest of dread, I moved back to New England to take up the fight to be acquitted of this false charge, clear my name and win back what reputation I could in the court's eyes. (Defamation of character as a result of the charge alone, even if acquitted, is a stain difficult, if not impossible to remove.)

My head was spinning. I could not even believe this was happening!

I wracked my brain for any sense of it. Had I sinned? Had I fallen foul of what the author of Hebrews writes in chapter 11, regarding the faithful of old… those whose eyes are **set on Yahweh** {God} in Heaven, and not looking for an earthly reward:

And, if, indeed, they remembered that from which they came out, they might have had occasion to go back.

Hebrews 11:15

So, I did ponder, since I had an "occasion to go back," whether I had sinned? Did I "remember (bring to mind and dwell on) that from which I came out" too much? Did I "look back" and think of my daughter too much? *(Dr. Tom Taylor speaks on this verse in Hebrews in detail in his study "167 – I see you.")*

Or... was it because Yahweh {God} knew all that I would learn? (I add today, while writing, and thus to help His other kids.)

Blessed is the God and Father of our Lord Jesus Christ, the Father of pities and God of all consolation, Who is consoling us in our every affliction to enable us to be consoling those in every affliction, through the consolation with which we ourselves are being consoled by God...

2 Corinthians 1:3-4

Yahweh {God} alone knows. However... I knew the Scriptures well, and consoled myself with these *repeatedly*... There is no condemnation:

Nothing, consequently, is now condemnation to those in Christ Jesus. Not according to flesh are they walking, but according to spirit, for the spirit's law of life in Christ Jesus frees you from the law of sin and death.

Romans 8:1-2

Trust in Yahweh {God}, when what you see in this physical world seems beyond human comprehension:

Be gracious to me, O Elohim, for a mortal gasps after me;
All day long this fighting man is oppressing me.
They gasp, those who lie in wait for me the entire day,
For many are fighting against me haughtily.
The day when I am fearing I am trusting in You.
In Elohim, I am praising His word;
In Elohim I trust;
I shall not fear;
What can flesh do to me?
All day long they are wresting my words;
All their devisings are against me for evil.
They are stirring up plots; they are lurking;
They are keeping track of my heel prints,
As though they expected to take my soul.
…
In Elohim I trust;
I shall not fear;
What can a human do to me?

Psalm 56:1-6 and 11

Now we are aware that <u>God is working all together for the good</u> of those who are loving God, who are called according to the purpose that, <u>whom He foreknew</u>, <u>He designates beforehand</u>, also, to be conformed to the image of His Son, for Him to be Firstborn among many brethren.

Romans 8:28-29

...in Him in Whom our lot was cast also, being designated beforehand according to the purpose of the One Who is operating all in accord with the counsel of His will...

Ephesians 1:11

When saying good-bye to Deborah and Daniel, who were both kind and encouraging... I sensed a slight, but still notable, heaviness in the spirit and in their energy.

I thought of Yeshua {Jesus} going to the cross after being falsely accused. Of course, though my predicament PALED in comparison to that, I did think of what Yeshua {Jesus} did amidst such persecution... "**Who, for the joy lying before Him, endures a cross...**" *(Read Hebrews 12:2)* My interpretation of that is... He thought of heaven, to be once again seated WITH His Father! Despite all He kept walking... And so, I too would think of heaven, imagining walking hand-in-hand with my Father and Yeshua {Jesus}! I would think of His glory... filling the temple so full no one could enter... my focus being firmly on the goal and the prize...

And the city has no need of the sun nor of the moon, that they should be appearing in it, for the glory of God illuminates it, and its lamp is the Lambkin.

Revelations - The Unveiling of Jesus Christ 21:23

...yet one thing -- forgetting, indeed, those things which are behind, yet stretching out to those in front -- toward the goal am I pursuing for the prize of God's calling above in Christ Jesus.

Philippians 3:13b-14

And buglers and singers were in unison to make one sound heard, to praise and acclaim Yahweh. And as they raised up their voice with the bugles and the cymbals and the instruments of song, and with praising Yahweh, saying:

> **For He is good,**
>
> **For His benignity** (mercifulness, kindness and bountifulness ~ *CLKC*) **is for the eon,**

then the House was filled with a cloud, the glory of Yahweh.

The priests were unable to stay and minister because of the cloud; for the glory of Yahweh filled the House of the One, Elohim.

2 Chronicles 5:13-14

The life of Corrie Ten Boom surfaced in my mind, a life forever marked by a period in which many were dealt afflictions beyond even the words inhumanely, abused, and tortured can describe, and in most cases then killed. I knew that the wicked afflictions in my life were NOT EVEN CLOSE to their sufferings and death… or as in Corrie Ten Boom's case, sufferings and *life*. I have seen some videos of her preaching, all with such a heart for Yahweh {God}! What forgiveness! What love of Yeshua {Jesus}! What a humble, joyful, devout follower whose faith held strong and true despite all! One of my favorite quotes of hers is:

> Worry does not empty tomorrow of its sorrow, it empties today of its strength.
>
> Corrie Ten Boom quote (gathered on June 7, 2021) at:
> EverydayPower.com/corrie-ten-boom-quotes

I had much time to think on my drive back to New England… I continuously re-focused my eyes on Yeshua {Jesus}, and tried desperately to be STRONG and FILLED WITH FAITH! I encouraged myself in Yahweh {God} *(1 Samuel 30:6)*, meditated on all His marvelous works *(1 Chronicles 16:9)*, and thought of the heroes of the faith including the account of David and Goliath:

David replied to the Philistine, You are coming against me with sword and spear and scimitar; yet I am coming against you in the Name of Yahweh of hosts, the Elohim of the arrays of Israel, Whom you have challenged today.

1 Samuel 17:45

Upon arriving in New England, I was kindly invited to move in again with a sister (a fellow follower of Yahweh {God}, Angelica). Thank You Father! Bless her!

...contributing to the needs of the saints, pursuing hospitality.

Romans 12:13

I met with the lawyer, and began the laborious process of clearing my name.

I also made contact with a therapist, as the divorce decree stipulated that *"following no less than four family therapy sessions, the parties shall confer to attempt to agree on resumption of unsupervised contact between the mother and daughter. In the event that they cannot agree, either party may file a Complaint for Modification in this regard."* I walked through every open door possible. Though, I should have known... (after the fabricated charges Red brought against me) that he would never **just agree** for me to have *any* unsupervised time with my daughter. Following the judge's orders, Red and I met with the therapist. I was relieved when the therapist asked me personally one day why Red was like that, why he exhibited such anger and emotions, and the therapist observed how stuck in the past he seemed. *"Finally,"* I thought, as I felt relief wash over me, *"someone sees the truth of his actions!"*

One positive, Praise Yah {God} for His mercy, was that in the midst of these different processes, I was able to see my daughter on the weekends again! (Though still under paid supervision.) However, when I did see her, something was definitely different about her mood. She was changing. A "shell" of protection was growing around her, and there was a distinct attitude of blame toward me. My heart was saddened, pierced. I should not have been surprised, as I was no longer a parental influence in her life having been a 24/7 mom to her. She now lived with Red. And that was that. Yahweh {God} bless everyone.

> **"You hear that it was declared, 'You shall be loving your associate' and you shall be hating your enemy. Yet I am saying to you, Love your enemies, and pray for those who are persecuting you…"**
>
> *Matthew 5:43-44*

His ways are not our ways:

> **Who gauges the spirit of Yahweh**
> **And is informing Him as a man of His counsel?**
> **With whom does He take counsel?**
> **And who is giving Him understanding,**
> **Is teaching Him in judgment's path,**
> **Is teaching Him knowledge**
> **And is informing Him the way of understanding?**
> **Or who has given to Him first,**
> **And it shall be repaid to him?**
>
> *Isaiah 40:13-14*

Still helping the "Sold-Out-Seekers" in Texas from a distance, doing as much as I could and mostly online, my presence was needed with Deborah in California for a few days. Unbeknownst to me, I was being probed (tested) again... tested to see if I would "hear and heed" the spirit. I did sense a leading of Yahweh {God} to check airline ticket prices... and, yet further, a sense that I was to purchase one for the trip. I felt a fear about spending over $500 on an airline ticket. All I had was a credit card. So, not confident it was the spirit, I held off charging it. A few hours later, Deborah asked me, *"Have you purchased a ticket for California?"* I responded, *"Not yet."* I was then shunned for *"not following the leading of the spirit."* Deborah always says, *"If you are looking at money, you are looking to low."*

My son, do not disdain the discipline of the Lord,
Nor yet faint when being exposed by Him.
For whom the Lord is loving He is disciplining,
Yet He is scourging every son to whom He is assenting.

For discipline are you enduring.

...

Thereafter, indeed, we had the fathers of our flesh as discipliners, and we respected them. Yet shall we not much rather be subjected to the Father of spirits and be living.

For these, indeed, disciplined for a few days as it seemed best to them, yet that One for our expedience, for us to be partaking of His holiness. Now all discipline, indeed, for the present is not seeming to be a thing of joy, but of sorrow, yet subsequently it is rendering the peaceable fruit of righteousness to those exercised through it.

Hebrews 12:5b-7a and 9-11

I had chosen fear over faith... I had sinned, *again*. Shunned. Shunned from the "Sold-Out-Seekers." Once again, no home, no job, no human spiritual guidance. Utter loneliness, lostness, anxiety and fearfulness overwhelmed my heart, already weighed down under the sexual abuse "GUILTY" stamp. Becoming a heap inside I just wanted to fall to the ground and cry. But, I could not. There was no time. I was given two days to move out.

While writing this, listening to worship music, the song *"Flawless"* from **MercyMe** came on... the premise being that, no matter what is happening in life, to keep our focus on Yahweh {God}, and Praise Him that Yeshua's {Jesus'} death on the cross makes us pure and white as snow in Yahweh's {God's} eyes. This is perfectly fitting with this chapter...

I had to walk on, no matter. I found a "room to rent" in a house on a short-term basis, *hoping* this entire appeal process would take only a month or two. Of course, it meant the immediate need of an income.

Most importantly... I did the ONLY thing I knew to do in all situations: I fell to my knees and PRAYED. I appealed, beckoned and pleaded to the Lord to be with me. I fasted often. In repentance, I slept on the floor often too. I thought to myself that IF David did it, and he had "a heart for Yahweh {God}" then I WOULD DO IT too. Help me, Father!

So David appealed earnestly to the One, Elohim, on behalf of the lad; David also <u>abstained for a fast</u>; he went and <u>lodged for the night lying on the earth</u>.

2 Samuel 12:16

> **"Request and it shall be given you. Seek and you shall find. Knock and it shall be opened to you. For everyone who is requesting is obtaining, and who is seeking is finding, and to him who is knocking it shall be opened."**
>
> *Matthew 7:7-8*

"Will this end?!?" I wondered. *"Yes, keep going. Stay strong. Stand firm.* ***WAIT PATIENTLY for Yahweh*** *{God}!"* (I gave myself many such pep-talks from the Word.)

> **Thus says Yahweh:**
> **In a season acceptable I answer You,**
> **And in a day of salvation I help You;**
> **I shall preserve You**
> **And give You for a covenant of the people,**
> **To set up the land, To allot the desolated allotments…**
>
> *Isaiah 49:8*

> **For a thousand years are in Your eyes**
> **Like yesterday's day when it has passed…**
>
> *Psalm 90:4*

WHY?!? "Why is this happening to me, Father?" I prayed. *"Do not try to 'figure it out,'"* were the wise words of Elena, the fellow follower of Yahweh {God}. I sinned in this area much, sadly, my mind attempting to figure out Yahweh {God}, to figure out why… instead of using my energy and focus on the positive and to simply Praise His Holy Name.

All be doing without murmurings and reasonings…

Philippians 2:14

The spirit recalled to my mind David, and how he suffered so much WORSE than I, four hundred of his men (his own followers) wanting to KILL HIM. And what did he do, under the pressure of these threats?

Yet David encouraged himself in Yahweh his Elohim.

1 Samuel 30:6

So, I too, humbling myself, encouraged myself in Yahweh {God} my Elohim, filling myself up full with the Word of Truth to stiffen my resolve!

For the rest, brethren mine, be invigorated in the Lord and in the might of His strength. Put on the panoply of God, to enable you to stand up to the stratagems of the Adversary, for it is not ours to wrestle with blood and flesh, but with the sovereignties, with the authorities, with the world-mights of this darkness, with the spiritual forces of wickedness among the celestials. Therefore take up the panoply of God that you may be enabled to withstand in the wicked day, and having effected all, to stand. Stand, then, girded about your loins with truth, with the cuirass of righteousness put on, and your feet sandaled with the readiness of the evangel of peace; with all taking up the large shield of faith, by which you will be able to extinguish all the fiery arrows of the wicked one. And receive the helmet of salvation and the sword of the spirit, which is a declaration of God.

Ephesians 6:10-17

Be steadfast, and be resolute! Do not fear, and do not be terrified because of their presence, for Yahweh your Elohim, He is the One going with you; He shall neither neglect you nor forsake you.

Deuteronomy 31:6b

"And lo! I am with you all the days till the conclusion of the eon!" Amen!

Matthew 28:20b

Now thanks be to God, Who is giving us the victory, through our Lord Jesus Christ.

So that, my beloved brethren, become settled, unmovable, superabounding in the work of the Lord always, being aware that your toil is not for naught in the Lord.

1 Corinthians 15:57-58

Let the word of Christ be making its home in you richly, in all wisdom…

Colossians 3:16a

And the spirit recalled to my mind Yeshua's {Jesus'} life, and ALL that He lived through, eyes fixed on His Father's purpose. I was reminded of the excerpt from Dr. Tom Taylor's incredibly moving book titled, **You Think YOU Have It Tough?**, previously quoted in the chapter on forgiveness, in which he recounts his vision with Yahweh {God} and

Yeshua {Jesus} where they brought him (Tom) step by step, through the last few days of Yeshua's {Jesus'} life. What could I have to complain about compared to Yeshua {Jesus}, whose cause was to save all but Himself? Not even in His most troubled moments did He falter.

And He is taking Peter and James and John aside with Himself, and He begins to be overawed and depressed. And He is saying to them, "Sorrow-stricken is My soul to death. Remain here and watch." And, coming forward a little, He fell on the earth and prayed… And He said, "Abba, Father, all is possible to Thee. Have this cup carried aside from Me. But not what I will, but what Thou!"

Mark 14:33-36

Now a messenger from heaven was seen by Him, strengthening Him. And coming to be in a struggle, He prayed more earnestly, and His sweat became as if clots of blood descending on the earth.

Luke 22:43-44

Now the chief priests and the elders and the whole Sanhedrin sought false testimony against Jesus, so that they should be putting Him to death, and they found it not. At many false witnesses approaching, they found it not…

Matthew 26:59-60

Then they spit into His face and buffet Him. Now they slap Him, saying, "Prophesy to us, Christ! Who is it that hits you?"

Matthew 26:67-68

And the men who are pressing Jesus, scoffed at Him, lashing Him. And putting a covering about Him, they beat His face and inquired of Him, saying "Prophesy! Who is it that hits you?"

Luke 22:63-64

Pilate is saying to them, "What, then, shall I be doing with Jesus, who is termed Christ?"

They are all saying, "Let him be crucified!"

Matthew 27:22

…Now, whipping Jesus, he gives Him over that He may be crucified.

Matthew 27:26b

…and, stripping Him, they place a scarlet mantle about Him, and, braiding a wreath out of thorns, they place it on His head, and a reed in His right hand, and, falling on their knees in front of Him, they scoff at Him, saying, "Rejoice, king of the Jews!" And spitting on Him, they got the reed and beat Him on His head. And, when they scoff at Him, they strip Him of the mantle and put His garments on Him, and led Him away to crucify.

Matthew 27:28-31

They took Jesus along, then, and led Him away. And, bearing the cross Himself, He came out to what is termed a "Skull's Place," which is termed, in Hebrew, "Golgotha"...

John 19:17

Now it was the third hour, and they crucify Him.

Mark 15:25

Now Jesus said, "Father, forgive them, for they are not aware what they are doing." Now dividing His garments, they cast the lot.

Luke 23:34

And at the coming of the sixth hour, darkness came over the whole land till the ninth hour.

Mark 15:33

Now Jesus, again crying with a loud voice, lets out the spirit. And lo! the curtain of the temple is rent in two from above to the bottom, and the earth quaked, and the rocks are rent, and the tombs were opened.

Matthew 27:50-52a

I still felt alone... though my *"complaining attitude,"* the murmuring mindset, was gone.

I believe Yahweh {God} was strengthening me all along... and showing me my own strength of character, ***when only depending on HIM... and Him alone.*** I was "out of the camp," shunned by the "Sold-Out-Seekers." And now I was stood in the lawyer's office revealing to him that I was going back to Texas, to serve Yahweh {God}, as soon as my name was cleared. He was horrified, attempting to convince me at all costs to change my mind. I stood strong, committed to my calling. I felt the eyes of Yahweh {God} upon me... probing me... watching for what I would do. Would I trip and people-please again? What would I choose? *Who* would I choose? Who would I truly follow... Him or man? I PASSED MY TEST! I held fast to my calling. PRAISE YAHWEH {GOD}!

Yet answering, Peter and the apostles say, "One must yield to God rather than to men."

Acts 5:29

"With men this is impossible, yet with God all is possible."

Matthew 19:26

I did the ONLY thing I knew to do: HOLD ON TO THE BIBLE... TIGHT. I made notecards of Scriptures, cue cards if you will, to carry with me in my purse and in my pocket, to pull out as a sword, a declaration of Yahweh {God}, to combat wandering thoughts and stray emotions. I also had at the ready documents on my computer consisting of "Favorite Scriptures," my own compilation of "Well-Pleasing to Yahweh {God} vs sin" and "Encouraging Psalms."

Consequently, faith is out of tidings (hearing, that which is heard ~ *CLKC*), yet the tidings through a declaration of Christ.

Romans 10:17

...but be filled full with spirit, speaking to yourselves in psalms and hymns and spiritual songs, singing and playing music in your hearts to the Lord, giving thanks always for all things, in the name of our Lord, Jesus Christ...

Ephesians 5:18b-20

Meditate on all His marvelous works!

1 Chronicles 16:9b

Light Up the Scriptures studies continued weekly, and it was truly a LIFELINE to me! My spiritual well from which to drink living water.

Yet He, answering, said, "It is written, 'Not on bread alone shall man be living, but on every declaration going out through the mouth of God.'"

Matthew 4:4

"What happens in the physical, happens in the spiritual," Deborah taught me, referenced from the **Old Testament** where Yahweh {God} told Jeremiah to buy a belt and bury it, and how, when ruined, it then represented the ruination Yahweh {God} would bring upon the pride of Judah and Jerusalem, *(read the whole account in Jeremiah 13:1-11).* Also, when Yahweh {God} told Jeremiah to go to the potter's house, Yahweh {God} said: **"…behold, like clay in the hand of the potter, so are you in My hand, house of Israel"** *(read the whole account in Jeremiah 18:1-10).* As well as when Yahweh {God} told Ezekiel to bind sticks together, signifying the convening of some of the nations of Israel *(you can read the whole account in Ezekiel 37:15-28).*

So, putting these learnings into practice in my own life, when I was by myself, I would lie flat on the floor and "die to myself and the world." I would imagine myself being buried. Dead. (The old humanity was dead, *read Ephesians 4:21-24.*) Then I would LEAP UP to my feet into my LIFE IN YESHUA {JESUS}, my new humanity put on… arms raised in the air, shouting, *"PRAISE YAHWEH {GOD}!"* I felt silly, and did not deep down believe that it would do any good. HOWEVER, I knew enough to NOT LISTEN to any "reasonings" in my mind (which is a **sin,** *read Philippians 2:14*), and so I "died" quite a few times! Hey, if Yahweh {God} works this way… so will I! I follow HIM!

One weekend afternoon of my allotted supervised visits with my daughter, she was feeling "under the weather." Years prior when she was around 3-years-old, we both began enjoying the health benefits of a dietary supplement. Having studied into health and nutrition more myself over the previous years, I gave my little girl extra vegetable supplements to regain her health. Now please understand, this means that I gave her EXTRA vegetables. VEGETABLES! Not over-the-counter medicine. Not sugar. Vegetables grown responsibly (some even organically), and then juiced and dried into chewable form for young children. No additives. No preservatives.

When Red arrived to pick up my daughter, I kindly asked if he would *please* continue to give her these supplements. *For years* I had shared the importance of health and nutrition with him, and described how these supplements bridge the gap between the amount of fruits and vegetables we should eat, and the amount we actually **do** eat. He had previously never listened, and for the eleven years prior his own food intake had consisted of rice, meat, tortillas and desert. Almost no fresh, raw vegetables and rarely any fresh fruit. I desired only for my daughter to be healthy and well again. He angrily took the bag, looked at it and left.

Not long after, the court appointed lawyer to represent my daughter learned about these world-renowned supplements and sceptically questioned me about them. I shared of the wonderful nutritional value, and asked if they would like me to bring a package to them. They graciously said no, they had one in their hands. (Wonderful, I thought!) I had researched this company much over the years, and KNEW they were not just some "bogus" supplement company. It was a reputable, world renowned corporation, which created this wonderful, chewable health product that consisted ONLY of responsibly grown fruits and vegetables!

Beyond, FAR BEYOND my surprise... after holding the actual package of these healthy and nutritious fruit and vegetable supplements, as well as reading the information I shared, the lawyer gave their professional opinion that my little girl was **not** to be allowed to consume them.

They advised in favor of Red. I actually laughed. How could this possibly be true?!? I was being "advised" to NOT give my daughter fruits and vegetables?!?

It took a few moments to sink in what had just transpired… WHAT!?! The world gone mad! Words cannot describe what is going on in my head while recalling this beyond ridiculous outcome! (*"Bless everyone,"* I remind myself.)

If I were to recount all that happened regarding my daughter, including custody and court proceedings, scripts and notes… my records would mount up to beyond the space around me, an entire home library not able to contain them.

Besides fighting to freely feed my little girl healthy foods… every other spare moment I had, I POURED over all the prior sexual abuse investigation paperwork and transcripts. I looked for every detail to prove, beyond a shadow of a doubt, that the investigation held was incomplete, fabricated. Knowing it was all lies… all I had to simply do was to PROVE it!

Yahweh's {God's} blessings were SUPERABOUNDING… even in the midst of "my training" (or "my breaking" as some call it), I had been BLESSED BEYOND my imagination; months before I had been invited on a trip to Israel (completely paid for by Deborah and Angelica,)! Bless them Father! (Since being a young GIRL I had *longed to go to Jerusalem!* To walk where Yeshua {Jesus} walked! To the temple Yahweh's {God's} robes filled!) While remaining on the travel roster, I was still considered shunned… and the trip to Jerusalem (with the "Sold-Out-Seekers") was in only a few days' time! In my spirit, I felt I was supposed to *go*!

"But, GO? How can I go on a trip across the globe with people who are not even speaking to me?" Yet... the spirit said, *"Go! Show up at the airport!"* I was learning to obey the spirit, (Praise Yahweh {God}), and so I both nervously, (my stomach doing SUMMERSAULTS), and excitedly shouted in my head with glee, ***"I AM GOING TO JERUSALEM!!!"*** I went to the airport. I boarded the plane, and found my seat had been moved away from the group. (I felt bad. However uncomfortable though, I remained excited about going to JERUSALEM... I tried not to let any other thought fill my mind.)

On the evening of the third day into the trip, I was invited *"back into the fold."* It comes to mind what Yeshua {Jesus} said to Peter:

Now the Lord said, "Simon, Simon, lo! Satan claims you men, to sift you as grain. Yet I besought concerning you, that your faith may not be defaulting. And once you turn back, establish your brethren."

Luke 22:31-32

I soaked in every moment of being in Israel, where our LORD, Yeshua {Jesus}, WALKED. I LOVED IT! Words are inadequate to convey the JOY and AWE in my SPIRIT... the sense of *belonging* there. In my heart, I wanted to move to Jerusalem! Where the spirit of the Lord is so strong...

A few places we walked in Israel included:

The Shrine of the Book

This is where the Dead Sea scrolls are located and presented for viewing. I was transfixed in utter silence and holy awe... so BLESSED to be so close to and even see with my own eyes the **original transcripts of the Scriptures!!!**

The Sea of Galilee

Where Yeshua {Jesus} walked on the water (twice)! Just off shore, preaching the Word from the boat… healing and feeding the thousands that flocked to His side. I awoke early one morning to put my toes into the Sea of Galilee, alone, just me and my Father! *(Scrunching my eyes shut, I prayed to walk on the water…)*

Synagogue in Capernaum

We visited an Ancient Synagogue where Yeshua {Jesus} had preached! The ancient, ornate stones and atmosphere of the temple were holy and awe-inspiring… knowing Yeshua {Jesus} was there. Right there! Healing. Preaching. Walking. Talking. My spirit was in holy awe, in reverent adoration, in quite stillness. So pure. So peaceful. I envisioned Yeshua {Jesus} Himself, standing there teaching.

The Jordan River

I was baptized (again). And where more significant than in the river where Yeshua {Jesus} was baptized, following which the Spirit descended as if a dove, and the Father Himself spoke to His Son in Whom He delighted! *(Read Matthew 3:13-17)* My spirit was on fire, knowing thousands of years prior, Yeshua {Jesus} Himself was there…

Rabbinic Tunnel and a tour of the Western Wall Tunnel

I thoroughly cherished walking in the underground tunnels in the Old City of Jerusalem, the closest you can physically get to where the Ark of the Covenant would have been located... in the Holy of Holies! Oh how my spirit *soared* in such proximity of where Yahweh {God} Himself would have been in the temple!

Jerusalem

Ohhh... Jerusalem! Such a holy place to walk. Exactly where Yeshua {Jesus} Himself walked... and David... countless others, "Fathers of the faith!" What an impartation!

We walked around the "separately owned quarters" of the Ancient "Old" Jerusalem. I cautiously walked out of the Jewish quarter boundary, and, literally, the second I did, all purity of spirit drained out of me, prevented from joining me on the other side of the line, blocked by an invisible, thick, guarding wall, a heaviness I could literally feel. Within only a few steps I knew I had to leave. NOW. Then, turning, the moment I stepped back into the Jewish quarter, my spirit's vibrance returned and I was immediately overwhelmed with the utmost PEACE, LOVE, LIGHT, LIFE and JOY again... I could literally feel **holiness** and **lightness**... The divinity of His presence once again my sanctuary.

The Wailing Wall

Even though this is not a Biblical tradition, I still partook. Standing at the Wailing Wall, I wrote *"my daughter's name"* on a pink sticky note, folded it up and placed it in a crevice in the wall, signifying the placing of my daughter into Yahweh's {God's} arms. She is His child. He is her Father. His will be done, His way. *"What happens in the physical, happens in the spiritual,"* was again ringing in my ears. (Just as lying on the ground represented my dying to the world spiritually, my physical act of writing her name and inserting it into the wall bore the same witness, of my giving my daughter into the hands of the Father.)

Bethlehem

BETHLEHEM… my second FAVORITE place in Israel! (That is, following my absolute favorite, the temple home of the Ark of the Covenant in Jerusalem.) Bethlehem… where the angels appeared to the shepherds near the birthplace of the Lord!

Oh my heart and spirit were singing… psalms and hymns and spiritual songs in my heart to my Father in Heaven *(read Ephesians 5:19)*, bursting with JOY and GLADNESS! Joyous childhood memories welling up inside me… tears of utter awe trickled down my cheeks.

Oh… I sat on the hillside and heralded Luke 2 to the celestials LOUDLY in my mind… multiple times! (Just as when I was growing up, heralding the joyous message in the little church on the hill!) What a sight! My spirit was alive and on fire!

And suddenly with the messenger there came to be a multitude of the heavenly host, praising God and saying,

> **"Glory to God among the Highest!**
> **And on earth peace,**
> **Among men, delight!"**

Luke 2:13-14

As I had learned in the **Light Up the Scriptures** studies, Dr. Tom Taylor spoke of his friend, Harold Smith, who has found himself living off and on in Israel as a testament to the faithfulness of *haEl haNeAman* (Hebrew for "the Faithful One"), to bear witness to the "Truth of Who He Is" and to be a support to His People (in Israel). Harold has learned the Hebrew culture, and thus assimilates it into the meaning of the Scriptures (instead of the "Western Culture" that I and so many others bring into our mis-understanding of the Hebrew writings).

Harold reveals that the teachings of the "birth of Yeshua {Jesus}" that I received as a child had many flaws… (Not too great a surprise, considering the mistranslations of many **Bible** versions now rectified by revelations in the **Concordant Literal** translation!) Yeshua {Jesus} was NOT born in a stable, and not because there was "no room at the inn." No. By "correctly cutting" the word of the Truth, Harold Smith writes in his article *"the Birth Series –* ***the Birth Revisited****"*:

> Micah, the Hebrew prophet who foretold of haMashiach's (the Messiah's) birth in Bethlehem, also prophesied, "And you, O Tower of the Flock (in Hebrew, Migdal Eder), the stronghold of

> the daughter of Zion, unto you shall it come, even the first dominion; the kingdom shall come to the daughter of Jerusalem" (Micah 4:8). Although obscure and often overlooked, Micah disclosed that the Messiah, who embodied the hope of the Kingdom of Israel, "was to be revealed from Migdal Eder – 'the Tower of the Flock'."
>
> **He That Has An Ear** - *"the Birth Series – the Birth Revisited"*
> by Harold Smith (gathered on July 29, 2021) at:
> HeThatHasAnEar.com/Birth.html

Astonishing! It is well worth reading Harold Smith's website (the link can also be found in the resources section at the end of the book) to discover the exact place where the flawless, unspotted sacrificial lambs were born (Migdal Eder), the intricate details to which are enlightening, and the true account of the events that occurred in and around the period of Yeshua's {Jesus'} birth! Only Yahweh {God} designs in such detail! Praise His Holy Name!

What an incredible blessing to sit on a hillside in Bethlehem. Our Father in Heaven DOES do superabundantly above all that we ask for... in HIS timing! Praise His Holy Name!

What a superabundant blessing... a ten-day trip to Israel!

One of my favorite prayers of Deborah's, which she prayed over me throughout my journey of faith (also called training or breaking) was: *"Father, show us Your strategy for the victory."* The "Sold-Out-Seekers" prayed this for myself and my daughter.

"Request and it shall be given you. Seek and you shall find. Knock and it shall be opened to you. For everyone who is requesting is obtaining, and who is seeking is finding, and to him who is knocking it shall be opened."

Matthew 7:7-8

So Moses said to them: Stand by and let me hear what instruction Yahweh may give for you.

Numbers 9:8

Yahweh {God}, in His goodness, also continued to bless me on my journey as well… I became very close to Deborah, she was both my spiritual mother and my physical mother for years. As I said, she is also a *kindred spirit!* Deborah flew to New England to spend time with me (and the other "Sold-Out-Seekers") for a few days, and to *support me* at the custody court hearing in November 2014. Bless her Father!

…even as you are aware how we were to each one of you, as a father to his own children, consoling and comforting you and attesting unto you to be walking worthily of God, Who calls you into His own kingdom and glory.

1 Thessalonians 2:11-12

For God is not unjust, to be forgetting your work and the love which you display for His name when you serve the saints, and are serving.

Hebrews 6:10

I was SO RELIEVED to have support in court for the trial, I cried tears of relief. I hated court. Absolutely hated it. It was so unfair and unjust. Thank You Father for sending angels to go walk with me into court that day. Both Deborah and Angelica, (such giving and kind servants of Yahweh {God}), came with me. Bless them! Thank You Father!!!

"...be giving, and it shall be given to you: a measure ideal, squeezed down and shaken together and running over, shall they be giving into your bosom. For the same measure with which you are measuring will be measured to you again."

Luke 6:38

Mere days before court, we all continued praying for Yahweh {God} to show His strategy for the victory in both my and my daughter's lives. Yahweh {God} answered our prayer! Praise His Holy Name!

Day after day is uttering a saying,
And night after night is disclosing knowledge.

Psalm 19:2

When His answer was revealed, it was a great surprise and even a shock to me, similarly I might imagine, as it would be to someone's first reading of the account of Abraham being instructed to sacrifice his son, Isaac.

However… I am in GOOD (even GREAT) company… if I am remotely similar to Abraham. I am humbled to even think this. Honored.

Then king David came and sat before Yahweh; he said: Who am I, my Lord Yahweh, and what is my house that You have brought me as far as hither?

2 Samuel 7:18

To me, less than the least of all saints, was granted this grace: to bring the evangel of the untraceable riches of Christ to the nations…

Ephesians 3:8

For I am the least of the apostles, who am not competent to be called an apostle, because I persecute the ecclesia of God.

1 Corinthians 15:9

Yahweh's {God's} revelation was: *"Go. Leave everything including your daughter, yes… give up your child completely, pick up your cross and follow Me."* It was as if He was saying, Stop fighting. Stop fighting a court system that does not listen to you. A corrupt court system that unjustly saw fit to label you guilty of sexual abuse. Follow your calling, Tamra. Serve Me as Yeshua {Jesus} served when He walked on the earth…

A little bewildered… yet now a whole lot stronger in my faith, I said the ONLY correct answer, the answer that came to me without hesitation:

"Yes Lord."

Today, writing this, the Scripture comes to mind of the rich young man speaking to Yeshua {Jesus}, asking what he must do to follow Yeshua {Jesus}. The "one thing" Yeshua {Jesus} told him, was to sell everything and follow him. He walked away saddened. *(Read Matthew 19:16-22)*

For that young man, that day, it was to relinquish his sizable wealth. For me? My "one thing," my only jewel on earth. But I would NOT walk away sad. DETERMINED to follow Yeshua {Jesus}, no matter the cost, I said: *"Yes Lord."*

There was a time when my declaration of surrender was, *"Lord, you can have ANYTHING, as long as my precious daughter comes with me."* (I had prayed for a child for five *long* years! BEGGED YAHWEH {GOD}! Cried… pleaded… continuously…) The "one thing" He wanted was the "one thing" I had left yet to surrender.

Thank You Father for giving me the STRENGTH to follow You! I am the MOST amazed! From a complete PEOPLE-PLEASER… to a complete YAH-PLEASER! (On the path at least… as I am still today, paying close attention to constantly please ONLY Him!)

I let my mind wander **far** into the future, to my deathbed, having often heard wisdom comes to those near life's end, beyond material worth and worldly opinions. I pondered on which choice I would be most content with (or even proud of…). **Instantly** I knew that obeying Yahweh {God}, doing something SO *"out of the box"* in worldly terms, was DEFINITELY THE RIGHT PATH to walk! It was the ONLY path lit by, and leading to, The Almighty Yahweh {God}.

I thought of Moses... how he was raised in a heathen palace, yet when he grew up he was sent to help Yahweh's {God's} people, and eventually SAVED a nation from captivity in Egypt! Oh Yahweh {God}... Your ways are perfect!

So, I obeyed Yahweh {God}. I prepared to place my daughter in a basket... and set her in the river always under the shelter and guidance of Yahweh's {God's} mighty hand. (See **Light Up the Scriptures** study *"88 - God's Calling, Are You Coming,"* where Barbara Brown shares much on this very subject also.)

Previously, (before Yahweh showed His new strategy for the victory), I had prepared for a court battle: proof piling in my corner to the heavens, proof of the manipulation of my daughter, proof of the defendant's irrational conduct (even before a court-appointed therapist). However, the said therapist was afraid to speak in court, the truth of what he knew, what he saw. (I could have subpoenaed him. However I did not see him being very open in court, since he was so afraid to speak the truth in conversation with me, and also refused to write a letter that I could read in court, stating his previous professional opinion to me that *"Red cannot go forward, he is stuck in emotions."*) Bless everyone Father. However, since the "sexual abuse guilty stamp" was STILL on my name, having not yet been cleared, the truth yet to prevail, the deck was again stacked against me... **Just as Yahweh** {God} **had shown** to stop fighting a court system that does not listen to you.

If I may be so bold as to compare myself to Yeshua {Jesus}, this reminds me of when Yeshua {Jesus} was questioned by Pilot, and "**He did not answer.**" *(Read Matthew 27:14 and Isaiah 53:7)* In my opinion, Yeshua {Jesus} knew that His words would not be listened to... everyone had had over three years to hear Him, and everyone had already made up their minds about Him. (It felt the same with me... and "the justice system.")

Again, I felt so RELIEVED and strengthened by the holy women of Yahweh {God} accompanying me in court on the day of trial. For the first time, I walked into the courtroom with family beside me, encouraging me, standing *with* me.

But entreat (exhort, comfort ~ *Thayer*) **yourselves each day, until what is called "today..."**

Hebrews 3:13a

Now we are entreating you, brethren; admonish the disorderly, <u>comfort the fainthearted</u>, <u>uphold the infirm</u> (weak ~ *CLKC*)**, be patient toward all.**

1 Thessalonians 5:14

I obeyed Yahweh's {God's} word of "strategy for the victory," the ONLY path to follow...

I spoke in court, knowing that my daughter's "blood" was on the hands of everyone there. I spoke my truth. (And I pointed at them all.) I felt like Yeshua {Jesus}, Paul, Peter, and Stephen, all of whom I always thought were SO VERY BOLD to speak the truth to others... to their face. *(Some examples to read about include: Yeshua {Jesus} in Matthew 12:22-50, Matthew 23, Mark 11:15-18, John 7:14-24, John 8:42-58; about Paul in Acts 13:14-49, Acts 14:1-7, Acts 19:8-12; about Peter in Acts 2:14-43, Acts 4:5-23; about Stephen in Acts 6:1 - 7:60; about David in 1 Samuel 24:8-15.)*

Here is **some** of the wording I spoke in the courtroom that day:

I relinquish parental rights of my daughter effective immediately.

It is heart-wrenching to sign away parental rights to the daughter that I gave birth to, but this situation is untenable.

These are the events that led to this decision:

- *My daughter was ripped from my arms in August of 2012.*
- *For the last 26 months, I have been unfairly treated like a criminal and constantly supervised during the short visits allowed with my (now) 7-year-old daughter. I have been permitted to see her a total of 85.5 hours. That is 0.133% (3.56 days / 2681 days) of her young life.*
- *I was wrongly accused of fraudulent charges, through the defendant's manipulation of my daughter.*
- *I was forced to take a leave of absence from my incredible job in order to fight the false charges.*

I choose not to live under the control and oppression of the defendant and this court system. I am going on with my life…

As long as my daughter is under the negative influence of the defendant, a meaningful relationship with her is impossible. I have a wonderful home waiting for her when she is freely returned to me. Until I am granted sole custody of my daughter with no strings attached, you will not see my face again.

All the hidden things will come to light. God will judge all that has happened here. One day my daughter will know the truth.

Respectfully submitted, Tamra Jean

"…the spirit of truth, which the world can not get, for it is not beholding it, neither is knowing it. Yet you know it, for it is remaining with you and will be in you."

John 14:17

The judge said there was an entire process to give up my daughter legally (as if for adoption), which could not happen that very day. So, the defendant's lawyer had the idea (insight I knew was from Yahweh {God}, as He speaks through anyone) to my signing of an agreement stating that I would not see my daughter until she was at least 13-years-old. Neither would I attempt to communicate with my daughter by any means, by any format. No contact whatsoever. I chose to obey Yahweh {God}, live my life HIS way, no matter the cost. HE is Yahweh {God}, not me. His ways are His, and not mine.

But Samuel said,
Does Yahweh have as much delight
in ascent offerings and sacrifices
As in hearkening to the voice of Yahweh?
Behold, to hearken is better than sacrifice,
To pay attention than the fat of rams.
For rebellion is like the sin of divination,
Insubordination, like the lawlessness of teraphim.
Because you rejected the command of Yahweh,
He has also rejected you from being king over Israel.

1 Samuel 15:22-23

See! I am setting before you today blessing and malediction: the blessing if you should hearken to the instructions of Yahweh your Elohim that I am enjoining on you today, and the malediction if you should not hearken to the instructions of Yahweh your Elohim, and you withdraw from the way that I am enjoining on you today…

Deuteronomy 11:26-28a

We walked out of the court room together, my mother and sister and I, my spiritual family. Walking out of court for the last time, my spirit at peace, yet still my mind in a whir in its vain attempts to fathom His ways with which I was still learning to flow.

"Who is My mother, and who are My brothers?" And stretching out His [Jesus'] hand over His disciples, He said, "Lo! My mother and My brothers! For anyone whoever should be doing the will of My Father Who is in the heavens, he is My brother and sister and mother!"

Matthew 12:48b-50

Now, onto the next battle, clearing my name… After presenting all my evidence and counterevidence at the child services department court hearing, it was CLEAR and indisputable, and now **substantially proven**, that the previous *investigation* was incomplete (to put it politely). Now, the waiting, waiting for the judge to state this legally, to sign the decree, and, in so doing, seal the final and absolute clearing of my name officially, to be wiped clean from all national records of all that had tainted my otherwise flawless character. (I say this NOW with confidence, however, even knowing the truth and praying the judge would be open to seeing the truth for what it was and clear my name officially, I tell you now that still my faith did waver, worrying much.)

After all court meetings were completed… Yahweh {God} was about to test me and search my heart, *though I did not know at the time that a test was coming.*

I am Yahweh Who investigates the heart,
Who tests the innermost being,
So as to give to each one according to his ways,
According to the fruit of his actions.

Jeremiah 17:10

Beloved, do not believe every spirit, but test the spirits to see if they are of God, for many false prophets have come out into the world.

1 John 4:1

The very next day, Deborah asked, "*Are you going to sue Red for defamation of character, wrongly accusing you of abuse charges, dragging you through court, slandering your name?*" I was shocked at the question. It had never occurred to me. In fact, I was repulsed at the thought. The very idea deflated my heart and my spirit slumped. "*More court? And what for?*" I thought. "*No. No lawsuit. Not for gain in the form of money nor for the purposes of 'getting him back…'*"

> **"You hear that it was declared, 'An eye for an eye,' and 'A tooth for a tooth.' Yet I am saying to you not to withstand a wicked person, but anyone who slaps you on your right cheek, turn to him the other also. And he who wants to sue you and obtain your tunic, leave him your cloak also."**
>
> *Matthew 5:38-39*

"I am done." I thought, *"I have turned my cheek and left my cloak. I am going on* ***with the call of Yahweh*** *{God}* ***on my life****. I am going to serve and help others."*

> **Be… of a humble disposition, not rendering evil for evil, or reviling for reviling, but, on the contrary, blessing, seeing that you were called for this, that you should be enjoying the allotment of blessing, for**
>
> **He who is wanting to love life and**
> **be acquainted with good days,**
> **Let his tongue cease from evil**
> **And his lips speak no guile.**
> **Now let him avoid evil and do good.**
> **Let him seek peace and pursue it,**
> **For the eyes of the Lord are on the just**
> **And His ears are for their petition,**
> **Yet the face of the Lord is on evil doers.**
>
> **And is there anyone who will be illtreating you, if you should become zealous of good?**
>
> **Yet if you may be suffering also because of righteousness, happy are you. Now you may not be afraid with their fear, nor yet be**

> disturbed, yet hallow the Lord Christ in your hearts, ever ready with a defense for everyone who is demanding from you an account concerning the expectation in you, but with meekness and fear, having a good conscience, that, in what they are speaking against you as of evildoers, they may be mortified, who traduce your good behavior in Christ.
>
> *1 Peter 3:8-16*

And so I answered, *"Yahweh {God} says in His Word that vengeance is HIS. He will deal with others as He sees fit. Yahweh {God} is judge, not me."*

> To no one render evil for evil, making ideal provision in the sight of all men, if possible that which comes out from yourselves. Being at peace with all mankind, you are not avenging yourselves, beloved, but be giving place to His indignation, for it is written, Mine is vengeance! I will repay! the Lord is saying. But "If your enemy should be hungering, give him the morsel; if he should be thirsting, give him to drink, for in doing this you will be heaping embers of fire on his head." Be not conquered by evil; but conquer evil with good.
>
> *Romans 12:17-21*

> For we are acquainted with Him Who is saying, Mine is vengeance! I will repay! the Lord is saying, and again, "The Lord will be judging His people" Fearful is it to be falling into the hands of the living God!
>
> *Hebrews 10:30-31*

I am going to serve Yahweh {God}:

Blessed is the God and Father of our Lord Jesus Christ, the Father of pities and God of all consolation, Who is consoling us in our every affliction to enable us to be consoling those in every affliction, through the consolation with which we ourselves are being consoled by God…

2 Corinthians 1:3-4

"Now these signs shall fully follow in those who believe: In My name they shall be casting out demons; they will be speaking in new languages; they will be picking up serpents; and if they should be drinking anything deadly, it should under no circumstances be harming them; they will be placing hands on those who are ailing, and ideally will they be having it (be healed)."

Mark 16:17-18

"Yet hoard for yourselves treasures in heaven, where neither moth nor corrosion are causing them to disappear, and where thieves are not tunneling nor stealing; for wherever your treasure is, there will your heart be also."

Matthew 6:20-21

Later Deborah told me that IF I had NOT walked away… I would have died. I would have completely died in spirit, which is *truly* **all** that matters!

This then brought to my mind two different **Light Up the Scriptures** studies where Barbara Brown shared about how the Father had made a promise to her years ago while on her own walk of fully and wholeheartedly surrendering all (including her own kids) and following Yeshua {Jesus}. (Now, please do note, her kids were in college at the time of this word from Yahweh {God}. However, I held onto this same promise for myself, just as I hold onto different promises of Yahweh {God} throughout the Bible, spoken to other people at the time.)

As you do for my kids, I [Yahweh] am doing for yours.

Light Up the Scriptures study "28 - *What if GOD Just Wants YOU*" by Dr. Tom Taylor. (Time: 27:07 - 27:11)

Light Up the Scriptures study "89 - *God Cuts Deep to get the Cancers Out*" by Dr. Tom Taylor. Time: 1:12:58 - 1:13:01)

I left New England, for good, feet dusted off, once for all time. I loaded up everything I owned into my car, and returned to my calling to help His kids, with the "Sold-Out-Seekers" in Texas.

I, Yahweh, I call You in righteousness,
And I shall hold fast to Your hand;
I shall preserve You
And give You for a covenant of the people,
For a light of the nations,
To unclose the eyes that are blind,
To bring forth the prisoner from the enclosure,
And those dwelling in darkness from the house of detention.
I am Yahweh; that is My Name,
And My glory I shall not give to another,
Or My praise to carvings.
The former things, behold, they came;
Now I will tell the new;

Ere they are sprouting I shall announce them to you.
Sing to Yahweh a new song,
His praise from the end of the earth…

Isaiah 42:6-10a

Not ten minutes south of my daughter's home, driving out of New England for good, my phone bleeped with a text message from my then 7-year-old daughter asking if I was going to her school concert. My heart broke again. I cried. (*WHAT?!?* I doubt that my little girl typed this message herself. She did not own a phone!) Was this a final test of my faith? I had made my decision. I had signed the court papers and was not going to be found in contempt of court! *I cried, again "lowing as I went."*

"And everyone who leaves houses, or brothers, or sisters, or father, or mother, or wife [or husband], or children, or fields, on account of My name, a hundred-fold shall be getting, and shall be enjoying the allotment of life eonian."

Matthew 19:29

Blessed is the master who trusts in Yahweh
So that Yahweh comes to be his trust.
He will become like a tree transplanted by the water,
That sends forth its roots by a canal;
It shall not fear when the bright warmth comes;
Its leaf remains flourishing;
And it shall not be anxious in a year of dearth,
Nor suspend from yielding fruit.

Jeremiah 17:7-8

As Yahweh {God} says through Paul and Barnabas:

> **…entreating them to remain in the faith and saying that, "Through many afflictions must we be entering into the kingdom of God."**
>
> *Acts 14:22*

My ONLY PRAYER is (and continues to be to this day):

Father,
Keep me faithful until my last breath.
Whatever it takes.
Amen.

I drove on to fulfill my calling and purpose, to serve Yahweh {God}.

> **"The infirm (weak ~ *CLKC*) be curing, the dead be rousing, lepers be cleansing, demons be casting out. Gratuitously you got; gratuitously be giving."**
>
> *Matthew 10:8*

Let your eyes look ahead,
And your eyelids be straight in front of you.
Balance the route of your foot,
And all your ways, let them be established.
Do not turn aside to the right or left…

Proverbs 4:25-27a

He sent from the height; He took me;
He removed me from many waters;
He rescued me from my strong enemy
And from those hating me;
For they were tougher than I.
They confronted me in the day of my calamity,
Yet Yahweh became my Stay.
He brought me forth into a wide place;
He liberated me, for He has delighted in me.

Psalm 18:16-19 and 2 Samuel 22:17-20

Chapter 14

MY BLIND WALK OF FAITH…

OUT OF THE BOX of lies, and into Yahweh's arms, the freedom of truth!

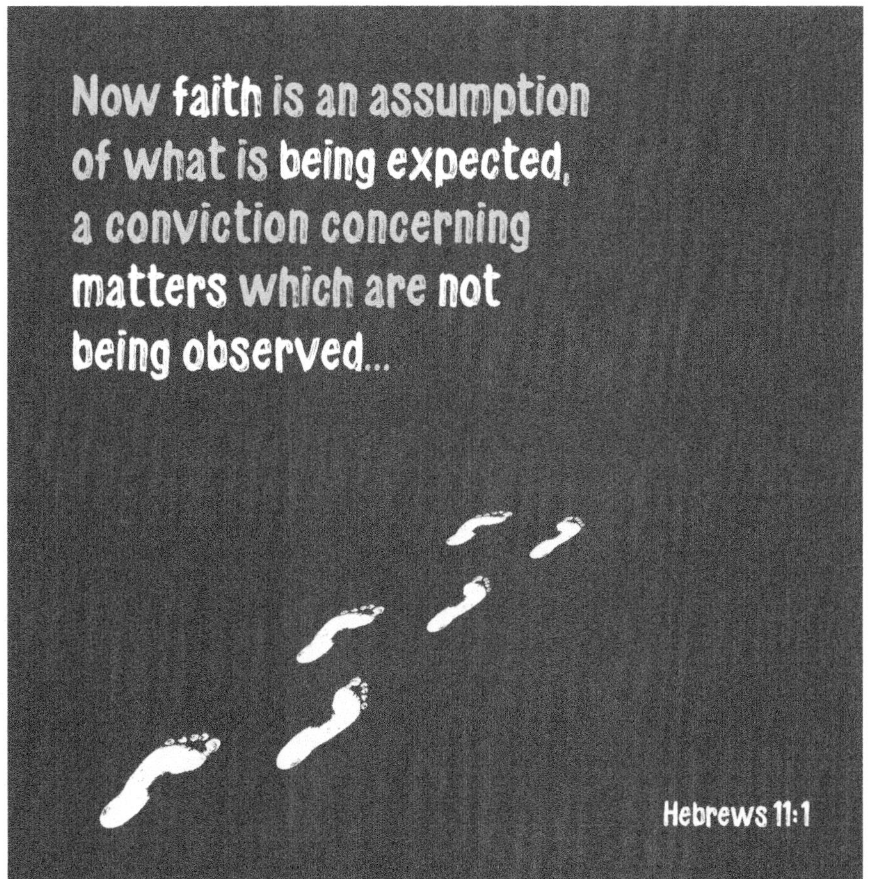

> **Now faith is an assumption of what is being expected, a conviction concerning matters which are not being observed…**
>
> *Hebrews 11:1*

My blind walk of faith…

Yahweh {God} is into even the finest of details… and He can change things in a heartbeat... and often *does*. His miracles are *not always*, nor often, grandiose, like the physical parting of the sea!

A pivotal turning point in my walk of faith was over one single, short email correspondence. Yes! Such a key moment in my life, over one seemingly simple act. Years ago, I was crafting an email, having had the most advanced training in how to write succinct, to the point, only what is needed to be said, emails. Devoid of bouts of familiarity, or needy people-pleasing, or **repeated** apologizing for ANYTHING (effectively bringing up the past, that which is not to be spoken of). And most important of all: always ending the correspondence on a relevant while positive note… that is, on the basis of the essence of, and reason for, the email itself, SPEAKING *(writing)* what is desired *into existence* AS IF it is already happening or happened.

> **"Therefore I am saying to you, All, whatever you are praying and requesting, be believing that you obtained, and it will be yours."**
>
> *Mark 11:24*

This last part, the "ending with a positive statement" was incredibly difficult for me. It felt like a complete LIE! I had always feared this approach would be viewed by others as being "pushy" or *even* "weird."

Charles Capps, describing this exact same feeling regarding prayer, writes (underline emphasis mine):

> Many people want to know why it won't work for them when they have not *meditated the Word* and would not dare say anything contrary to their *sense knowledge*. They would not dare say, "My God has supplied all my need according to His riches by Christ Jesus," when the rent is due and they don't have the money. Sense knowledge would say that would be telling a lie.
>
> But how can you tell a lie when you say the truth?
>
> GOD'S WORD IS TRUTH.
>
> **The Tongue, A Creative Force** by Charles Capps, pages 76-77.

However, when switching the focus from pleading for an outcome (to the point of begging) to the expression of the expectation *of* it, it had dramatic effects. Up to this point, I had not yet built up the confidence to prophesy, to "speak things into existence" in communications. I was still a people-pleaser, living by what I thought other people wanted to hear or read, instead of a Yah-pleaser, living by *the ways* of the Almighty Creator Himself, Yahweh {God}.

> **And Elohim said: Let light come to be! And light came to be.**
>
> *Genesis 1:3*

So, having grown sick and tired of my own choice of words missing the mark, I **finally** chose to do something different, to leap *"out of Tamra's box"* of the norm and breach the walls of my comfort zone (look where THOSE previous choices had got me, ugh). I wrote the last sentence of the email *as* a prophecy.

> Let me explain by way of example. Let's say you are inviting (via email) a business owner for a meeting. The final sentence, before the closing, would previously have been: "If you have time to meet, please do let me know as soon as you can so I can organize something so we can discuss what you need. I hope this week will work for you. Please let me know." And has now become: *"I look forward to our meeting to discuss how together we will achieve a remarkable growth in your business!"* This is prophesying, speaking (writing) your desires INTO existence, not only the meeting, but also the positive outcome of it!

It was VERY DIFFICULT for my finger, wavering above the "SEND" button, to click the email onto its destination. Oh man! But I did it...

I felt like I had just *walked OFF a steep cliff*,
and was falling DOWN the side,
falling... falling... soon to hit the ground, dead.

I was so nervous. As you know, once sent, the control you have over that email and how it is received is completely out of your hands. I was CONVINCED I would receive an angry response, or worse still, be ignored completely with no response at all.

However, to my complete and utter amazement... I did not SPLAT on the ground below at the bottom of that cliff! NO! I flew... I had spread my wings (without even knowing it) and was now FLYING!!!

Yahweh {God} must have been pleased with my email, how short, concise and to the point it was, without needy people-pleasing, profane babbling (fluff) or countless apologies. So much so, that I received a response *in accord with my prophecy.* (I honestly do not remember what the prophecy was... but I DO distinctly remember the feelings of utter dread in sending the email followed by a JOYOUS CONFUSION and DELIGHTFUL RELIEF when the response was favorable!)

Brother Lawrence shares this too, that new learnings take time and effort, yet it is above and beyond being well worth it (emphasis mine):

> … we must at first apply to Him with some diligence: but that **after a little care** we should find His love… **without any difficulty**.
>
> **The Brother Lawrence Collection – An Christian Classic – Practice and Presence of God, Spiritual Maxims, The Life of Brother Lawrence**
> by Brother Lawrence, Kindle page 13 of 139.

I share this all with you to give you a practical analogy, and a "real-time" example of how this really works. How to put Yahweh's {God's} principles into practice today! (Ooooh, that is a good title for a book!)

This just came to mind as I describe the feelings of over-riding my previous subconscious programming to achieve the above… it is like eating salad on your plate, with a fork… in your OPPOSITE HAND. Try it! Strange does not even begin to describe the feeling… right? (Unless of course you are ambidextrous!) The same applies with anything you do anew for the first time… it feels "strange," but **only** at first!

Or, try writing with pen on paper, again with your OPPOSITE hand! The strokes and shapes of the letters you know oh so well suddenly become alien to you. What seemed so natural, something at which you had become very proficient, becomes the scribblings of a 4-year-old.

People-pleasing is (a wisdom) of the world, not of the spirit. Precisely as the Scripture states:

> **…for the wisdom of this world is stupidity with God.**
>
> *1 Corinthians 3:19a*

The "wisdom" I learned in the world, (people-pleasing, the importance of a "5-year life plan," to know where your life is heading, etc.), is NOT how Yahweh {God} wants us to live... He wants us to trust Him in ALL THINGS *(read Isaiah 26:3-4),* to "not worry about tomorrow" *(read Matthew 6:34)* and to care ONLY what HE thinks of us and what HE directs us to do in the now *(read Psalm 118:8).* As He told Abraham:

Yahweh said to Abram: Go by yourself from your land, from your kindred and from your father's house to the land that I shall show you.

Genesis 12:1

If I were Yahweh {God}, my life would have been walking through fields of lovely roses that sing happy tunes... past soft bubbling brooks... joyously watching wild horses galloping by as I snack on pistachios and chocolate hanging from a nearby tree! However, since I am NOT Yahweh {God}, and HE planned my life (perfectly), and since I have humbled myself to accept this fact, I no longer cry out to Yahweh {God}, *"Why is this happening?"* nor do I try to figure out (so much) *"What or Why..."* anything! Yahweh {God} does miracles... He has miraculously changed me, He will certainly change you also, my fellow traveler!

Not three days ago... storm clouds began forming. The wind picked up. All of a sudden, it began to hail. Slowly at first, (as if in slow motion), a small light "plunk" on the roof, then another, then larger with a heavier "plunk," and more often. I immediately began praying, asking Yahweh {God} for RAIN ONLY (instead of hail), asking angels to guard and protect the solar panels on the roof. I prayed in tongues... I felt the spirit leading me to go outside and stand under the front door awning.

So, I went outside and continued to pray. I felt the spirit telling me to take the next step, *"stick your hand out into the hail."* I did not, my mind *reasoning* (ugh) that it was not safe to do that, the hail now larger than the size of regular marbles. I kept praying, PRAYING FOR RAIN ONLY. Praying for the air above to warm up, and melt the hail. I felt the spirit again telling me to *"stick your hand out into the hail, and catch some in your hand."* My mind reasoned again (double ugh) that it was now even less safe than before to do such a thing.

FINALLY… after about two long minutes of PRAYING and BEGGING Yahweh {God} to protect my solar panels, I remembered all I had learned in my life. I remembered ALL I am writing about in this book! And I obeyed, I stuck my hand out into the hail and caught some in my hand. Immediately, as soon as I obeyed, Yahweh {God} (His spirit) then showed me what to do next. (One step at a time… just as I have been writing in this book!) He showed me a vision of myself closing my hand around the hail, melting it, and as I do, Him melting the hail above my home, turning it to rain, and thus protecting the solar panels. And as I obeyed the vision, He did *precisely* what He had shown me. Instantly. As soon as the hail melted in my hand, the hail from the sky melted back into mere rain! RAIN!

Incredible! Awe-inspiring! Yahweh {God} did a miracle RIGHT before my eyes! As SOON as I obeyed, He gave me another step "to do," and as SOON as I obeyed, He showed up! PRAISE HIS HOLY NAME! PRAISE YOU FATHER!

I am finally listening! Hearing and heeding! And Yahweh {God}, my Father in Heaven, is blessing my obedience with signs and wonders… right before my eyes! Thank You Father!

…granting signs and miracles to occur through their hands.

Acts 14:3b

> **… the Lord working together with them and <u>confirming the word by the signs following them up</u>.**
>
> *Mark 16:20*

I am most surprised at all the quicksand Yahweh {God} has graciously helped me clamber out of before it completely swallowed me up…

- OUT of "big box religion" and all of its lies.
- OUT of the "medical model box" and all of its lies.
- OUT of "family systems" and superficial life, and all the lies that go with them.

I did not have a CLUE that I was entrenched in SO MANY LIES. Everywhere I turned, my eyes were being newly opened to the truth, new realizations flooding in, coming to terms with the fact that I had been taught and had then subsequently chosen to live *in… lies!*

Now, would you like to see or *live in* a miracle? Climbing OUT of and abandoning all this worldly web of deception and into Yahweh's {God's} arms of faith and truth is completely miraculous!

Accepting the truth renders all the falsehoods transparent and powerless and puts Yahweh {God} back in the driver's seat, where I had no right to be. Obeying His instructions, along with applying all the learnings and principles I have shared in this book, *made* the difference... *created* the change.

As I shared in a previous chapter, the **Concordant Literal Version's** accurate translation from the original texts of *Hebrews 11:1* reads…

> **Now faith is an assumption of what is being expected, a conviction concerning matters which are not being observed…**
>
> *Hebrews 11:1*

I always admired Daniel's spiritual walk and His inviolable* faith when he told people regarding Yahweh {God} and the **Bible** (which he did often), *"Believe it. Don't believe it. Your choice. It will not change the fact of it being THE truth."*

I just came across that word, *'inviolable.'* Isn't that a great word! It means:

> * inviolable
>
> In a divine sense - sacrosanct, holy, sacred;
>
> And also: prohibiting violation; secure from destruction, violence, infringement, or desecration.
>
> Thesaurus.com and Dictionary.com

How else would you want your faith to be? I had craved that firm, steadfast, deep-rooted faith myself. I longed for it… I dreamed of it, I *prayed* for it. (I had had such a poor view of myself though, that I truly did not think it was possible for me to ever have *that* level of faith.)

Even after all I had lived through, I still did not know Yahweh {God} *personally*, I had simply "**learned obedience through all I suffered.**" *(Read Hebrews 5:8)* Enduring the unthinkables, armoring up to the unimaginables and getting passed the "punch-the-steering-wheel" exclamations of, "*Why is this happening?*" I finally submitted to the fact that Yahweh {God} will do what He wants, for the delight of His will, *always* for the good of those who are loving Him *because* He always knows better than my wistful ways and sees beyond my logical agenda.

… for it is God Who is operating in you to will as well as to work for the sake of His delight.

Philippians 2:13

PRAISE YAHWEH {GOD} FOR MIRACLES
and for HIS FAITHFULNESS.

Today, years later, in His (Yahweh's {God's}) graciousness, I now have and walk in that faith I dreamed of. I also now *know* the Lord more personally and know to not try to understand His ways, only to *accept* them as they are… HIGHER.

Some four years ago, I spoke that exact same declaration… "*Believe it. Don't believe it. Your choice. It will not change the fact of it being THE truth,*" to someone who was beginning their own walk of faith. When I spoke the declaration myself, firm and unwavering, in that moment I *knew that I knew that I knew* that I believed it in every cell of my being!

This gives me confidence… the confidence in Yahweh {God} that He can and does change hearts! Miraculous! Thank You Father!

Even when I did not have the faith… Yahweh {God} still extended His grace, love and mercy to me! Bless His Holy Name!

May I encourage you, as I myself was encouraged so very many times:

KEEP GOING!

You WILL learn to hear Yahweh's {God's} voice. You WILL learn discernment. You WILL learn His ways. Yahweh {God} promises:

> **For I Myself know the designs that I am designing for you, averring is Yahweh, designs for your well-being and not for evil, to give you a hereafter and an expectation. When you call Me and you come and pray to Me, I will hearken to you. When you seek Me, you will find Me, for you shall seek after Me with all your heart, and I will be found by you, averring is Yahweh.**
>
> *Jeremiah 29:11-14a*

(Read also Deuteronomy 4:29, Proverbs 8:17, and Matthew 7:7-8.)

Going for prayer walks on the weekends (while going through all the horrendous court proceedings), I would see many caterpillars crossing the road (or, I should more accurately say, that Yahweh {God} had many caterpillars cross the road in front of me… there are no happenstances). It was Yahweh {God} saying to me… you are a caterpillar now, but keep going, daughter of Mine, one day you will become a butterfly. (I did not have MUCH faith of that actually happening, but I DID hope and pray.)

And it came true. I re-read this book (as I am writing it), looking at all that I have lived through and am now in awe of how I even kept walking sometimes…

Dogged determination,
and DEEP FAITH in Yahweh {God}.
PRAISE HIS HOLY NAME!

I could not have walked this on my own. I would have buried my head in the sand, rather than face the giants I faced... I think of the ten lepers whom Yeshua {Jesus} healed, and the single one grateful among them who sought Him out to thank Him. I, likewise, RUN to Yahweh {God} and THANK HIM for all the angels he sent me and continues to send!

Now one of them, perceiving that he was healed, returns, glorifying God with a loud voice. And he falls on his face at His feet, thanking Him [Jesus]... And He said to him, "Rise, go. Your faith has saved you."

Luke 17:15-16a and 19

(Read the entire story Luke 17:11-19.)

It was quite difficult at first for me to "get" this new walk of life, "the Yeshua {Jesus} walk!"

I was such a people-pleaser... I distinctly remember learning to remove seventy-five-percent of my use of the word "please" from conversation and written correspondence. (I was completely mortified at first, thinking it was so incredibly rude to NOT say "please" *at least once* in every single sentence of every single subject!)

I do not even recognize myself now *(chuckling out loud to myself as I write this)...* years later, and after many "classes" from my Heavenly Father. As I said, Deborah calls it "**H.S.U. ~ Holy Spirit University**" and each of our lives are specifically laid out with our very own classes! I have, thankfully, finally learned to say only what need be said, not to be "friends" with business clients, not to "go out to eat" with others just for fun, nor be friends with (or joke with) anyone at all, frankly! To live on purpose, making every breath count, walking hand-in-hand with my Father in Heaven above!

"Now I am saying to you that, for <u>every idle declaration</u> which men shall be speaking, they <u>shall be rendering an account concerning it</u> in the day of judging. For by your words shall you be justified, and by your words shall you be convicted."

Matthew 12:36-37

Remember Deborah's wise words:

"It's an alone walk, but never lonely."

Ponder on how Brother Lawrence lived his entire peaceful life, focused on Yahweh {God} alone, His grace and spirit emanating from him as others attested to (emphasis mine):

You must know his (that is, Brother Lawrence's) continual care has been... to be always with GOD, and **to do nothing, say nothing,** and **think nothing which may displease Him**; <u>and this without any other view than purely for the love of Him</u>, and because He deserves infinitely more.

The Brother Lawrence Collection - An Christian Classic - Practice and Presence of God, Spiritual Maxims, The Life of Brother Lawrence by Brother Lawrence, Kindle page 39 of 139.

Learning to "walk blind" (meaning in faith, trusting, not seeing the whole path, and sometimes not even seeing much further than the next step) was one of the hardest parts of my journey. I had to "get real" on the true understanding of what "the walk" looked like. Just as Dr. Tom Taylor teaches in his study *"104 - Don't look behind when God is redetermining your life ahead"*:

Don't think this is some cushy, "God-will-do-everything-for-me-and-I-have-it-made" kind of life. Now, that is actually true, but our human expectations may meet with stark disappointment, because following after the Lord is full of uncertainty when our certainty has been rooted in ourselves. We are on a need to know basis, know as you go. And it's uncomfortable - it might even be harsh - and not necessarily restful. So, look at the pattern Son here, Who has nowhere to lay His head. And, then, look at all who followed Him: every one of them was martyred!

Light Up the Scriptures study *"104 - Don't look behind when God is redetermining your life ahead"* by Dr. Tom Taylor. (Time: 3:02 - 3:56)

Climbing out of "the box of religion" and out of "the medical model box" and learning something NEW, *never mind applying it*, all of which FLEW in the face of almost EVERYTHING I had learned and adopted in my life up until then, was a mountainous and rocky climb. Lutheran faith, being that which dictates to NOT QUESTION ANYTHING, not even teachings by your pastor, rendered even the first step of "questioning why I believed what I believed" a cliff-climb for me in itself.

I Praise YAH {GOD} for the Scripture that I held onto often, that *what* He began in me... *He would complete*:

...having this same confidence, that He Who undertakes a good work among you, will be performing it until the day of Jesus Christ...

Philippians 1:6

I was a very "habitual" being (or *"habitual doing,"* more accurately...) brought up eating dinner at 5:30 pm sharp every single day, as well as following strict routines for chores, school... everything. I had taken an accounting class in high school, and absolutely loved it! I loved the methodical, step-by-step factualness of it. It fit perfectly with how I had been molded. So, I then acquired a College Degree in Accounting. My life was very organized, structured and yes, *habitual*, thus (especially in the beginning of this walk) it was incredibly difficult to *"break out of the norm box"* for me. Difficult yes, but **utterly** DOABLE.

PRAISE YAHWEH {GOD} for changing me.

"You are doing better than you know," Deborah used to say to me. (I honestly thought she was crazy because all I could see was a scroll unraveling in my mind to reveal all the countless times I had "missed the mark," and a catalogue of all my failures.) I now understand that to even STAY on this path takes strength in itself, to "get up every time you trip or fall." (This is just like one of Barbara Brown's chapters in ***GOD is* GOD *and* We Are Not** so aptly titled, *"Faith Isn't For Sissies."*)

Now, when I first heard the Scripture below, I thought it was completely crazy and honestly impossible to achieve. I thought, in my immaturity, that ONLY the "rock-solid-mature" followers would receive this truly deep in their hearts:

> **All joy deem it, my brethren, whenever you should be falling into various trials, knowing that the testing of your faith is producing endurance. Now let endurance have its perfect work, that you may be perfect and unimpaired, lacking in nothing.**
>
> *James 1:2-4*

I have definitely come a long way… as I now understand and resonate with this Scripture, and in many instances even embrace it. Other times, I'll just say I am a work in progress…which, by the way, we all are and always will be.

Brother Lawrence comes to mind, in his humility and grace, as he shares how he understands and LIVES according to the fact that knowing, loving, and serving Yahweh {God} with every breath is the ONLY thing he (Brother Lawrence) desires to do. No rewards. No blessings. Simply to place a smile on Yahweh's {God's} face. ***(Read The Brother Lawrence Collection – An Christian Classic – Practice and Presence of God, Spiritual Maxims, The Life of Brother Lawrence** by Brother Lawrence, Kindle page 12 of 139.)*

Chatting with a friend (as I shared in an earlier chapter), *"In these last few months I see myself as if I am walking in a wheat field… No set path. And I do NOT KNOW THE WAY!!! Ahhhhh!! I thought there was a PATH to life! THE PATH to Yahweh {God}. ONE PATH."* And my friend responded with such an encouraging word when I shared this vision, *"Good! I am glad you do not know the way. That means Yahweh {God} is guiding. This is how He guides."* And you can be sure, He does know the way. His way!

What if we trusted Him… in everything. What would that look like? I shall tell you from experience…

Peace…Utter peace.

"Peace I am leaving with you. My peace I am giving to you. Not according as the world is giving to you, am I giving to you. Let not your heart be disturbed, neither let it be timid."

John 14:27

Which opens the door to the final Scripture topic…

Chapter 15

PEACE… TRUE PEACE

Finally living in the Presence of Yahweh!

> **"Peace I am leaving with you. My peace I am giving to you. Not according as the world is giving to you, am I giving to you. Let not your heart be disturbed, neither let it be timid."**
>
> *John 14:27*

Have you ever felt peace...
Peace flowing through every cell of your body?
True peace?

Like the kind of peace enveloping you as a large blanket wrapped around you, sitting in the most comfortable recliner chair, drinking hot chocolate, with not the single, minutest thought of anything going through your mind... **even while, say, for example:**

- much of the entire world is fearful of dying of the flu and continue with glued-eyes to watch the news (propagated to make us fearful, as Bruce Lipton Ph.D. would say, as previously quoted).
- you are "stuck" at home (ordered by the government) and not even able to go for a walk to exercise and stretch your legs in fresh air or clear your mind of any clutter.
- you are not allowed (again by the government) to travel to work (if that is the requirement of the job or career you are in).
- wars are continuously happening in Israel, Gaza, Palestine, Afghanistan, Iraq, Nigeria, Ukraine, etc.
- famine, storms, earthquakes and fires that are ravaging the nations are all being constantly broadcast on the news.
- memories of past events in your life attempting to invade your mind.
- believing in Yahweh {God} is becoming ever increasingly unpopular and persecution seems to be on the rise in America.

etc...

Yet do you choose to keep watching all this, possibly NOT EVEN QUESTIONING why news stations do not report on the positives and all the good that people are doing across the globe?

Or do you know someone who seems oblivious, preferring to live in Yahweh's {God's} unshakable peace even with all of life's goings on? (Do you *wish* you had that deep a level of peace in your life?)

What does your life look like today? Are you at peace, right now? Truly?

What if… you could read these Scriptures below, with conviction, knowing in your heart of hearts that they are true!

Knowing… that no harm shall come close to you!

You shall not fear the alarm at night,
Or the arrow that flies by day,
Neither the plague that walks in gloom,
Nor the sting that devastates at high noon.
A thousand may fall at your side,
And ten thousand at your right hand;
It shall not come close to you.

Psalm 91:5-7

Not becoming distressed… when battles and turbulences are happening!

Now He said, "Beware that you may not be deceived, for many shall be coming in My name, saying that 'I am!' and 'The season is near!' You may not, then, be going after them. Now whenever you should be hearing battles and turbulences you may not be

dismayed, for these things must occur first, but not immediately is the consummation."

Then He said to them, "Roused shall be nation against nation, and kingdom against kingdom. Besides, there shall be great quakes and, in places, famines and pestilences. There shall be fearful sights besides great signs also from heaven."

Luke 21:8-11

Shared in the book **The Practice of the Presence of God**, Brother Lawrence wisely wrote to a friend saying (emphasis mine):

> God knows very well what we need and that all He does is for our good. If we KNEW how much He loves us, **we would always be ready to face life** – both its pleasures and its troubles.
>
> You know, the difficulties of life do not have to be unbearable. IT IS THE WAY THAT WE LOOK AT THEM THROUGH FAITH OR UNBELIEF. We must be **convinced that our Father is full of LOVE for us** and that He only permits trials to come our way for our own good.

The Brother Lawrence Collection – An Christian Classic – Practice and Presence of God, Spiritual Maxims, The Life of Brother Lawrence
by Brother Lawrence, Kindle page 104-105 of 139.

It sounds to me like Brother Lawrence lived, breathed and deeply believed what Paul wrote to the Romans, a verse I personally memorized as a child… today, an ever greater understanding has taken hold of me:

Now we are aware that God is working <u>all</u> <u>together</u> for the good of those who are loving God, who are called according to the purpose…

Romans 8:28

As I follow the leading of the spirit, walking my path in serving Him alone, His home in me is deepening… Praise His Holy Name! Living on a pig farm, (not able to go ANYWHERE during the COVID-19 pandemic for months and months, as with the rest of the world), here on a tiny spot of land on Yahweh's {God's} great green earth… here, I have surrendered to a **deeper level**, leaning on and trusting in my Father, the Creator of the entire universe!

Yahweh shall bless every undertaking of your hand,
And bless you in the land He is giving you.

Deuteronomy 28:8

And behold, I am with you; I will keep you in all the way you are going…

Genesis 28:15a

Have I not instructed you? Be steadfast and be resolute. Do not be terrified, and do not be dismayed, for Yahweh your Elohim is with you wherever you go.

Joshua 1:9

Bless You Yahweh {God}, and THANK YOU for Your Patience, Father! Because here… I have learned TRUE PEACE… even in the midst of what most of the world calls chaos, and I have chosen to live in peace in this secluded sanctuary.

I continue to "**become grateful**" for all I have lived through, and am living in… (as I shared in the beginning, in chapter one). I have found at least one reason (if not more) to be truly grateful for each and every life experience I have shared in this book, for this leads to true peace. ALL life events including: raped at knifepoint, walked through horrific divorce, daughter stolen from me, shunned multiple times, defamed character, COVID-19 pandemic, etc… yes, ALL the events in my life. I release the past, and Praise Yahweh {God} for ALL that I learned. I would not be who I am today without each and every one of those events. I learned to "**become grateful**" for ALL things, and to WATCH and LISTEN for Yahweh's {God's} voice. I learned this (sadly) through *ignoring* His spirit, living through a horrific rape, and finally looking back and finding SOMETHING to be thankful for! Praise Yahweh {God} for bringing me into Barbara Brown's life… for her to be BOLD enough to say, *"Find one thing you are grateful for, truly grateful for… Tamra."* Peace in my life has come from "**becoming grateful.**"

And let the peace of Christ be arbitrating in your hearts, for which you were called also in one body; and become thankful.

Colossians 3:15

I learned to SEEK ONLY Yahweh {God} and His voice alone… though I mainly only learned it when I HAD *(literally)* ONLY HIM to turn to, and HIM to ask. I used to look to both Deborah and Daniel, for I could see them, I could physically speak to them… and so I would not SEEK Yahweh {God} directly for myself, I would seek Yahweh {God} through them. And so, Yahweh removed me from their lives… multiple times…

Through this, I have finally learned, (many years later), to SEEK YAHWEH {GOD} ALONE, and I have found HIM! Bless Him! Praise Him for His patience with me!

I thank Yahweh {God} for EVERYTHING in life, and focus only on today and the purpose for which I was created… including helping ALL of His kids to find His peace also, to immerse ourselves in YAHWEH'S {GOD'S} PEACE.

"Peace I am leaving with you. My peace I am giving to you. Not according as the world is giving to you, am I giving to you. Let not your heart be disturbed, neither let it be timid."

John 14:27

Years ago… I turned off the television in my home. (Disregarding the taunts that I was *"completely crazy."*) I chose to STOP watching the news which instills fear – spreading it rampantly (being "filtered" and influenced by the advertising companies who fund them, by large corporations and by "big brother," such that it is **not** a "neutral party" deciding what YOU watch, but one driven by greed). I chose to STOP watching movies (mostly Disney movies: Aladdin, Beauty and the Beast, The Princess Diaries, etc.), that filled both my and my daughter's heads with LIES of "happily ever afters" to make our minds believe what life SHOULD look like (with actors who "look perfect" and thus influenced our minds to think we must look like that also…). I chose to STOP watching "game shows" that spread the belief that you could become a millionaire in mere minutes! I chose to stop the lies. I chose to STOP wasting my time watching others "recite a script of what someone envisioned that life SHOULD look like…" I chose to LIVE MY OWN LIFE! I chose to take control of my LIFE AND PATH, instead of being brain-washed into habitual pointlessness.

I cannot believe I am about to say this... I absolutely dislike movies now, however, I must say that the idea behind the movie The Matrix is **true**. Most people in the world are programmed (as I myself was by LIVING in front of the television) to see a lie, to be brain-washed into a "non-reality" society portrayed as being REALITY, a society that is self-serving!

I do so appreciate much of how Caren and Roger raised me... there was NOT ONE television in the house until I was 7-years-old and we only had two or three channels until I was a teenager! Bless them! Caren believed that "fresh air" was a necessity every day, no matter the weather, come rain or shine, hot or cold, and even in Minnesota's freezing cold... *"Bundle up!"* she would say!

Deborah encouraged me to read the book **The Dream Giver** when I first met her. I could NOT put it down! It is an easy to read, wonderfully analogical story of what the path of life looks like when leaving "the mainstream rat-race" that so many of us are raised to believe as "normal" (I was anyway), to face what is ahead outside of our comfort zone, conquering all to follow our hearts and spirits and to **find** TRUE LIFE! Life in the NOW! Living every breath for Yahweh {God} to fulfill His purpose in our lives! The book describes the journey out of "ordinary" and into "true purpose" in a refreshingly simple manner. It warns to not abandon your true purpose when hardships arise (which they WILL), and teaches just as the Scriptures do that Yahweh {God} works ALL things in life, for our good!

Now we are aware that God is working all together for the good of those who are loving God, who are called according to the purpose...

Romans 8:28

I admit, I embarrassingly confess on my knees, that Yahweh {God} offered to give me His peace, to teach me **to live in His peace** *years ago.* I said no. I blatantly said no. (Words do not describe the sadness my spirit feels remembering this… writing this.)

I clearly remember Deborah asking me (at least three times) before I would go to court, *"What if you felt God's peace* **now***, in the midst of this?"* Every time she said it I replied with the same answer, *"No. There is no way I could feel peace now. Maybe after all of this is over."*

Oh, the CURSE I SPOKE OVER MYSELF! (My head and spirit hanging low now, just remembering **this very curse I spoke over myself.**)

Death and life lie in the grip of the tongue,
And they who love it shall eat its fruit.

Proverbs 18:21

This is precisely what Charles Capps speaks of in his book of wisdom, **The Tongue, A Creative Force**:

> You can see that the words work for or against you. He said you are going to be justified or condemned by the words of your mouth.
>
> **The Tongue, A Creative Force** by Charles Capps, page 96.

I noticed Deborah stopped asking. (I noticed it, but I did not SAY anything about it, nor ask for her wisdom. Ugh.)

This is the very same reason that Elijah got "fired" by Yahweh {God}, answering His question with the SAME answer… twice. Wrong answer!

(IF Yahweh {God} asks any question, Tamra... speak as Ezekiel did: ***"Oh Sovereign Lord, You alone know!"*** Correct answer!)

Throughout the 19+ times I appeared in the three different courts... not only did I NOT FEEL at peace, I REFUSED to believe that I *could* feel any peace. I was in fear of man (meaning humans). I was in fear of the court system. I was in fear of most everything it seemed...

> Fear, by the way, is a current-day "idol." An idol is NOT only a visible "god" like Baal in the Old Testament or Greek gods of their day, but an "idol" can also be money (greed, security, worry, fear), a spouse, a child, a pet, a reputation. As Barbara Brown would say, *"Anything that gets your time, your money, and your attention (and what you talk about). THAT IS YOUR 'god'!"*

On top of that, I was a people-pleaser. I would do EVERYTHING to suit EVERYONE ELSE's opinion, literally. I remember one day Christina saying to me, *"I love going shopping at the mall with you."* And I thought to myself, *"Yes, because I rarely ask to go to any store that I WANT... I simply **follow you** around all day!"* This thought STUCK in my mind. It dawned on me that day how unhappy I was... and it was the cause and effect of MY OWN choices. Not anyone else's choices! People-pleasing does NOT bring peace. (I say this from personal experience, from almost my entire life. The above is only one teeny-tiny example.)

What DOES bring true peace, you may ask? Yah-pleasing!

*Caring **only** about what*
the Creator of YOU thinks of you,
*and **not** what the world thinks of you.*

I tried it "the world's" way... for over thirty years... and as you have read throughout this book how that worked out for me, *all* of the HELL

I created for myself! (And I did not even write about one quarter of the horrendous details throughout these pages.)

Now that I am further along the Yeshua {Jesus} walk, living and caring ONLY what my Father, (our Creator), thinks, says, shows, and does…

NOW my life is a JOY and my insides are in PEACE!

I live in TRUE PEACE, in every cell of my being. (Not every moment, as I am repenting from still sometimes sins of worry, reason, fear, etc.) However, I am becoming MORE and MORE completely Yahweh's {God's}. I am dying to myself. I am giving up all rights to myself. I am living for Him and Him alone!

He must be growing, yet mine it is to be inferior.

John 3:30

Praise Him! ONLY HE ALONE could cause this deep change in me. To HIM be all the glory!

"Worthy art Thou, O Lord, our Lord and God,
To get glory and honor and power;
For Thou dost create all, And because of Thy will they were, and are created."

Revelations - The Unveiling of Jesus Christ 4:11

Relax and know that I am Elohim…

Psalm 46:10a

Bless Yahweh, my soul,
And all within me, bless His holy Name!
Bless Yahweh, my soul,
And do not forget any of His well-dealings,
Who is pardoning all your depravity,
Who is healing all your ailments,
Who is redeeming your life from ruin,
Who is crowning you with benignity (mercifulness, kindness and bountifulness ~ *CLKC*) **and compassion,**
Who is satisfying your future with good,
So your youth is renewed...

Psalm 103:1-5

Trust in Yahweh with all your heart,
And do not lean to your own understanding.
In all your ways acknowledge Him,
And He Himself shall straighten your paths.

Proverbs 3:5-6

While I still have room for growth in living in peace... I am definitely further along in my journey. At the beginning of writing this book, I felt anxious with many nervous visits to the toilet ... I also felt gas and bloating. So, I turned to my "medicine-free cabinet" and looked up "gas" in Louise Hay's book, HEAL YOUR BODY, to its explanation of what negative feelings and emotions (sins) I was allowing, and then the positive affirmation that, once applied through thought or speech, replaced the feelings of fear that I had felt.

So, I would have little chats with myself... to calm (or cure) any feeling of "fear" and "undigested ideas" regarding writing this book. I questioned myself, *"Am I crazy? Am I attention seeking?… Or do I truly want to share my journey to help others, as I have always desired to do?"* Since Yahweh {God} had sent me SO MANY angels to help me along my own journey, I reminded myself of the **truth**, renounced-rejected-and-rebuked any lies, and returned to **peace in His arms**… the physical symptoms ebbing away.

It is written:

> **Do not worry about anything, but in everything, by prayer and petition, with thanksgiving, let your requests be made known to God, <u>and the peace of God</u>, that is superior to every frame of mind, <u>shall be garrisoning</u> (protect with a military force ~ *CLKC*) <u>your hearts</u> and your apprehensions in Christ Jesus.**
>
> *Philippians 4:6-7*

It is written:

> **Yahweh will guide you continually,**
> **And He will satisfy your soul in sun-glaring places;**
> **He shall invigorate your bones,**
> **And you will become like a well-watered garden,**
> **And like a flowing well of water whose waters are not defaulting.**
>
> *Isaiah 58:11*

It is written:

> **…he (King Jehoshaphat) recruited singers for Yahweh praising His holy effulgence, as they went forth <u>before</u> the vanguard, saying, Acclaim Yahweh, for His benignity (mercifulness, kindness and bountifulness ~ *CLKC*) is for the eon.**

> **Now as they started off with jubilant song and praise, Yahweh set ambushers against the sons of Ammon, Moab and Mount Seir who had set out against Judah, and they were struck down.**
>
> *2 Chronicles 20:21-22*

Also, during the times I would pendulum from one end of the emotional spectrum, joy and peace, to the other, gripping fear (as I am sure you have felt at times too), the wisdom of Barbara Brown and Dr. Tom Taylor would come to my mind, speaking what they *so very often* said:

> It Happened.
> It's Over.
> It's OK Now!
>
> **It Happened, It's Over, It's OK Now! How to Let Go of the Past and Heal Your Mind, Memory and Emotions**
> by Barbara Brown, MSE and Dr. Tom Taylor, page 79.

"Is it happening to you RIGHT NOW, Tamra?" I ask myself. *"No"* is OFTEN the answer. *"Well then,"* my learned voice of wisdom says, *"…it is over. STOP THINKING ABOUT THE PAST (or future). Everything is OK NOW! Look around you, name five things you are grateful for that you can SEE right now!"* This helps bring me back **into the present**. (A helpful tip shared by Elena, years ago, while in the midst of court proceedings.)

Dr. Tom Taylor also teaches on peace in multiple **Light Up the Scriptures** studies, one of particular pertinence being *"180 - Pause for further instructions"* where he reads Psalm 60: 1-2 and 5-8 (see below) and shares what the spirit showed him regarding David's inspired words (emphasis mine):

*So, look with me at the same **Psalm 62** in the Concordant Literal Version (CLV), again beginning in verses 1-2 and then we will jump down to 5-8:*

Psalm 62:1-2, 5-8

1 Only in Elohim is my soul stilled;
From Him comes my salvation.
2 He only is my Rock and my Salvation,
My Impregnable Retreat;
I shall not slip more.
…
5 Only in Elohim be still, my soul,
For from Him comes my expectation.
6 He only is my Rock and my Salvation,
My Impregnable Retreat;
I shall not slip.
7 On Elohim rest my salvation and my glory;
The rock of my strength, my refuge is in Elohim.
8 Trust in Him at all time, people;
Pour out your heart before Him;
Elohim is our Refuge.

*…Verse 5 reads, "**Only in Elohim, be still, my soul.**" Now David is addressing his own insides – his own self-talk, we might say; he's speaking to his mind, his awareness as a human being, who has the noise of dying clamoring for attention, clamoring for attention all the time. Most people are numb to this inevitable and continual survival alarm.*

He goes on to say my favorite piece which gives me a "*temperature gauge*" of how close I truly am to Yahweh {God}, to living in His presence (emphasis mine):

> *In addition, the only way we CAN be in His presence is by "stilling" our souls – our thoughts, emotions, our preoccupations, our priorities, our agenda. And I would suggest further… because of the way David has phrased this Psalm, that* ***if we are not experiencing silence in our minds – we are not in His presence;*** *it is like, if your mind will not shut down, you are not in His presence. And conversely, when we ARE experiencing that stillness, that quiet, or peace – when nothing of our lives occupies even a shred of our awareness – then we are ABLE to appreciate… and* **only then** *are we able to appreciate His presence.*
>
> Light Up the Scriptures study "*180 - Pause for further instructions*" by Dr. Tom Taylor. (Time: 5:43 - 6:45 and 7:49 - 8:19 and 10:51 - 11.44)

This lovely Scripture comes to mind:

> **…the disposition of the spirit is life and peace…**
>
> *Romans 8:6b*

Remembering just how bone-chillingly FEARFUL I felt for months and months after I was raped at age 17… I compare that to how I feel today. Feeling peace, TRUE PEACE even in the midst of "the propagated COVID-19 pandemic," wars and ALL the "crazy chaos" in the world.

I am in tearful awe at
the MIRACLES YAHWEH {GOD}
has performed in my life!

May I encourage you, dear reader, to keep walking. Keep Going! All that you are living through… all of which Yahweh {God} knows is happening, (just as He did throughout EVERYTHING in my life), just as

He knew all that was happening to Job... know that He will NOT give you, nor allow you to live through, more than you can handle. I PROMISE YOU! It is written! It may not feel like it to you... if I had written my life, I would definitely have STOPPED many of the "trials and tribulations" LONG BEFORE they actually ended. However, I am who I am today because of all that I have endured. I appreciate every step. I choose to appreciate every step... without them I would not be where I am today. PRAISE YAHWEH {GOD}!

I always used to think that events would NEVER END... literally never. Now, today, I KNOW BETTER! And I want to encourage you, from the depths of my heart... to keep going. I have often thought of the unspeakable and beyond horrendous life events that Corrie Ten Boom lived through during the Holocaust. She is an inspiration to me. I watch some videos of her preaching... and her faith (even with ALL she lived through) encourages me. As Joseph and Job in the Old Testament, she has also surrendered her life, past, present and future, completely to Yahweh {God} and you can sense it, watching her flow in serenity.

I especially like when she shares how her dad taught her just how deep Yahweh's {God's} love and caring arms are:

> *And also, when the ways (life) went through depths he (her dad) knew, A PIT CANNOT... BE SO DEEP... ALWAYS DEEPER ARE THE EVERLASTING ARMS!*
>
> *"Surrender - Corrie Ten Boom"* video found at:
> YouTu.be/rXoGTP5NoR8
> (Time: 36:24 - 36:40)

What peace and joy she lived in, during the many following decades since living through "hell," literally. Even as she recounts and teaches others through horrendous events in her life, she smiles and seems to be

IN peace, all forgiving and thanksgiving... IN Christ {the Messiah}! Truly an inspiration! Bless her Father!

And most importantly, as I have discussed previously in this book... is the life and example of Yeshua {Jesus}. ***"Thy will be done."*** I echo Him and His words in my life. And the Scripture comes to mind when Yeshua {Jesus} said:

> **"These things have I spoken to you that <u>in Me you may have peace</u>. In the world you have affliction. But <u>courage</u>! I have conquered the world."**
>
> *John 16:33*

In the mornings, and throughout the day when I remember to... I LOVE to "go to heaven" with my Father!

Climbing up into heaven, out of and away from THIS WORLD (the pointless happenings of this "chaotic planet"), I sit next to my Father. He is in a big, comfortable double-seated recliner, and I sit right next to him. I am enveloped in His strength, His power, His glory! I see what He sees from His perspective, *Heaven's View*, and I think what He thinks... Simply watching while detached from the earth below. I pray to live in this perspective 100% of the time.

> **For, as regards Yahweh, His eyes go to and fro through all the earth to reinforce the heart of those who are at peace with Him.**
>
> *2 Chronicles 16:9a*

"…will He be finding the faith on the earth?"

Luke 18:8b

I agree whole-heartedly with Brother Lawrence's perspective of the presence of Yahweh {God}, (and eagerly train my mind in this):

> That we should establish ourselves in a sense of GOD'S Presence, by continually conversing with Him. That it was a shameful thing to quit His conversations, to think of trifles and fooleries.
>
> The Brother Lawrence Collection - An Christian Classic - Practice and Presence of God, Spiritual Maxims, The Life of Brother Lawrence by Brother Lawrence, Kindle page 10 of 139.

Other times, I am holding hands with my Father, walking down the streets of gold. Seeing myself as a young girl, skipping and swinging my hand in His… Giddy with joy and excitement about how perfect life is in heaven! Joy exuberating from EVERYTHING! (No glum faces on anyone!) Father, I await that day with joy and anticipation!

Yahweh {God} alone knows what heaven will be like… This is what I see, with my Father and elder Brother, the Firstborn, Yeshua {Jesus}.

Yet the righteous, they shall rejoice;
They shall be glad before Elohim,
And they shall be elated with rejoicing.

Psalm 68:3

Be rejoicing in the Lord always! Again, I will declare, be rejoicing!
Philippians 4:4

In addition to all you have previously read and, perhaps, the helpful notes you highlighted in your own mind as you went (and here in this book too!)... here are **12 Tips and Tools** I continue to use myself on the journey, and gladly share with you... how I bring myself from nervousness or a sense of complete and constant TURMOIL and FEAR, to more continuous PEACE, TRUST and DELIGHT!

12 Tips and Tools
to finding TRUE PEACE

1 ~ Prophesy! Prophesy! Prophesy!

- Speak purposefully. Every word. Speak what you DESIRE... not what you have or have not.
- Stop joking. You are ONLY speaking negativity into your own life! (Notice the next time you joke. Were your spoken words to come true, joking or otherwise, would the outcome be positive or negative? Is this *truly* what you desire?)
- The law of the spirit is real and operating... just like the law of gravity. Believe it. Don't believe it. It does not change **the fact** that *words create.*

And Elohim said: Let light come to be! And light came to be.
Genesis 1:3

2 ~ Do what Yeshua {Jesus} did!

- Quote Scriptures with: It is written… It is written… It is written.
- Write a list of "favorite Scriptures." Write notecards of Scriptures and carry them around in your pocket. Any time a negative thought, worry, or fear comes into your mind or is spoken around you, pull out your notecards and speak them (either in your mind or out loud), "It is written…" It may take over fifty times a day at first… but you will unlearn fear, and embed Yahweh {God} into you! Amen!

3 ~ Gratitude is the Secret Key!

LOOK for the Positive and FOCUS ON IT!

- Remember chapter one… EVEN IN THE WORST OF events, how I FOUND something I was grateful for! (IT WORKS!)

> **And let the peace of Christ be arbitrating in your hearts, for which you were called also in one body; and become thankful.**
>
> *Colossians 3:15*

- I sometimes think, and have said to my friend… what if Yahweh {God} allowed me to live through all this so that I may teach and encourage others to be grateful in all things? In this way, others can no longer use the excuse, *"Well, you do not understand, I have been through something HORRIFIC, I cannot find something positive in that."* Yahweh {God} alone knows…

  a. I pray for a heart of *"Yes, I will do it"* for us all, and a death to any spirits of pity or *"I can't."*

  b. Daniel and Deborah always say it is *not ever* that someone "CAN not," it is that they "WILL not."

4 ~ Miracles Study

- Over a year ago, I was helping guide a precious child of Yahweh {God} on this path, through the cramped gate and narrow way… to "be seated among the celestials!" This person had quite the OPPOSITE upbringing to myself. They had almost NEVER read the **Bible**, and did NOT believe in it either, none of it. So, it came to me (by the spirit) to do a "Miracles Study" of the **Bible**. To read about all of the AWE-INSPIRING miracles that Yahweh {God} has ever done! (Well, recorded anyway.)

  I have found there are **509 miracles** in the Old Testament alone! In fact, in my opinion, MOST of the Old Testament is *entirely about miracles*! The document I created to account all the miracles in the Old Testament alone is 362 pages! (And it is not even completed yet…) We would read a miracle, and then discuss it, write our insights from it, and write how we can apply any learnings of Yahweh {God} to our lives today. (I LOVED doing this!) I pray it becomes a book someday… this is "my plan," **His will be done**! Amen.

5 ~ Tapping into the Subconscious

- After reading **The Biology of Belief** by Bruce Lipton Ph.D., and knowing a little about NLP and the subconscious… an idea came to me, (Praise Yahweh {God}!), how helpful it would be to create a video with Scriptures, in between which inserting subliminal embedded messages that flash so quickly that only the subconscious has time to read them, each containing positive and Scriptural beliefs that I want to EMBED IN MY SUBCONSCIOUS, ones I may not totally believe in my conscious at the time. (For me, for example, *"Yahweh {God} loves you right now. Today. Where you are and who you are."* Or *"Yahweh {God} delights in you!"* etc.)

While writing this book, sharing my journey, I realized that the "Be quiet Tamra" embedded belief from a young age was still programmed into me. SO... I created a video to help DELETE this negative, harmful program. Praise Yah {God} it helped! I wrote MUCH of this book in joy, health and peace, despite most of the memories that I had to temporarily revisit... grateful to be fulfilling my calling and deep desire to help others... just as Yahweh {God} sent others to help me!

Go to WhereTheSpiritOfTheLordis.com/book-bonuses-KTF and view or download **The Practice of PEACE** video!

6 ~ No Condemnation

- Oh I **loved** the results of this study when I dug into it… deep!

I had memorized this Scripture as a child… however I had not SEEN examples of it lived out in my life. Certainly not that I remember… not toward me anyway.

> **Nothing, consequently, is now condemnation to those in Christ Jesus. Not according to flesh are they walking, but according to spirit…**
>
> *Romans 8: 1*

Dr. Tom Taylor would quote this Scripture often also… however the "old program" of knowing the words but not living the feeling of freedom still ran rampant throughout my body. So… I sat down at my computer, and studied the entire chapter of *Romans 8*. (This is suggested at the end of **Light Up the Scriptures** study

"70 - To Whom Are We Living.") So, I finally did it, after being prompted again in this study...

I looked up EVERY SINGLE word in the first verse alone and wrote about them. I wanted to *immerse myself in this*, in "no condemnation." I wanted to FEEL IT in every cell of my body. I wrote down all that I found for EVERY WORD of this first verse. (Then, I proceeded to do the same for almost the entire chapter.)

It was WELL WORTH IT. *I finally got it!* Yahweh {God} cleansed my cells of fear, doubt and guilt with a bristle brush… and I FELT PEACE flowing through every cell of my being! Yahweh {God} opened my eyes! He did "surgery" on me, and removed the religious teaching from the past. Bless Him! NO CONDEMNATION! *So lovely, beyond words!*

This feeling of COMPLETE PEACE stayed with me for months. And, every time I revisit the study it comes flowing back over me! Praise Yah {God}!

Brother Lawrence, in his gloriously peaceful way of living, shares (emphasis mine):

> That he was very sensible of his faults, but not discouraged by them; that he confessed them to God, but did not plead against Him to excuse them. When he had so done, he peaceably resumed his usual practice of love and adoration.
>
> The Brother Lawrence Collection - An Christian Classic - Practice and Presence of God, Spiritual Maxims, The Life of Brother Lawrence by Brother Lawrence, Kindle page 15 of 139.

- Ask, seek, knock.

  Yahweh {God} ANSWERED my prayer… my prayer to KNOW what "no condemnation" *felt* like… when I took the time to seek, truly seek, study, "get knee deep" in the Word. (I pray you know what I mean.)

> **When you seek Me, you will find Me, for you shall seek after Me with all your heart, and I will be found by you, averring is Yahweh.**
>
> *Jeremiah 29:13-14a*

  I did my part… and then Yahweh {God} did His! Thank You Father!

  Just as the Scriptures state:

  a. Ask, seek, knock.
     (Read Matthew 7:7-8)

  b. Seek as your most treasured possession.
     (Read Matthew 13:44-46)

  c. Store up for yourself treasures in heaven.
     (Read Matthew 6:20-21)

7 ~ Read, Listen and Think.

Read, Listen to, and Think of ONLY What is Positive and Inspiring.

- Listen to the **Bible** audio recordings

  ~ CONCORDANT LITERAL NEW TESTAMENT, completely FREE audio recording at Concordant.org

- Listen to **Light Up the Scriptures**
- Listen to "Christian" worship music. Be selective. Some OFTEN only speak of pain, woes, hardships, etc. THE TONGUE BOOK STATES, do NOT speak about what IS happening... speak about what you WANT TO HAPPEN! Speaking (and singing) IS creating! (So, let us all please be careful when choosing the words we sing... including the song lyrics of "Christian" artists.)
- Thoughts are ALSO creating! Let's all think positive and inspiring thoughts... Again, Daniel teaches that everything is about energy, and Deborah continuously says, *"Thoughts are things."*
  - ~ IF you truly believed that every word you spoke would CREATE THE EXACT EXPERIENCE that you are speaking about... *would you speak differently?!?*
- Monitor what OTHERS around you speak about... Who do you spend your time with? EVEN if it is family members, YOU can stand up for yourself and ASK them to NOT speak negatively in front of you! And... IF they do not listen, guard your ears: *LEAVE.*
  a. I TAUGHT my daughter, at age 3+ to be HAPPY when leaving a park! Yes, HAPPY! (It took TIME to teach her this... and my own discipline of following through with what I said: *"If you cry, we are not coming back to the park tomorrow."* Guess what. One day she cried. So, I KEPT MY WORD and DID NOT GO TO THE PARK THE NEXT DAY. I reminded her why. I calmly taught her that what I said, I would follow through with! And you know what... SHE LEARNED! SHE LEARNED to be as happy when we left the park, as when we arrived!
  b. Stand up to blood relatives, even spouses. Yes. GUARD the ideal thing committed to you *(read 2 Timothy 1:14)* – this means YOU DO SOMETHING. Set boundaries. Set limits. WALK AWAY if/when your boundaries are not being respected and they are being crossed.

c. This includes GOSSIP! One day I was speaking with two followers of Yeshua {Jesus}, and one of them and myself began speaking about another person. (Yes, it was sin.) The third person got up and left. He did NOT want to partake in gossip, in sin, in wasting time, nor "preach" to us nor judge. He simply got up and walked out of the room. What strength of character! What OBEDIENCE to Yahweh {God}! Praise Yahweh {God} for his strength, example and life!

8 ~ The Victory March and Bio-Energetic Treatments

- Victory March: I learned how to give myself a "FREE neurological upgrade" from Dr. Tom Taylor and Barbara Brown. My definition of this includes: bringing yourself up to another level energetically, and clearing yourself from emotional "garbage." It is simple and easy, and takes mere minutes to do! (Please see the resources section for more information.)
- Bio-Energetic Treatments: **The QUICKEST** way to "bust through and out of" old programming, according to Bruce Lipton Ph.D., Barbara Brown and Dr. Tom Taylor (and many *many* others) is with bio-energetics. I have helped others with this life-changing treatment, (and I used to give treatments to my young daughter also).

9 ~ Positive Visualization

- Olympic athletes use it… WHY NOT FOLLOWERS OF YESHUA {JESUS}!?!
- Let's learn from "the best" as Paul writes, run as to WIN the prize!

- Some personal examples of how I use positive visualization include:
  a. During the rare times when I feel pain in my head… using the book, **HEAL YOUR BODY – The Mental Causes for Physical Illness and the Metaphysical Way to Overcome Them**, by Louise Hay, I visualize what I would be doing and how happy I will be when my head feels 100% healthy!
     ~ The feeling of pain in my head would completely disappear. (Sometimes only for a few minutes at a time… and sometimes FOR GOOD!) I am a work in progress in this journey called life!
  b. Once, years ago, when I applied for an apartment, the paperwork stated if you had filed for bankruptcy in the previous two years, you would be ineligible to live in this upscale complex. Well, I would not lie, (and due to the divorce court judgment appointing me alone responsible for paying off all the debt that Red and I had both accrued, I had no choice but to file for bankruptcy), so I told the truth on the rental application… and prayed and prayed for Yahweh's {God's} favor, dancing around with GREAT levels of joyous excitement and energy, thanking and praising God for my new apartment! *(Read 2 Chronicles 20:22, the account of first Praising Yahweh {God} for victory, and THEN Yahweh {God} fighting the battle for Israel.)*
     ~ Within a few days, I was granted the "stamp of approval" to live in the apartment complex! COMPLETE MIRACLE! PRAISE YAH {GOD}! (I am convinced angels sat on my paperwork, covering up the bankruptcy information I truthfully disclosed.)
  c. Today, (during the continuing COVID-19 pandemic and complete chaos, including hold-ups in many governmental offices), I waited 16 long months for the paperwork of my 1998 vehicle to get on the road. I visualized myself JOYFULLY

driving over hills and through valleys and mountains... with the said paperwork of course! **His will be done!**

~ During many of these months, I would ride my bicycle to the grocery store, and carry back all of my food and oat milk. I determinedly REMAINED joyful... happy... grateful for strong legs and healthy bones to be able to ride a bike!

~ Yahweh {God} SAW my faithfulness, and blessed me. One day... when it was GETTING QUITE HOT in the summer, (and I was not looking forward to carrying groceries on my back in the heat), Yahweh {God} placed it on someone's heart to DRIVE 2+ hours to me and let me borrow their car until mine was legal. THEN they took the train back to their own home. Bless them Father.

~ I am now driving again, my own older vehicle!!! PRAISE HIS HOLY NAME! I have a NEW appreciation for cars now! And the simple things in life, driving to the grocery store and back!

10 ~ Stop Praying

- Yes, you read that correctly! Stop praying.

  TRUST Yahweh {God}, He KNOWS what I need even BEFORE I ask Him...

> **"...aware is God, your Father, of what you need before you request Him."**
>
> *Matthew 6:8*

- I have prayed for things, THINKING I KNOW BEST... and later realized that because I continued asking and asking and asking, Yahweh {God} gave it to me... though it MAY NOT have been the best thing for me. (Some even turned into NIGHTMARES... what I perceived as a "dream come true," turned into completely the opposite! Ugh.)

  a. Read the parable of the friend at midnight, *Luke 11:5-13*.

  b. Read the unjust judge and the persistent woman, *Luke 18:1-8*.

  c. As Barbara Brown shares from an event in her life:

> One night, as I was taking my eight year-old nephew home from a restaurant in his hometown, I asked, "Adam, how do we get to your house from here?"
>
> He answered very innocently, "I don't know, Aunt Barbara, my mom or dad always drives."
>
> "How simple," I thought. All little Adam does is sit in the car and know, without a shadow of a doubt, that his parents will take him where he needs to go, with no concern on his part. That's their job. Why don't we do that with our Heavenly Father, Who made this whole world and keeps it going?
>
> *GOD is* GOD *and* We Are Not
> by Barbara Brown, MSE, page 119.

- IF you *must* pray:

  a. ALWAYS END ANY AND EVERY PRAYER AS YESHUA {JESUS} DID, especially when feeling "strong emotions" about something, ***"Your will be done!"***

  b. MOST importantly, do NOT pray the PROBLEM!

  As Charles Capps writes:

In Mark 11:24 the Word says, "What things soever you desire when you pray, believe you receive…" Defeat is not what you desire, *so don't pray it or say it.* You can see how the wrong choice of words can cause even your prayers to work against you. You have prayed, "Lord, I've got this problem and it's getting worse."

The Tongue, A Creative Force by Charles Capps, page 2.

11 ~ Write the Scriptures on the Jambs of Your House!

- I have LOVELY Scriptures EVERYWHERE throughout my humble abode with Yahweh {God}. On ALL the cupboards, the walls, the doors… I am SURROUNDED by HIS WORD!
    a. Images taken by a cell phone of LOVELY nature, places and scenes I love, have become the backgrounds to Scriptures I live by (and that is also the case with the majority of the Scripture images included in this book)! Mountains, green pastures and puffy clouds, a palm tree with the PERFECT BLUE SKY behind it, a daisy in focus with puffy clouds in the background, sunsets, sunrises, an old church ruin at the top of a small mountain, budding olive trees, flowers, a wall of the city of Jerusalem, and more! All hanging in my home, my home with my Heavenly Father!

Hence you will place these my words in your heart and in your soul, and you will tie them as a sign on your hand, and let them come to be as brow-bands between your eyes. You will teach them to your sons, speaking of them when you sit in your house, when you walk on

> **the road, when you lie down and when you arise. You will <u>write them on the jambs of your house</u> and on your gates…**
>
> *Deuteronomy 11:18-20*

b. You can view some of the very images in my home at WhereTheSpiritOfTheLordis.com/book-bonuses-KTF (Download them for yourself OR a friend for FREE and hang them on the walls, cupboards and doors in your homes also!)

12 ~ Remember…

Remember How Yahweh {God} Has Helped Me In The Past… *and thus KNOW TODAY that HE WILL CONTINUE TO HELP ME!*

- Guard yourself!

> **… then guard yourself, <u>lest you should forget</u> Yahweh your Elohim Who brought you forth from the land of Egypt, from the house of servants.**
>
> *Deuteronomy 6:12*

~ I can hear Dr. Tom Taylor's voice on one of the **Light Up the Scriptures** saying, more loudly than normal, *"Yahweh {God} SAID this because it IS POSSIBLE to forget!"*

- Meditate on all His marvelous works!

> **Make melody to Him!**
> **Meditate on all His marvelous works!**
>
> *1 Chronicles 16:9*

a. Now, if you were raised in religion, before you get "weird" with the word "meditate" (like I used to…), let us remember what meditate means: to engage in thought or contemplation; reflect. (Dictionary.com)

b. To me, meditate does NOT mean be like a "hippie," sitting cross-legged with your thumb and forefinger tips touching, or in a yoga studio with candles, etc. NOTICE the first sentence of the Scripture, "Sing… make melody…" When you sing, you are thinking of something, so… SING to Yahweh {God}! And ponder on ALL His marvelous works! This *is* meditating.

- I keep a "miracles" journal. When something GOOD happens, meaning miraculous and from Yahweh {God}, I **write it down**! And, GIVE YAHWEH {GOD} THE GLORY!
- I then READ my "miracles" journal when/if I ever feel fear, doubt, worry… REMEMBERING all that Yahweh {God} has done and can do. *He is big "into" doing miracles! (Read Genesis through Revelations… you will see for yourself!)*

Dear reader, here are some Scriptures I speak out loud to this day, bringing peace into my life. I pray they do the same for you:

"Peace I am leaving with you. My peace I am giving to you. Not according as the world is giving to you, am I giving to you. Let not your heart be disturbed, neither let it be timid."

John 14:27

Now may the God of expectation be filling you with all joy and peace in believing, for you to be super-abounding in expectation, in the power of holy spirit.

Romans 15:13

Relax and know that I am Elohim…

Psalm 46:10a

"These things have I spoken to you that in Me you may have peace. In the world you have affliction. But courage! I have conquered the world."

John 16:33

Furthermore, brethren, rejoice, adjust, be entreated, be mutually disposed, be at peace, and the God of love and of peace will be with you.

2 Corinthians 13:11

(Be encouraged by the following Scriptures of peace also: Isaiah 55:12, Philippians 4:6-7, Psalm 4:7-8, Matthew 6:25-34, 2 Thessalonians 3:16, Psalm 94:17-19, Galatians 5:22-23a, Colossians 3:15, Romans 5:1-2, Romans 8:6, Matthew 5:9, Psalm 121:1-2, Psalm 34:14, 1 Peter 5:6-7, Ephesians 6:15 and all vs 13-17, Isaiah 26:3-4, Psalm 29:11, 2 Chronicles 16:9a, Proverbs 12:20b, James 3:18, Proverbs 16:7, Romans 12:18b, Psalm 37:37, Ephesians 4:3 and all vs 1-6, Isaiah 26:12, 1 Corinthians 14:33, Proverbs 29:25, Isaiah 54:10, Romans 14:17-19, Hebrews 12:14, 1 Thessalonians 5:23, and more...)

Look what happens WHEN we are at peace with Yahweh {God}...

For, as regards Yahweh, His eyes go to and fro through all the earth to reinforce the heart of those who are at peace with Him.

2 Chronicles 16:9a

Thank You Father for reinforcing our hearts!

Father in Heaven, Abba, Papa,
I pray for your child, reading this book that You inspired, this life You planned and designed for me to write about today...
I pray You open their eyes to see YOU!
To know Who You really are!
I pray You strengthen them, to see NEW things, to believe in the REAL YOU, the all-powerful, delighted, strong, glorious, compassionate, benign (and disciplining) Father that You are! Wrap Your big arms around them, hold them close.
Walk with Your dear child, send angels to them to guide them on their path!
Thank You Father for being faithful...
even if/when we are not.
Thank You Father for Your kindness...
even if we do not feel deserving.
Thank You Father for showing us Your secrets, as You did to the Apostle Paul.
Thank You Father for giving us a heart of flesh, and removing a heart of stone.
I break (and renounce, reject and rebuke) any agreements made and any words spoken, (known or unknown), with spirits of religion, ancestral curses, anything that is not from You, Father in Heaven.

Open our eyes and overtake any feelings of unforgiveness, ingratitude, doubt, anger, fear toward You and/or any person on the face of this earth.
Open our eyes to see the Truth,
The Word, You!
Open our ears to hear You and You alone!
Open the floodgates of heaven over us… flowing down ALL YOU have for us…
Your wisdom, Your secrets and
Your treasures in HEAVEN!
Keep us faithful, I pray, until our last breath… or until Yeshua {Jesus} descends, as we ascend!
Keep us faithful, no matter what it takes… for it WILL be worth it as we are walking in the city square of gold with YOU!
(Read Revelations 21:21)

Thank You.
Thank You for everything in life…
Thank You for EVERYTHING we have ever experienced, and will experience!
Thank You for ALL we are learning…
today and every day!
Thank You for Your grace,
patience and love!
Thank You that You are our Father,
and we are Your children.
Thank You!
Thank You for Yeshua {Jesus}, for His life, His death and His resurrection!
Thank you for the price You and He paid for our freedom!

Thank You for ALL the prophets and saints
of old (and Your followers alive today)…
to inspire us and teach us…
Thank You for Your spirit, guiding us
into ALL the truth!
Thank You for living in us,
Father and Yeshua {Jesus}!
Thank You!
Bless You Father!
In Yeshua's {Jesus'} Holy Name I pray,
Amen. Amen and Amen.

Blessings beyond…
Tamra

נמראָה

Hebrew for "Tamra"
(received in Israel).

REMEMBER TO GET YOUR

FREE BOOK BONUSES

WhereTheSpiritOfTheLordis.com/book-bonuses-KTF

The Practice of Peace Video

Embed peace Scriptures into your subconscious to dwell in peace daily

Scripture Inspirations for your Walls & Screens

LIVE in Peace, True Peace!

WhereTheSpiritOfTheLordis.com/book-bonuses-KTF

May Yahweh
bless you and keep you;

May Yahweh
light up His face toward you
and be gracious to you;

May Yahweh
lift His face to you and
appoint peace for you.

Numbers 6: 24-26

APPENDICES

SECTION 1

TIMELINE OF EVENTS

Since I "jump around" a bit throughout this book, I decided to write a timeline for you, in case you ever wonder what I lived through... and when (or the chronological order).

FINDING YAHWEH {GOD}
in the midst of life...

Age 7 ~ Yahweh {God} spoke to me at the Little Lutheran Church on the Hill, "*You are the **only one** here who means every word you say.*"

Age 17 ~ Horrific event of being raped at knifepoint.

~ Moved to New England, joined a big conglomerate "big box church" (which my sister Christina attended).

Age 19 ~ Began attending college.

~ After having left church (and Yahweh {God} actually), Yahweh {God} gave me a dream with a candle almost completely burned out.

Age 20 ~ Met and dated Red

Age 22 ~ Married Red

Age 23 ~ Returned to the "big box church" (where *I believed* Yahweh {God} was…)

~ Diagnosed with depleted disk in my sacrum… *"No cure,"* said the doctors. *"None."*

Age 24 ~ Received an Accounting Degree (graduated with honors from a four-year college).

Age 29 ~ Gave birth naturally to my precious daughter.

Age 32 ~ Yahweh {God} spoke to me, *"Everyone here is dead."* And I thus left "big box religion" and followed Yahweh {God} and the **Bible** (with no man-made rules).

~ Learned about bio-energetics and energy… how it works in our bodies, the way YAHWEH {GOD} made us!

~ Attended *"Live the Victory"* seminar with Dr. Tom Taylor and Barbara Brown, MSE.

Age 33 ~ Heard "the call" from the Father, (the first time).

~ Word of Yahweh {God} spoken over me, *"You are the head, and not the tail."*

~ Yahweh {God} spoke to me again saying, *"Light cannot live with darkness."*

Age 34 ~ On my birthday, I finally decided to get a divorce. And IMMEDIATELY my depleted disk in my sacrum was completely healed! (A condition to which the doctors had said, *"There is NO cure!"*)

~ Officially filed paperwork for a divorce.

Age 35 ~ My daughter was ripped out of my arms while at the holistic treatment center in Texas...

~ Unjust and bias court, trial and judgments, gave my daughter legal custody to the dad!?!

Age 36 ~ My prayer for the opportunity to visit Jerusalem was graciously granted. Praise Yah {God}!

~ Followed the CALL OF YAHWEH {GOD} on my life, left everything to serve at the "Sold-Out-Seekers" in Texas!

Age 37 ~ Red (the biological dad of my daughter) filed fabricated sexual abuse charges against me.

~ Incomplete and one-sided investigation... I was found GUILTY of the charges!?!

~ I moved back to New England to clear my name... LONG ARDUOUS task.

Age 38 ~ I left New England for good... to return to Texas, following the CALL OF YAHWEH {GOD} on my life!

Age 42 ~ COVID-19 pandemic began.

Age 43 ~ Lived on a farm, and finally chose to live in PEACE (Yahweh's {God's} PEACE)!

~ Authored this book, ***KEEPING THE FAITH through the UN-thinkable...***

Age 44 ~ Birthed **Where The Spirit of the Lord is**

~ Created and launched the website: **WhereTheSpiritOfTheLordis.com**

SECTION 2

REFERENCE GUIDE

Listed below, in order of the first appearance of each in this book, are quoted references:

Books

- **Concordant Literal New Testament with the Keyword Concordance**, Concordant Publishing Concern, P.O. Box 449, Almont, MI 48003-0449, www.Concordant.org
- **Your Personal Roadmap to Whole Body Cleansing** by Dr. Tom Taylor and Barbara Brown, MSE, 2021, Whole Life Whole Health, 201 S. Shady Shores Drive, #1952, Lake Dallas, Texas 75065, www.WholeLifeWholeHealth.com
- **Concordant Version of the Old Testament**, Concordant Publishing Concern, P.O. Box 449, Almont, MI 48003-0449, www.Concordant.org
- ***GOD is* GOD *and* We Are Not** by Barbara Brown, MSE, 2013, Victory Publishers, 201 S. Shady Shores Drive, #1952, Lake Dallas, Texas 75065, www.WholeLifeWholeHealth.com
- **The Shack** by William P Young, Copyright © 2008. Reprinted by permission of Windblown Media, an imprint of Hachette Book Group, Inc., 53 State Street, Boston, Massachusetts 02109 (Pages referenced from the Kindle version.) www.TheShackBook.com
- **The Biology of Belief – Unleashing the Power of Consciousness, Matter & Miracles** by Bruce Lipton Ph.D. (10th Anniversary Addition, Kindle version), 2015, Hay House, Inc., Carlsbad, California, www.BruceLipton.com

- **Rescuing God From the Rubble of Religion** by Dr. Tom Taylor and Barbara Brown, MSE, 2018, Whole Life Whole Health, 201 S. Shady Shores Drive, #1952, Lake Dallas, Texas 75065, www.WholeLifeWholeHealth.com
- **The Dream Giver – Following Your God-Given Destiny** by Bruce Wilkinson with David and Heather Kopp (Kindle version), Multnomah Books, 12265 Oracle Boulevard, Suite 200, Colorado Springs, Colorado 80921
- **The Brother Lawrence Collection – An Christian Classic – Practice and Presence of God, Spiritual Maxims, The Life of Brother Lawrence** by Brother Lawrence (Kindle version), 2012, Start Publishing LLC, 221 River St, 9th Floor, Suite 9137, Hoboken, NJ 07030
- **God's Eonian Purpose** by Adlai Loudy, 1991, Concordant Publishing Concern, P.O. Box 449, Almont, MI 48003-0449, www.Concordant.org
- **It Happened, It's Over, It's OK Now! How to Let Go of the Past and Heal Your Mind, Memory and Emotions** by Barbara Brown, MSE and Dr. Tom Taylor, 2018, Whole Life Whole Health, 201 S. Shady Shores Drive, #1952, Lake Dallas, Texas 75065, www.WholeLifeWholeHealth.com
- **HEAL YOUR BODY – The Mental Causes for Physical Illness and the Metaphysical Way to Overcome Them** by Louise Hay, 1988, Hay House, Inc., Carlsbad, California
- **The Tongue, A Creative Force** by Charles Capps, 1995, Capps Publishing, P. O. Box 69 England, Arkansas 72046
- **You Think YOU Have It Tough?** by Dr. Tom Taylor, 2018, Whole Life Whole Health, 201 S. Shady Shores Drive, #1952, Lake Dallas, Texas 75065, www.WholeLifeWholeHealth.com

Listed below, in order of the first appearance of each in this book, are quotes from websites, YouTube videos and music or audio recordings:

Websites and Audio Recordings

- **Concordant.org**
- **BlueLetterBible.org** – Contains *Thayer's Greek Lexicon* information for definitions.
- **LightUpTheScriptures.com**
- **Dictionary.com**
- **DomesticShelters.org – Domestic Shelters** *"Men Can Be Abused, TOO"* article written in September 2015 (copied from this link on November 10, 2021) www.domesticshelters.org/articles/statistics/men-can-be-abused-too
- **Who.int – World Health Organization** *"Devastatingly pervasive: 1 in 3 women globally experience violence"* Published on March 9, 2021 (copied from this link on July 7, 2021) www.who.int/news/item/09-03-2021-devastatingly-pervasive-1-in-3-women-globally-experience-violence
- **BruceLipton.com** – *"The Frontier Sciences: Evidence-Based Practices & Principles Guiding You To Transform"* with Bruce Lipton Ph.D. interviewed by Guy Lawrence on March 23, 2021 (downloaded from this link on May 13, 2021) www.brucelipton.com/the-frontier-sciences-evidence-based-practises-principles-guiding-you-to-transform
- **ChrisKresser.com (Chris Kresser, M.S., L.Ac.)** – *"Natural Childbirth V: Epidural Side Effects and Risks"* Last updated on February 21, 2019 (copied from this link on June 9, 2021) chriskresser.com/natural-childbirth-v-epidural-side-effects-and-risks/#Epidural_also_have_side_effects_for_babies

- **Mercola.com (Dr. Joseph Mercola)** - *"The Amazing Benefits of Breastfeeding"* Published on January 2, 2016 (copied from this link on June 7, 2021) articles.mercola.com/sites/articles/archive/2016/01/02/amazing-benefits-breastfeeding.aspx
- **USA Today** - *"Arsenic, toxic metals found in baby food including Walmart, Gerber, Beech-Nut brands,"* article by Dee-Ann Durbin, Associated Press, on February 4th, 2021 (copied from this link on June 15, 2021) https://eu.usatoday.com/story/money/food/2021/02/04/baby-food-toxic-heavy-metals-fda-congressional-report/4379474001/
- **JuicePlus.com** – Quoted information (copied from this link on December 16, 2021) JuicePlus.com/es/en/franchise/about-the-juice-plus-company/juiceplus-company
- **Kathryn Kuhlman** teachings - *"Knowing the Holy Spirit"* teaching at Oral Roberts University in 1972 (YouTube video viewed on July 10, 2021) https://www.youtube.com/watch?v=q3hfHeGZyfg
- **Child Welfare Monitor** – *"Family court crisis: courts placing children with abusive parents with tragic results"* published on October 15, 2019 (copied from this link on July 14, 2021) childwelfaremonitor.org/2019/10/15/family-court-crisis-courts-placing-children-with-abusive-parents-with-tragic-results/
- **GW Law Faculty Publications & Other Works** prepared the following report titled, *"Child Custody Outcomes in Cases Involving Parental Alienation and Abuse Allegations"* by Joan S. Meier (George Washington University Law School, jmeier@law.gwu.edu), Sean Dickson, Chris O'Sullivan, Leora Rosen, and Jeffrey Hayes, 2019 (copied from this link on July 14, 2021) scholarship.law.gwu.edu/cgi/viewcontent.cgi?article=2712&context=faculty_publications
- **The Journal of Social Welfare and Family Law** prepared the following report *"U.S. child custody outcomes in cases involving parental alienation and abuse allegations: what do the data show?"*

by Joan S. Meier at George Washington University Law School, Washington, D.C. (received on September 17, 2021) and can also be found at: https://doi.org/10.1080/09649069.2020.1701941

- **Corrie Ten Boom** quotes – (Including a few found online at everydaypower.com/corrie-ten-boom-quotes/)
- **He That Has An Ear** – *"the Birth Series, the Birth Revisited"* by haRold Smith, (copied from this link on July 29, 2021) hethathasanear.com/Birth.html
- **Thesaurus.com**
- **Corrie Ten Boom** quote – *"Surrender - Corrie Ten Boom"* video (viewed at this link on June 30, 2021) YouTu.be/rXoGTP5NoR8
- **WhereTheSpiritOfTheLordis.com**
  - ~ **The Practice of PEACE** video downloads from Tamra's website WhereTheSpiritOfTheLordis.com/book-bonuses-KTF
  - ~ **Scripture Inspirations for Your Wall** to download from WhereTheSpiritOfTheLordis.com/book-bonuses-KTF

Worship Song Titles Mentioned

- **Martin Nystrom** (1984) *"As the Deer."* Maranatha Praise Inc.
- **MercyMe** (2014) *"Flawless."* [Title of the album: Welcome to the New.] INO Records.

SECTION 3

RESOURCES

"The Stuff that will change Your Life!"

You can find links and the beneficial reasons for all of these items below on my website at WhereTheSpiritOfTheLordis.com/other-resources:

BOOKS

- Concordant Literal New Testament with keyword concordance and Concordant Version of the Old Testament

- Rescuing God From the Rubble of Religion by Dr. Tom Taylor and Barbara Brown, MSE

- *GOD is* GOD *and* We Are Not by Barbara Brown

- You Think YOU Have It Tough? By Dr. Tom Taylor

- The Brother Lawrence Collection – An Christian Classic – Practice and Presence of God, Spiritual Maxims, The Life of Brother Lawrence by Brother Lawrence

- HEAL YOUR BODY – The Mental Causes for Physical Illness and the Metaphysical Way to Overcome Them by Louise Hay

- The Biology of Belief, Unleashing the Power of Consciousness, Matter & Miracles by Bruce Lipton, Ph.D.

- The Tongue, A Creative Force by Charles Capps

- **Your Personal Roadmap to Whole Body Cleansing** by Barbara Brown, MSE and Dr. Tom Taylor
- **It Happened, It's Over, It's OK Now! How to Let Go of the Past and Heal Your Mind, Memory and Emotions** by Barbara Brown, MSE and Dr. Tom Taylor
- **God's Eonian Purpose** by Adlai Loudy
- **The Dream Giver – Following Your God-Given Destiny** by Bruce Wilkinson with David and Heather Kopp

WEBSITES

- **Concordant.org**
  - ~ FREE online New Testament version
  - ~ FREE downloadable Old Testament version
- **LightUpTheScriptures.com**
- **WholeLifeWholeHealth.com** and **BarbaraBrown.com**
  - ~ *"Barbara's Ultimate Power Breakfast"* shakes
    (Bonus with purchase of the book **Your Personal Roadmap to Whole Body Cleansing** at CleansingRoadmap.com)
  - ~ Victory March
    (Bonus with purchase of **Power Shake PLUS+** at PowerShakePLUS.com)
  - ~ *"Non-Negotiable 5"*
    (Free e-book: ga1536514f3.pages.infusionsoft.net/)
- **JuicePlus.com**
- **BruceLipton.com**
- **HeThatHasAnEar.com** (Harold Smith)
- **Mercola.com** (Dr. Mercola)

YAHWEH'S HELPING HAND *(through Tamra)*

- **The Practice of PEACE** video downloads from Tamra's website WhereTheSpiritOfTheLordis.com/book-bonuses-KTF
- **Scripture Inspirations for Your Wall** – Download and print quality images of my favorite Scriptures on peaceful nature from Tamra's website: WhereTheSpiritOfTheLordis.com/book-bonuses-KTF
- **WhereTheSpiritOfTheLordis.com** – for a "host of help" that will literally change your life, being added continually…
- **Join our Community of Truth-Seekers** on Facebook at Facebook.com/KeepingTheFaithThroughTheUnthinkable.
- **And much much more…**

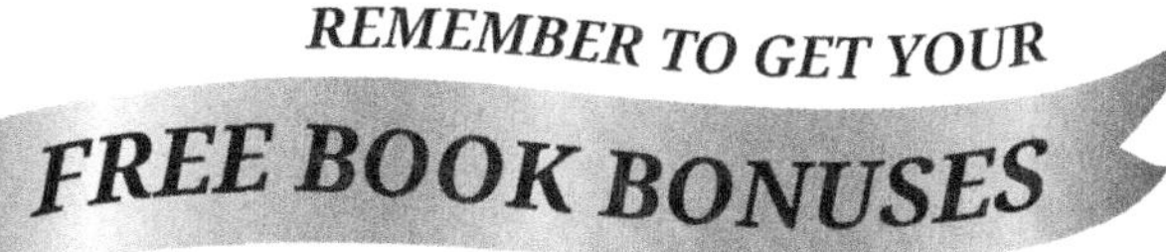

WhereTheSpiritOfTheLordis.com/book-bonuses-KTF

Printed in Great Britain
by Amazon

86057133R00261